WOMEN'S ACTIVISM
AND SOCIAL CHANGE

WOMEN'S ACTIVISM AND SOCIAL CHANGE

Rochester, New York, 1822–1872

Nancy A. Hewitt

CORNELL UNIVERSITY PRESS

ITHACA AND LONDON

First published 1984 by Cornell University Press.
Published in the United Kingdom by Cornell University Press Ltd., London.

International Standard Book Number 0-8014-1616-7
Library of Congress Catalog Card Number 83-45940
Printed in the United States of America
Librarians: Library of Congress cataloging information
appears on the last page of the book.

The paper in this book is acid-free and meets the guidelines
for permanence and durability of the Committee on Production
Guidelines for Book Longevity of the Council on Library Resources.

For Mom and Dad

Contents

Acknowledgments

In 1973 I took a course entitled "History's Outcasts: Women, Children, and Criminals," during which I first realized the potential of combining feminist politics and historical scholarship. The possibility of this book began then, under the guidance of Robert Smith and Susan Stuard of Brockport State College: without their encouragement, I would not be a historian. My research was begun during my graduate training at the University of Pennsylvania. Discussions with many faculty members there, especially with my adviser, Carroll Smith-Rosenberg, and with Lynn Lees, clarified and strengthened my arguments. Many of those arguments were first framed among friends at Walsh's Tavern and at Middle Atlantic Radical Historians Organization meetings. For their enthusiasm, wit, and unstinting support, I especially thank Susan G. Davis, Roma Heaney, Daniel Schiller, and Steven Zdatny. To Roma and to Andrew Feffer I owe a very special debt for keeping me healthy and sane during my last summer in Philadelphia as I completed the work upon which this book is based. I also thank those friends who sustained me over many years and often over long distances. I hope that Deborah Drechsler, Valerie Jaworski, Ann Repplier, Katherine Kobayashi, and Ardis Cameron will find in these pages the values that have kept the cords of friendship close about us for so long. This wish also extends to Marcus Rediker, who has participated in every phase of this project. That the book and the friendship prospered through recurring rounds of criticism is testimony to his commitment to both.

Research for the book was facilitated by many archivists, librarians, and interested Rochesterians, including those at Haviland Records

Room, New York, Presbyterian Historical Society, Philadelphia, Rochester Public Library, and at the Central Presbyterian, St. Luke's Episcopal, First Unitarian, and Asbury First United Methodist churches. I also appreciate the assistance of Mrs. Thomas Gosnell, who not only allowed me access to the Rochester Female Charitable Society Papers in her home but also supplied me with many glasses of lemonade while I worked on them. Fellowships from the University of Pennsylvania and the Woodrow Wilson Foundation allowed me to spend many additional hours pursuing such documents. Much time was spent at the University of Rochester Rare Books and Manuscripts Room, where an enthusiastic staff and comfortable working conditions made research pure pleasure. Mary Huth, in particular, flawlessly guided me through existing collections and continually unearthed new ones. My trips to Rochester were always enriched by her interest, her knowledge, and her dinner invitations.

The development of this book was aided by many. Ann Firor Scott and Ellen DuBois read the entire manuscript: I thank them for their incisive criticisms, which were generous not only in number but in tone. The staff of Cornell University Press minimized the trauma of completing this project. Lawrence Malley, my editor, encouraged me to do more and do it better and faster than I thought possible. Carol Betsch, through her copyediting skills, contributed greatly to my meeting these expectations. So too did Robert Ingalls of the University of South Florida, who by easing my transition from graduate student to faculty member enabled me to concentrate on research and writing. To the staff of USF's Word Processing Center—Michael Copeland, Gregg Gronlund, Robin Kester, Cecile Pulin, and, especially, Marian Pittman—I am grateful for bringing laughter as well as skill to the typing and retyping of the manuscript. The members of the history department, faculty and staff, and of the Lust for Theory study group also offered essential motivation and assistance.

A few individuals, despite my recent arrival in Tampa, provided support comparable to that of lifelong friends. Etta Bender Breit, Marilyn Myerson, and Barbara Ogur have demonstrated time and again that sisterhood is still powerful: they have offered collective sustenance while crediting me alone with each achievement. Louis Pérez has alternately nudged and nurtured me into being a better scholar. His ability to combine political commitment and scholarly excellence renews my faith in the vision of history I conceived a decade ago. My deepest thanks go to Steven Lawson, who has sustained me through crises both personal and intellectual. Through his generosity, his humor, his counsel, and his empathy, he has shown me what a real *mensch* is.

Finally, I thank my family—my grandmothers for their perseverance and their love; my brothers Will and Tom for believing in me and treating me as an equal; and my parents for instilling in me respect for the past and for the abilities of women.

NANCY A. HEWITT

Tampa, Florida

Abbreviations

AKPF	Abby Kelley Foster Papers, American Antiquarian Society, Worcester, Massachusetts
BFFP	Benjamin Fish Family Papers, University of Rochester, Rochester, New York
CGFP	Charles Grandison Finney Papers, Oberlin College Archives, Oberlin, Ohio
CS	Rochester Female Charitable Society
CSP	Rochester Female Charitable Society Papers, University of Rochester, Rochester, New York
FASS	Rochester Female Anti-Slavery Society
FHP	Rochester Friendly Home Papers, University of Rochester, Rochester, New York
FMRS	Rochester Female Moral Reform Society
GSP	Gerrit Smith Papers, Gerrit Smith Collection, George Arents Research Library for Special Collections, Syracuse University, Syracuse, New York
GYMWF	Genesee Yearly Meeting of Women Friends
HCCP	Hillside Children's Center Papers, University of Rochester, Rochester, New York
HF	Home for Friendless and Virtuous Females
HRR	Haviland Records Room, New York, New York
IAPFP	Isaac and Amy Post Family Papers, University of Rochester, Rochester, New York
IS	Industrial School
JHF	*Journal of the Home*
LASS	Rochester Ladies' Anti-Slavery Society
LWTAS	Ladies' Washingtonian Total Abstinence Society
NYSWTS	New York State Women's Temperance Society
OAA	Rochester Orphan Asylum Association
PPWP	Phebe Post Willis Papers, University of Rochester, Rochester, New York

SAS	Soldier's Aid Society
SDPFP	Samuel Drummond Porter Family Papers, University of Rochester, Rochester, New York
WHSP	William Henry Seward Papers, University of Rochester, Rochester, New York
WNYASS	Western New York Anti-Slavery Society
WPU	Working Women's Protective Union
WTA	Women's Taxpayers Association
YMCF	Yearly Meeting of Congregational Friends

WOMEN'S ACTIVISM
AND SOCIAL CHANGE

Introduction

In 1822 fourteen women met at the home of Mrs. Everard Peck in the new village of Rochesterville and formed the Female Charitable Society to aid the "sick poor." Envisioning themselves as community caretakers and sources of social stability, they signified the entry of women into organized civic activity in this western New York community. Fifty years later Susan B. Anthony led fourteen friends and kinswomen to a local newstand, Rochester's eighth ward registry, to vote. Confronting one of the most formidable barriers to women's public influence and authority, these women announced the entry of their sex into national electoral politics. In the half century separating these events, thousands of women in Rochester as elsewhere joined in a vast array of campaigns to ameliorate social ills and gain civil and political rights for themselves and others. They performed these myriad public labors at a time when the segregation of the sexes supposedly heightened as well as tightened the bonds of womanhood. Yet relations among Rochester's female activists were characterized as often by sibling rivalry as by sisterhood. Where members of the Female Charitable Society were pleased to be described as "almoners of Heaven" working "noiselessly, economically, and consistently," a woman's rights advocate was proud that a man "should know [she] was from the Gennesee [*sic*]" by her "too strong" opinions.[1] Between 1822 and 1872

[1] *Rochester Telegraph,* 4 March 1823; CS, Minute Book, 1 March 1859, CSP; Ann Pound to Amy and Isaac Post, [1840], IAPFP.

Female activists also differed in the forms by which they wished to be addressed, particularly in the use of titles of marital status. I employ as far as practicable the forms of names—Mrs. Everard Peck, Susan B. Anthony, Amy Post—that appeared in organizational records and published reports.

women in these two movements as well as those in many others vied for leadership in the cause of social change.

Historians of nineteenth-century women have generally been more attentive to struggles between the sexes than to those among women themselves. They have also been more attentive to the private than the public sphere. While recognizing the achievements of a few publicly prominent women reformers and the large network of female societies that supported their efforts, historians of women, particularly those studying the decades before the Civil War, have focused the greatest attention on female experience within the domestic arena. These historians have claimed that the defining characteristic of that experience in Greater New England was the separation of men's and women's spheres. In the colonial era, shortages of women and of labor, the small scale of community life, and the frontier environment temporarily blurred the lines between public and private and male and female domains. But in the first half of the nineteenth century, men once again firmly grasped the reigns of public economic and political power while simultaneously cloaking women in a mantle of spiritual and moral guardianship that was rhetorically expansive but pragmatically restrictive. Viewing early nineteenth-century women as increasingly relegated to home and church and the domains themselves as increasingly relegated to the periphery of social power and authority, women's historians have elaborated women's private lives in fine detail. The tenets of "true womanhood"—piety, purity, domesticity, and submissiveness—which accompanied the privatization of female experience were initially interpreted as signs of woman's defeat at the hands of the Jacksonian era's "true man," who was aggressive, virile, competitive, and domineering. Gradually, however, true womanhood was recast as a source of female bonding and strength, and sorority was added to the list of mid-nineteenth-century woman's virtues.[2] Scholars, faced with the problem of explaining the nearly simultaneous but seemingly contradictory emergence of "true womanhood" and women's public activism, then devised an intricate argument to account for the

[2]On the definition of woman's proper role, see Barbara Welter, "The Cult of True Womanhood, 1820–1860," *American Quarterly* 18 (Summer 1966): 151–66, 171–74, and Ann Douglas, *The Feminization of American Culture* (New York: Knopf, 1977). On female bonding, see Carroll Smith-Rosenberg, "The Female World of Love and Ritual: Relations between Women in Nineteenth-Century America," *Signs* 1 (Autumn 1975): 1–29, and Nancy Cott, *The Bonds of Womanhood: "Woman's Sphere" in New England, 1780–1835* (New Haven: Yale University Press, 1977).

transformation of pious, pure, domestic, submissive, and sororal women into social, and specifically feminist, activists by 1848.

According to the now widely accepted scenario, women's path to public prominence began at the hearth of the privatized family and the altar of religious revivalism. Within the family, women became inculcated with a sense of their moral superiority, while the churches, to which they flocked in far larger numbers than their male kin, assured them of their spiritual superiority. The forces that pushed women into domesticity also gave birth to increasingly visible social ills—poverty, crime, delinquency, intemperance, prostitution, and vagrancy. When evangelical ministers of the 1820s and 1830s began citing irreligion and materialism, both fostered by male-dominated economic and political institutions, as the causes of such problems, they inspired women's entrance into the public realm. Inspiration was translated into action as the tenets of the Second Great Awakening spread across the country, demanding that all Christians apply their material and moral resources to public ills. Initially concerned only with ameliorating the plight of the old, the ill, the orphaned, and the destitute, urban women became the bearers of prayers for the profligate and alms for the poor. They soon discovered deeper and more extensive social problems, however, and gradually expanded their sphere of activity. Seemingly without economic or political power and therfore armed only with humanitarian motives, women moved beyond the confines of local charity to seek the universal abolition of vice, intemperance, and slavery. It was in these pursuits that women encountered debilitating barriers to their efforts based on the very femaleness that inspired their public labors. Some women were thereby led to initiate campaigns for their own social and political rights. The historical image thus emerges of a relatively homogeneous body of women—white, middle class, Yankee, urban, and evangelical—who left their private havens to purify the world under the banner of revivalism: they followed a lengthy, sometimes circuitous, but essentially singular path from benevolent associations through moral reform crusades to woman's rights campaigns.[3] At

[3]On the emergence of women activists from the privatized family via evangelical religion, see Cott, *Bonds of Womanhood;* Keither Melder, *The Beginnings of Sisterhood: The Women's Rights Movement in the United States, 1800–1840* (New York: Schocken, 1977); Carroll Smith-Rosenberg, *Religion and the Rise of the City: The New York City Mission Movement, 1812–1870* (Ithaca: Cornell University Press, 1971); Blanche Glassman Hersh, *The Slavery of Sex: Feminist-Abolitionism in America* (Chicago: University of Illinois Press, 1978); Barbara Berg, *The Remembered Gate: The Origins of American*

each step, even when demanding certain forms of equality with men, women activists confronted the masculine values of material progress with the feminine tenets of moral perfection.

This interpretation has provoked few challenges. First, it attests to the success of male-directed economic and political expansionism even while illuminating the seamy underside of the process. Second, it affirms women's collective strength in preserving both personal identity and moral values through the espousal of female virtues. Third, it bears witness to the dynamism of the urban environment as providing the necessary preconditions for progressive politics. Thus it simultaneously appeals to urbane modernization theorists and feminist scholars. Two historians, Ellen DuBois and Mary P. Ryan, have questioned significant aspects of the scenario. DuBois claims that the woman's rights advocates of the pre–Civil War era were a distinct group within the plethora of women reformers because they alone challenged the right of men to control the most powerful of all public domains, politics. Yet, while arguing that the woman's rights program was distinct, DuBois assumes that the program's advocates shared the Yankee, urban, evangelical heritage of their sister activists and that they similarly confronted men across the chasm of separate spheres.[4] Ryan alone argues that men and women did not occupy wholly separate spheres and that they did work together, particularly for familial and economic goals. In her study of Oneida County, New York, she details how men and women of the emerging urban bourgeoisie joined their efforts and devised family strategies to achieve material success, strategies that embraced Christian morality—sobriety, honesty, and faithfulness—as one means to upward mobility. Nevertheless, Ryan sees middle-class women as only temporary voyagers in the public pursuit of material and moral progress. She claims that "new domestic values, practices, and functions" were "incubated" in the public voluntary associations of the 1830s and 1840s, but that "the veterans of the reform era and their progeny" soon withdrew into "the conjugal family," which in the industrial age "itself became the cradle of middle-class individuals."[5]

Feminism, the Woman and the City, 1800–1860 (New York: Oxford University Press, 1978).

[4] Ellen DuBois, *Feminism and Suffrage: The Emergence of an Independent Women's Movement in America, 1848–1869* (Ithaca: Cornell University Press, 1978).

[5] Mary P. Ryan, *The Cradle of the Middle-Class: The Family in Oneida County, New York, 1780–1865* (Cambridge: Cambridge University Press, 1981), pp. 238–39.

To evaluate the dominant thesis and its challengers, I explore here three aspects of women's activism: the extensiveness, permanence, and position of women's public labors within larger processes of social, political, and economic change; the extent to which women activists identified with or challenged men of their own social and economic circles; and the social and economic characteristics of various groups of women activists and their relations to the forms of activism pursued. These concerns can be analyzed best in a community setting: here one can capture the localized character of mid-nineteenth-century women's activism and can explore the finite links among ideological prescriptions about female behavior, the social and economic circumstances of women's daily lives, and the translation of both into public forms.

Rochester, New York, is an ideal location for such an inquiry. The city embodied economic, social, and political transformations that swept across the country in the first half of the nineteenth century. It was a burgeoning commercial center at the hub of an increasingly specialized agricultural hinterland and the fastest-growing boom town in the nation between 1825 and 1835.[6] With the opening of the Erie Canal in 1822, Rochester became a depot for goods, for people, and for social and political movements as they traveled between eastern urban centers and frontier communities. At the heart of the Burned-over District, the town was illuminated (or ravaged, depending on one's perspective) by the fires of religious and reform enthusiasms in each of the decades from 1830 to 1870.

These changes reordered women's worlds in the nineteenth century, replacing eighteenth-century dependencies—embodied in extended kin groups, informal networks of community control and welfare, and the family as the locus of men's and women's labors—with more highly structured, stratified, and segregated social formations. In Rochester, these changes nurtured a varied and vital community of women reformers. Evangelical, Quaker, and Unitarian; affluent, upwardly mobile, and marginally middle-class; married and single; pioneer and

[6]On Rochester's early history, see Whitney Cross, *The Burned-over District: The Social and Intellectual History of Enthusiastic Religion in Western New York, 1800–1850* (Ithaca: Cornell University Press, 1950); Blake McKelvey, *Rochester: The Water-Power City, 1812–1854* (Cambridge: Harvard University Press, 1945); Paul Johnson, *A Shopkeeper's Millennium: Society and Revivals in Rochester, New York, 1815–1837* (New York: Hill and Wang, 1978); and James McElroy, "Social Control and Romantic Reform in Antebellum America: The Case of Rochester, New York," *New York History* 58 (January 1977): 17–46.

newcomer: Rochester women activists represented a wide range of social experiences and voiced a wide range of responses to social change. Not even poor white or free black women were entirely excluded from reform activities. Through more than a dozen associations and movements, Rochester women addressed the disruptive influences of geographic mobility, technological change, and urban growth; the physical, economic, and moral vulnerability of nineteenth-century women; and the place of women, family, and church in the changing social order.

Because social change, social activism, and women's activism converged in particularly vivid forms in mid-nineteenth-century Rochester, patterns are visible here that are obscured in quieter towns or in national surveys. Those patterns, forged in the material glow and spiritual fires of the Burned-over District, challenge many of historians' previous arguments about the relations between the changing parameters and experiences of women's lives and their entry into social movements. Rochester women activists emerged in a community where the segregation of work and home, public and private life, and men's and women's spheres was incomplete. They emerged at the junction of, rather than bridged a gap between, these spheres. They entered public associational activities, as founders of the Female Charitable Society in 1822, eight years before the local arrival of the Second Great Awakening, and justified their activities as often in secular as in spiritual terms. Moreover, a significant minority of local women activists forged their tactics and goals in agrarian rather than urban environments, extended their voluntary associations and labors into rural communities, and allied themselves with congregations that ignored or opposed revivalistic preachings and techniques.

Finally, Rochester women did not follow a straight or singular path from benevolent work through evangelicalism and abolition to woman's rights. Rather, three self-consciously competing networks of women activists followed three different paths. Women of each network proclaimed themselves the directors of the forces of social change in tandem with men of their own economic, social, and family circles and in opposition to women and men of competing circles. The women in these three networks did share some broadly defined characteristics: they were predominantly white, Protestant, and middle class and pursued activism in addition to rather than as a substitute for familial and domestic duties. Yet within this broadly defined typology of the woman activist, differences in material resources, ties to local political power, alliances with white men, free blacks, or working-class women, and denominational affiliation shaped distinct forms and styles of activism. In each case, these distinctions separated women activists from each other more rigidly than distinctions in spheres separated them from male kith and kin. Women did play sex-specific roles within the public realm based on their exclusion from economic independence and political authority, but the direction of material and moral progress would be decided not by a battle between the sexes over these roles but by a struggle among various segments of the new urban middle classes for economic and political domination. In the process, divisions among women would become more sharply defined; more women would become publicly active; and contention over women's proper public role would eclipse contention over the right of women to any public role.

[1]

Material and Moral Progress

In the mid-1840s British traveler Alexander McKay declared, "There is no other town in America the history of which better illustrates the rapid rise of material and moral progress in the United States than that of the city of Rochester."[1] While McKay apparently saw material and moral progress moving in tandem, most of Rochester's resident nineteenth-century chroniclers placed primary emphasis on the former. Growth in population, flour milling profits, and canal tonnage were the key indices of boom-town success. In the 1827 village directory, editor Elisha Ely claimed that the opening of the Erie Canal "together with the vast waterpower [of the Genesee River] conspire to give the village its commanding position for trade . . . as well as manufactures."[2] The village's hinterland, settled a decade or more before the village itself, already held a commanding position in agriculture, and it was the commercialization of this farming district that gave Rochester its financial supremacy in the pre–Civil War decades.

Pioneer Rochesterians constructed flour mills, warehouses, docks, and banks along the Genesee to which their country cousins delivered wheat, apples, vegetables, wool, hides, and lumber for processing. Barrels of flour shipped from the city's port were the clearest index of local prosperity in the early years and their numbers multiplied rapidly. In 1816, 26,000 barrels of flour left the Genesee port and that amount more than doubled by 1820. But it was the completion of the Erie

[1] Quoted in Blake McKelvey, *Rochester: The Water-Power City, 1812–1854* (Cambridge: Harvard University Press, 1945), p. vii.
[2] *A Directory for the Village of Rochester* (Rochester: Elisha Ely and Everard Peck, 1827), p. 86.

Canal, in 1822 to Rochester and 1825 to Buffalo, that created the most dramatic increase in local prospects. By 1831 local merchant-millers manufactured some 240,000 barrels of flour; four years later, twenty-one mills demanded 20,000 bushels of wheat a day to maintain their five-thousand-barrel capacity.[3]

Prosperity brought people, and New Englanders especially flocked to the falls of Rochesterville. By 1825 the village had some twenty-five hundred inhabitants; in the next decade, it gained another ten thousand, making it the fastest growing urban area in the country. Moreover, as many people moved through Rochester as to it. Directories became historical documents almost before they were off the press. Seventy percent of those who appeared in Ely's first village listing of 1827 had moved on when a second directory, containing the new city charter, was printed in 1834. The pace slowed, but only slightly, between 1838 and 1844 when 60 percent of the residents left town, and the city must have seemed almost static when it lost only half of its inhabitants in the five years before mid-century.[4] Despite the rapid appearance and disappearance of settlers, Rochester contained over thirty-six thousand citizens by 1850.

Rochester first attracted farmers, merchants, shopkeepers, and artisans rather than factory owners or their employees since the Genesee falls were quickly monopolized by millers who required agricultural products and commercial services but few laborers. Paper mills, woolen and cotton factories, tanneries and boot and shoe workshops appeared in these same years. Only the last, however, maintained a continuous foothold in the village, and most work for enterprises such as the Gould Boot and Shoe Factory was contracted on a piecework basis to women and children.[5] Farm labor and construction work kept itinerant males employed and gave men with few means a chance to gain a stake in the new community. The building of the Erie Canal increased demands for manual workers, providing both casual laborers and commercial speculators with new opportunities.

[3] Neil Adams McNall, *An Agricultural History of the Genessee Valley, 1790–1860* (Philadelphia: University of Pennsylvania Press, 1952), pp. 119–120.
[4] McKelvey, *Rochester*, pp. 165, 229. Rochesterville was the original name given to the settlement by its proprietors, three gentlemen from Maryland led by Nathaniel Rochester. While the proprietors brought many family members from Maryland with them to settle in the village, the predominant group of villagers came from New England and eastern New York. The dates for the mobility figures are based on the publication of city directories; the statistical analysis of these directories is from McKelvey, noted above.
[5] Ibid., pp. 87–90.

The route of the Erie Canal also determined the fate of hinterland communities. Canandaigua to the south was settled long before Rochester, and its leading men assumed the canal would pass their way. Rochester's lobbyists in the state capital prevailed, however, and the more northern route was selected. As a result, those towns surrounding Rochester—Greece, Henrietta, Perinton, Spencerport, Brockport, Gates, and others—made rapid advances toward commercialization of farming in the decade after the canal's completion. Meanwhile, those villages to the south—Darien, Bath, Lima, Bloomfield, and Farmington—retained the family farms of earlier eras, being too distant to profit from the Genesee River and Erie Canal crossroads. Canandaigua remained a genteel country town and central New York was dotted with sleepy villages while Rochester continued on its boomtown path, carrying neighboring communities with it.

In lobbying for the canal's passage through the village and throughout the boom-town era, city fathers, local politicians, and editors along with travelers and clergymen extolled the virtues of the Flour City. Elisha Ely was one of the many who seemed most impressed by "its superabundant wealth." Yet he also praised "the scenes of intellectual and moral felicity" played out "in the homes of its present and enlightened occupants."[6] Bureau of Indian Affairs chief Thomas L. McKenney passed through Rochester on his way west in 1826 and pronounced it "a wonderful town" with "some of the finest and most commodious public houses; an eye and ear institute; a bank; *six* churches, Episcopalian, Presbyterian, Methodist, Quaker, and Catholic; a court house and jail; and public baths! . . . [and] extraordinary pretensions" to being a full-fledged city.[7] On Thanksgiving Day 1828, Presbyterians flocked to the Third Church of that denomination in the city to hear Rev. Joel Parker celebrate "The Signs of the Times." He began by announcing that "God designs *especially* to bless us" and then detailed the cultural, economic, and political advances of the region. Parker was particularly impressed with the "multiplication of labour-saving inventions," with the press, which poured "a flood of light upon the whole community," and with the great "increase of wealth" among the population.[8]

[6] *Directory for the Village,* 1827, p. 76.
[7] Thomas L. McKenney, *Sketches of a Tour to the Lakes,* excerpted in Dorothy Truesdale, "American Travel Accounts of Early Rochester," *Rochester History* 16 (1954): 8–9.
[8] Joel Parker, *The Signs of the Times: A Sermon, Delivered in Rochester, December 4, 1828, Being the Day of Publick Thanksgiving* (Rochester: Everard Peck, 1828), n.p.

The Reverend Mr. Parker admitted that sins did still exist, including slavery, intemperance, and freemasonry, yet he claimed they were "opposed by such a combination of moral means, as promises their utter extinction." Indeed, the very wealth of the community enabled "a host of good men to devote time, money, and influence to the advancement of sound morals and pure religion."[9] Most of Parker's parishioners nodded in agreement. The path to moral and religious improvement had been set in the 1810s by the leaders of First Presbyterian and St. Luke's Episcopal churches who had donated time and money to missions among the poor, intemperate, and ungodly. The problems of frontier life were known before settlement began, and neighbors were prepared to help neighbors survive brutal winters, crop failures, fires, the ague and other diseases, and plain bad luck. As the town grew, more and more unfamiliar faces peered out from newly constructed huts and shanties, and those who found fortune in Rochester began to provide more systematically for those who did not. Much of the aid was moral—Bibles and tracts were circulated freely, Sunday and charity schools were opened, and temperance societies flourished. Some material assistance was provided through the county alms house, opened in 1826, but in Rochester itself the only formal vehicle for relief was the Female Charitable Society. The benevolent women who established the society in 1822 went from house to house, seeking out the needy and providing them with medical care, food, clothing, and bedding. During the 1820s most Rochesterians applauded these efforts and believed them sufficient to alleviate the wants of those left behind by the town's success.

Yet a few citizens became more and more alarmed with what they viewed as the moral and spiritual deterioration of the village. To them, material and moral progress seemed increasingly antithetical, and it appeared that the latter was losing out to the former. In 1804 a Methodist lay preacher, John B. Hudson, had visited the Genesee frontier and was shocked to find "whiskey and Sabbath desecration . . . notoriously prevalent." The local inhabitants, he reported, were "certainly not noted for morality, and still less so in regard to religion."[10] Ely, McKenney, and Parker notwithstanding, there was abundant evidence that the region still contained the progeny of Hudson's acquaintances. Liquor licenses, nine-pin alleys, and billiard tables multiplied along with the

[9] Ibid.
[10] McKelvey, *Rochester*, pp. 26–27.

population; casual laborers and fly-by-night adventurers constantly crowded the city and quickly moved on; and boatmen and travelers added instability as well as excitement to the town.

Many families who entered Rochester in the mid-1820s, especially those who planned to settle permanently, found the opportunities more restricted and the dangers as prevalent as the pioneers. They praised the city's material progress but sided with those who feared its (im)moral correlates. To them, western New York appeared as "the Waterloo of the world" where "a mighty contest is commenced & must be carried on . . . untill [*sic*] the great interest of Zion shall triumph" over the evils of "the 'world, the flesh and the Devil.' "[11] Probing beneath the profits carried by canal boats, these Rochesterians found captains who dismissed "women from their boats in a state of pregnancy" and boy drivers who claimed they "might as well be sent to state prison as to the Canal."[12]

Concerned citizens first tried to impose order by economic boycott and legislative fiat. Headed by pioneer flour miller Josiah Bissell of Third Presbyterian Church, a Sabbatarian movement emerged in the late 1820s that fought to close the canal locks and stop the mails on Sunday and prohibit the sale of liquor on every day. Bissell founded the Pioneer packet line, whose boats would not ply the canal on the Sabbath and whose captains would only hire teetotaling workers. Yet the citizenry was not convinced. Some feared a loss of profits; others believed the dangers were not sufficient to warrant such extreme measures; a few argued on constitutional grounds for a separation of church and state; and many believed that stranded boatmen and travelers would flock to the city on Sundays to "drink grog and court Venus."[13] Unsuccessful in gaining significant community support in these endeavors, Bissell and his coconspirators pleaded for help from Charles Grandison Finney. They succeeded in bringing the fledgling Evangelist to the youthful city, and where economic and political pressures had failed, Finney prevailed. His revivals rocked the city and brought hundreds of new converts into the churches. Daily sermons, prayer circles, and protracted meetings brought business to a near

[11] Josiah Bissell to Charles G. Finney, 15 September 1829, Microfilm, Roll 2 and James K. Livingston to Charles G. Finney, 7 December 1832, Roll 3, CGFP.

[12] Josiah Bissell to Charles G. Finney, 15 September 1829, Roll 2, CGFP.

[13] Paul Johnson, *A Shopkeeper's Millennium: Society and Revivals in Rochester, New York, 1815–1837* (New York: Hill and Wang, 1978), p. 84; on the Sabbatarian movement generally, see pp. 83–88.

standstill; economic and political strife were suspended; temperance became a symbol of salvation; and "a new impulse was given to every philanthropic enterprise."[14]

Finney's revivals were long remembered in Rochester, and the convergence of sin, confession, and rebirth provided endless small dramas for recounting by local conversationalists and chroniclers. Yet the fires of revivalism burned brightly for only a brief time, while the problem of sustaining both material and moral progress reemerged quickly. Those people most affected by the revivals included many from the new commercial classes, particularly those who were second-generation settlers and thus the most firmly gripped by the uncertainties of a boom-town economy.[15] While the connections were complex and not always self-conscious, men and women in this sector of society assumed there to be a certain resonance between gaining spiritual and moral control of themselves and gaining economic and social control in the larger community. Thus as the flush of revival faded, they sought new ways to institutionalize the evangelical tenets of industry, honesty, sobriety, and moderation in their own lives and those of their neighbors. Combining associational models developed before Finney's arrival with a new zeal for perfection, the converts of 1830 initiated campaigns for the abolition of vice, intemperance, and slavery and extended earlier efforts to provide for the ill, the uneducated, and the unconverted. Men's tract, temperance, moral reform, and antislavery societies flourished in the early 1830s, limited only by the multiple demands of business, family, and social service. The female kin of these activists joined evangelical efforts more slowly. They were urged by fathers, husbands, and clergy to form maternal associations and prayer circles, and they followed their female predecessors into benevolent works, but their role in the great moral campaigns of the day was unclear.

Throughout the Northeast the development of commercial and industrial centers was accompanied by revivalism, reform movements, the growth of voluntary associations, and the redefinition of women's roles. Poorer women and farmers' daughters whose hands were idle

[14] Susan Marie Ogden-Malouf, "American Revivalism and Temperance Drama: Evangelical Protestant Ritual and Theatre in Rochester, New York, 1830–1845," (Ph.D. diss., Northwestern University, 1981), p. 146. Quote is by Finney convert, Rev. Charles Bush. For general coverage of Finney's revival, see pp. 99–109 and below, Chapter 4.

[15] Johnson, *Shopkeeper's Millennium*, pp. 102–115.

were encouraged to leave home and boost the nation's manufacturing potential by entering the ranks of industrial workers. Simultaneously, women of middling or affluent circumstances, especially once they were married, were cautioned to remain within the home circle, devoting their energies to providing a haven for world-weary husbands and sons.[16] This latter role was not entirely new. The first book published in Rochester, for instance, was an old England and New England favorite from the 1790s, William Kenrick's *Whole Duty of Woman*.[17] Its alphabetical listing of attributes and advice counseled women to be modest, pious, chaste, industrious, frugal, and submissive. After one hundred pages of aphorisms, Kenrick summed up his wisdom with poetic aplomb: "Seek to be good, but aim not to be great/A woman's noblest station is retreat:/Her fairest virtues fly from sight,/Domestic worth still shuns too strong a light."[18] What was new was the proliferation of literature demanding in ever more florid and fervent phrases women's adoption of the pious, pure, domestic, and submissive tenets of this cult of true womanhood.[19]

The Erie Canal brought literally tons of sentimental novels, popular magazines, advice books, and spiritual publications to the doors of Rochesterians. This literature was sold in the village's finest bookshops, including those of Everard Peck, who printed the local edition of Kenrick's work in 1819, and Edwin Scrantom, who entered his name among the publishers of popular magazines for ladies in 1829. The *Rochester Gem and Ladies Amulet* combined excerpts from sermons, romantic poetry, moral tales, domestic advice, literary reviews, and local news. Scrantom advocated companionship in marriage and promoted temperance and abolition. He was a strong supporter of Finney's labors in Rochester and a believer in woman's natural spiritual superiority. Nonetheless, he sided with women's use of private influence over public authority and concluded that the weaker sex's place was in the home. In the May 1832 issue, he counseled *"Married Ladies"* that their "peculiar" influence resulted from "their connexion and intercourse with their husbands and children." Although the man

---

[16]Gerda Lerner, "The Lady and the Mill Girl: Changes in the Status of Women in the Age of Jackson," *Mid-Continent American Studies Journal* 10 (Spring 1969): 5–15.

[17]William Kenrick, *The Whole Duty of Woman, To Which Is Added Edwin & Angelina, A Tale* (Rochester: Everard Peck, 1819).

[18]Ibid., "Vanity," p. 100.

[19]Barbara Welter, "The Cult of True Womanhood, 1820–1860," *American Quarterly* 18 (Summer 1966): 151–64, 171–74.

wore the "breeches," Scrantom assured his female audience that no husband could withstand a woman's arguments if she possessed "the usual charms of her sex"—"gentleness of manner, sweetness of disposition, and a well-cultivated mind."[20]

Mrs. Edwin Scrantom had joined the Female Charitable Society in 1822 as Miss Mary Ann Sibley. After her marriage, she continued her benevolent labors and, encouraged by revival zeal, joined her evangelical sisters in founding the Rochester Orphan Asylum Association. Yet Mrs. Scrantom never strayed far from the boundaries of benevolence. Her signature on an 1837 antislavery petition is the only sign that she contemplated a wider public role for women. Hundreds of her female neighbors left similar evidences of such contemplations, but only a few, generally the most devoted Finney converts, ventured to form antislavery, moral reform, and temperance associations. Like their male counterparts, though several years later, these women advocated the eradication rather than amelioration of the vices they fought. They linked themselves to national campaigns and parent associations in New York City and Boston and distributed petitions, pledges, and reform journals published in these eastern urban centers.

The extralocal resources that reinforced female Finneyites' entrance into a larger public sphere revealed a shift among Rochesterians to a more cosmopolitan perspective. Assured that their new home was permanent, local citizens began looking outward to keep their town in the flow of new social and cultural currents. Millers, shippers, and commercial agents had already developed trading networks that stretched across the state and into New England and the Midwest. Some of the most successful had brought the material perquisites of cosmopolitan life—carpets, drapes, tea services, china, and carriages—to the village in the first decades of settlement. Singers, lecturers, and other entertainers began putting Rochester on their tour routes in the 1820s. Quilting bees, tea parties, and visiting provided women with social forays outside their own households, as dances, weddings, and church socials brought them into contact with village men.[21] Although the vast majority of the town's citizens lived in four-room frame or even less substantial domiciles, wealthier families began moving into rather grand residences with two stories, front and back staircases, porches, a fur-

---

[20] *Rochester Gem and Ladies Amulet,* 26 May 1832. The *Gem* enjoyed widespread popularity in Rochester from 1829 to 1843, when it ceased publication.

[21] McKelvey, *Rochester,* pp. 136–39.

nace or Franklin stove, glass windows, and perhaps a piano, which could be rented in Rochester.[22]

Spiritual concerns may have slowed the pace of material accumulation in the early 1830s, but Rochester remained a whirlwind of activity with its face to the future, be that the millennium or mere earthly prosperity. In the late 1830s, however, extralocal influences brought an end to Rochester's boom years, making the underside of urban expansion suddenly visible. The Panic of 1837, the worst financial crisis to hit the young nation, did not affect Rochester seriously for nearly two years. From 1839 to 1842, though, economic gloom settled over the town. Rochester was not as hard hit as some cities, but several of the city's leading businessmen lost their fortunes, vast numbers of poorer folk were unemployed and unable to move farther west, and the common council was forced to provide aid to over three hundred families as the CS suffered serious setbacks in donations and membership.[23] Among those needing public relief, the vast majority were immigrants, and Rochesterians who already feared licentiousness, intemperance, and irreligion among the poor now saw those fears personified in the newly visible underclass of destitute foreigners.

Simultaneously, Rochesterians became more aware than ever of the eruption of debates in northeastern cities over women's public activities. Ministers, educators, physicians, and popular authors were shocked when Sarah and Angelina Grimké began speaking out against slavery in "promiscuous" assemblies of men and women, and reform associations themselves battled over the propriety of such behavior. The *Advocate of Moral Reform* and the *Liberator,* circulated in Rochester by female Finneyites, covered both sides of the debate while arguing for women's continued participation in public labors.[24] Among local clergy and male kin, arguments for women's withdrawal from worldly endeavors prevailed, however, and many withdrew their earlier support from women's participation in antislavery, moral reform, and temperance campaigns. At the same time, the deepening depression turned Rochesterians attention away from campaigns for the millennium and toward more mundane matters of protecting family finances. The return of Finney to Rochester in 1842 renewed evangel-

[22] Ibid., p. 202.
[23] Ibid., pp. 213–221.
[24] For examples, see *Advocate of Moral Reform,* 1 August 1836, 15 September 1836, 1 January 1837, 15 October 1837, and 15 December 1837; see *Liberator,* 2, 16, and 23 June 1837, 5 January 1838, 27 July 1838, 10 April 1839, 22 May 1840, and 17 November 1842.

ical enthusiasm just as the economic cloud began to lift, convincing many that spiritual salvation was vital to economic prosperity. Nevertheless, even evangelical converts focused less on universal perfection than on personal and familial devotions. Moreover, Finney himself made it clear that he now saw woman's role in primarily domestic and maternal rather than public terms.[25] Some women refused to comply with the call to retreat, pursuing moral reform and temperance campaigns into the 1840s. Only benevolent women in the CS and the OAA were able to gain sustained and substantial support from the community, however, as the recession ebbed.

Not all of Rochester's downtrodden and poor citizens awaited relief from above. Immigrants turned to the church for support, Germans to the Lutherans and Irish to the Catholics. Free blacks, of which there were a few hundred in the city, also organized on their own behalf and to aid their enslaved brothers and sisters in the South. They protested against colonization schemes, formed an African Methodist Episcopal Zion Church, aided fugitive communities north of the border, and established a free school for black children. Although they were the most successful when they were assisted by wealthier white abolitionists, Rochester's black residents initiated numerous programs to help themselves.[26] Workers also formed associations to promote their own interests; joiners, carpenters, and cordwainers organized unions, and other journeymen formed libraries and mutual aid societies. In 1844 a "Women's Sewing Association" first brought women into the public domain on their own behalf. Comprised of "about thirty widows, who make their living plying the needle," the society sought "to protect themselves from the rapacity of employers" by opening a shop for the sale of their own goods.[27]

Rochester was no longer a frontier village, a homogeneous community where face-to-face encounters could resolve political as well as personal disputes and where neighborliness was sufficient to meet any

[25] Carroll Smith-Rosenberg and Nancy Hewitt, "The Cross and the Pedestal: The Perimeters of Women's Power in American Religion," paper presented at the Charles Grandison Finney Sesquicentennial Conference, 13 October 1981, Rochester, New York.

[26] On efforts of free blacks in Rochester, see Howard W. Coles, *The Cradle of Freedom: A History of the Negro in Rochester, Western New York, and Canada* (Rochester: Oxford Press, 1941), pp. 20–28, 45, 77–83, 97, 127–138; and *Liberator,* 3 September 1831, 29 October 1831, 8 March 1834, 30 April 1834, and 25 August 1837.

[27] *Liberator,* 19 April 1844 on Women's Sewing Association. On general developments in local labor organization, see Alan H. Gleason, "A History of Labor in Rochester, 1820–1880" (Master's thesis, University of Rochester, 1941).

crisis. The churches and charitable societies could no longer reach all the needy, nor could revivals and reform associations reach all the unconverted. Moreover, problems such as slavery had no local solution but nevertheless commanded the attention of local citizens. Yet the continuation and expansion of ameliorative and reform efforts were encouraged as prosperity returned to a few and beckoned to many.

The restoration of community order after the Panic of 1837 seemed both possible and essential to local elites. Those who lost Greek Revival homesteads in the early 1840s built Gothic Revival– and Queen Anne–style mansions at the end of the decade.[28] As business once again boomed, the children of the pioneers began weaving a web of marital ties that bound the elite ever more tightly together. Eastern furniture, foods, and clothing became more prevalent in local shops, *Godey's Lady Book* and *Peterson's Magazine* appeared more regularly on the glass-topped tables of the affluent, and foreign travelers like Alexander McKay reinforced Rochesterians' own vision of their present prosperity and future prospects.[29]

The mobility, vibrancy, and adventure of the early settlement period had slowed somewhat and even many evangelical enthusiasts no longer viewed western New York as the Waterloo of the world. Men in these upwardly mobile families turned increasingly to legislative means of asserting moral control, and they gained far more adherents than the Sabbatarians of the 1820s. Their female kin gradually carved out roles for themselves in the public domain by adopting benevolent models of activity or forming women's auxiliaries to support husbands' campaigns. Thus by mid-century the cult of true womanhood and the ideology of separate spheres for men and women, which had seemed to relegate women to a wholly private domain, had been modified. Among middling and affluent families, men's and women's roles were distinct, but both were allowed to perform public services fitting their different natures. Indeed, the bonds between men and women of the same family and social circles were strengthened as each sex was assured that only through a partnership with the other could all familial and community needs be met.

The signs of maturity among the elite and stability among the emerging bourgeoisie that so impressed McKay formed only part of the pic-

[28]Martha Montague Ash, "The Social and Domestic Scene in Rochester, 1840–1860," *Rochester History* 18 (1956): 1, 7.
[29]Ibid., 1–2.

ture, however. Benevolent ladies carrying alms to the poor encountered increased numbers of intemperate and dissolute characters who seemed unworthy of charity. Female Finneyites, having abandoned campaigns to eradicate social evils did not therefore deny the existence of those ills. The moral reformers who established the Home for Friendless and Virtuous Females, for instance, believed that without such a refuge, women without friends and family in the city would be subject to "the snares [of] the designing" and the advances of villainous men.[30] These same men were pointed to as the perpetrators of an increasing number and variety of crimes, including robberies, assaults, and even a murder or two. Immigrants flooded the city in ever larger numbers, increasing the proportion of the poor and the working classes in the city's population and raising further the middling classes' fears of a city bogged down in destitution, crime, moral turpitude, and ungodliness (or Catholicism, which some citizens considered little better).[31] Laborers, especially the more skilled and educated, continued to organize on their own behalf and, though they rarely sustained association beyond a single grievance or strike, they were clearly gaining experience in this field. Finally, within the midst of the middle class itself, movements were afoot to overthrow the existing order of society.

Rochester had always had its share of antiestablishment leaders. Obadiah Dogberry began publishing the *Liberal Advocate* in Rochester in 1832 to denounce revivalism and its attendant "sectarian dogma and prejudice."[32] The evangelical press, led by the *Observer* and the *Genesee Evangelist*, seemed more concerned with the circulation of tracts by Robert Owen and Fanny Wright than the vituperous outpourings of Dogberry.[33] The "disciples of Tom Paine packed the Court House in 1828" to cheer on Benjamin Offen, the New York shoemaker-deist, in his debate with a local Methodist preacher.[34] Freethinkers, "Friends of a Free and Liberal Conscience," "Friends of Liberal Principles," deists, Universalists, Millerites, Mormons, and spiritualists all appeared within Rochester's borders, proclaimed their doctrines, and attracted various and sundry followers for a time. Some of these groups faded; others moved west; and a few sustained small coteries of

[30] *Daily Democrat* (Rochester), 12 April 1851.
[31] On anti-Catholic sentiments as they affected women's activism, see Chapter 5 below.
[32] *Liberal Advocate*, 23 February 1832.
[33] McKelvey, *Rochester*, pp. 196–97.
[34] Ibid., p. 131.

followers in the city. Not until the early 1840s, however, did a group of grassroots radicals emerge who would reshape community attitudes by sustaining their critiques of society over an extended period. Beginning with the reformation of their own religious meetings, this circle of Hicksite Quaker farming and shopkeeping families initiated campaigns for the abolition of slavery, for prison reform, Indian rights, coeducation, the integration of the public schools, land reform, spiritualism, and woman's rights. By mid-century they had withdrawn from Quaker meetings to pursue the reorganization of society as a whole.

Women as well as men joined these ventures and, although they never gained broad support in Rochester, they kept issues of race relations, economic reform, and sexual equality before the public for three decades. Settled at the bottom rungs of the city's new middle class, they challenged their more affluent neighbors to consider and respond to the problems they raised while encouraging those below them—free blacks and working men and women—to organize themselves. Rochester's Quaker radicals also brought extralocal influences to bear on the community. Seeking neither the material accoutrements of cosmopolitan life nor the moral culture adopted from eastern urban centers by bourgeois evangelicals, the city's newest activists brought political education to their fellow and sister citizens from Boston, New York City, and Philadelphia. William Lloyd Garrison, Abby Kelley, Frederick Douglass, Lucretia Mott, Elizabeth Cady Stanton, Sojourner Truth, John Brown, Wendell Phillips, Ernestine Rose, and other advocates of racial and sexual equality and kindred concerns were beckoned to the city by these Quaker emigrants to western New York. Rochester hosted more antislavery, woman's rights, dress reform, and spiritualist conventions and rallies than did neighboring cities, primarily as a result of the migratory patterns of some two dozen Hicksite families, and local citizens took note, be it in honorific or horrorific tones.

After mid-century, Rochester would grow more slowly. It would become further entwined in regional and national economic and political networks. It would be revisited periodically by revivals and recessions. Larger numbers of its citizens would be foreign-born and working class. These new settlers would live in more segregated neighborhoods and only rarely venture into the third ward that housed the city's elite. The affluent still sought out those they considered worthy among the poor and offered them relief, primarily through the offices of

benevolent ladies. The new middle class continued campaigns to alleviate the worst sins of urban growth and spread evangelical doctrines
throughout the community while attempting to legislate morality for
those who refused moral precepts. These evangelical reformers would
be constantly challenged to seek more fundamental changes by a small
circle of men and women who themselves sought to reconstruct in the
larger world the egalitarian bonds of community left behind in Quaker
farming villages.

In 1827 Elisha Ely had sat at his editorial desk in a frontier village of
eight thousand and pondered the future: "We look forward to this place
at some distant day as a flourishing city," he wrote, "flourishing not
merely in wealth and power, but in knowledge and virtue, an honour
and a blessing to sister cities around, and the home of a great people,
enlightened and happy."[35] In the 1840s McKay suggested that
Rochesterians had attained the future envisioned by Ely. On into the
1870s the city would remain the home of wealth and power. Whether it
made equal progress in virtue and honor, whether its citizens were
sufficiently happy and enlightened would continue to be contested,
however—not only by workers, free blacks, and immigrants but also
by various segments within the city's middling and affluent circles.
Both in the amelioration and reform of Rochester's problems and in the
contest among pioneer elites, bourgeois evangelicals, and agrarian
Quaker radicals, women would play crucial roles. They would reach
beyond their families, their churches, their neighborhoods, and their
appointed spheres to offer assistance, salvation, and organization to
other members of the community. At the same time, the changes
women sought and the means of attaining these changes would be
determined largely by the experiences and expectations of their
families and social circles, experiences and expectations they shared
with men.

[35] *Directory for the Village,* 1827, p. 141.

[2]

A Profusion of Pathways

The Female Charitable Society invited "all classes of citizens" to "lend a helping hand" in its work and to "share impartially in its benefits."[1] The Orphan Asylum Association was founded by "a general meeting of the Ladies, in which all the different religious societies of the city were represented."[2] The Female Anti-Slavery Society of 1835 encouraged any "lady who approves of the [Society's] principles" to become a member merely "by signing its Constitution," while the Ladies' Anti-Slavery Sewing Society founded in 1851 sought the cooperation of "all whose love for the slave rises superior to . . . any particular party or sect. . . ."[3] Congregational Friends, in their search for racial, sexual, and spiritual equality, called on all who desired to see the " 'fruits of the spirit' . . . dispensed by and to every member of the human family" to join their efforts.[4] This rhetoric of cooperation, expressed by every public association of women, was often belied by forms of organization and action that appealed to various sectors of Rochester's population: female activism carried with it an ideology that spoke as clearly to women's own social and economic concerns as

[1] CS, *Charter Constitution, By-Laws, and Officers of the Rochester Female Charitable Society (for the Relief of the Sick Poor), Together with Its History and Annual Reports for the Year 1860* (Rochester: C. D. Tracy, 1860), p. 4.
[2] OAA, *History of the Rochester Female Association for Orphan and Destitute Children, Together with Its Organization, By-Laws, &c.* (Rochester: Shepard and Strong, 1839), p. 3.
[3] FASS, Constitution, (1835), SDPFP; LASS, "Circular, the First Report of the Rochester Ladies' Anti-Slavery Sewing Society, 1852," SDPFP.
[4] YMCF, *Proceedings of the Yearly Meeting of Congregational Friends, held at Waterloo, N.Y., from the Third to the Fifth of the Sixth Month, Inclusive, 1850* (Auburn, N.Y.: Henry Oliphant, 1850), p. 6.

38

to those of the persons whom they pledged to aid or organize. As the city itself became more socially and economically diverse, it spawned distinct networks of women activists that often struggled against each other even as they all commonly struggled for a better society and a larger role for women.

The vast majority of Rochester's female activists shared many features with nonactivists and with each other. They were predominantly white, Anglo-Saxon, Protestant, and, broadly speaking, middle class. They shared with nonactivists a general social and economic context that was framed by the dynamics of commercialization, urbanization, and revivalism. These forces fostered a cultural redefinition of gender roles, consisting of economic as well as ideological imperatives, that was most accessible to and formative for the new urban bourgeoisie.[5] While female activism implicitly challenged the tenets of domesticity and submission that characterized the nineteenth century's "true woman," many female activists sought to work within rather than challenge these bonds of womanhood. Even those who boldly declared their discontent with women's sphere recognized the power and popularity of the "true woman" ideal and attempted to use some of its tenets to justify a wider domain for women. Nor were Rochester's women activists set apart from their neighbors, male or female, by their awareness of the problems that accompanied rapid social and economic change. Rather their distinctiveness lay in the choice to act upon that awareness in public and collective ways.

The decision to act was shared by women activists as was their reliance on spiritual justification, domestic skills, and volunteer labor. Yet despite broad similarities in background and resources, women who chose activism differed from each other as much as they differed from nonactivists. Rochester women devised multiple forms of public action that often placed them in competition with each other for the moral and material resources to affect social change. It was this competition among women, rather than a quieter female solidarity, that

[5] On cultural redefinition of gender roles in this period, see Barbara Welter, "The Cult of True Womanhood, 1820–1860," *American Quarterly* 18 (Summer, 1966): 151–66, 171–74; Ann Douglas, *The Feminization of American Culture* (New York: Knopf, 1977); Carroll Smith-Rosenberg, "The Female World of Love and Ritual: Relations between Women in Nineteenth-Century America," *Signs* 1 (Autumn, 1975): 1–29; Nancy Cott, *The Bonds of Womanhood: Woman's Sphere in New England, 1780–1835* (New Haven: Yale University Press, 1977); and Mary P. Ryan, *Cradle of the Middle Class: The Family in Oneida County, New York, 1780–1865* (Cambridge: Cambridge University Press, 1981).

limited the power of ideological prescriptions that sought to contain the effects of change by relegating women to a private and subservient domain. By the very diversity of their claims, women activists built the platforms from which later generations would declare an ever wider sphere for women.

Five clusters of women pursued social change in nineteenth-century Rochester. Two of these groups—free black and working-class women—rarely competed with white middle-class women for material resources, nor in this period did they expect to direct the forces of social change. They emphasized instead self-help programs that sometimes benefited from the concern of their more affluent female neighbors. The three networks of bourgeois women activists emerged in different decades and from different segments of the community. Female benevolence appeared in the 1820s, within a decade of Rochester's settlement. As woman's contribution to the emergence of a village elite, benevolent women actively shaped Rochester's initial and long-dominant conception of women's proper public role while providing the community with its major social welfare institutions for half a century. A second pattern of women's activism was forged in the fires of Evangelicalism. Campaigns for moral and social perfection—seeking to rid the world of vice, intemperance, and slavery—were convergent with the wave of revivals that swept through Rochester's middling classes during the 1830s. Female perfectionists, so named because they sought to eradicate rather than ameliorate social ills, introduced new issues and new forms of public activity to the community but were never able to reproduce the social acceptability and stability of female benevolent societies. A few perfectionists found allies within a third activist network. Making their public debut in the mid-1840s, this third group of women advocated, among other things, complete legal, social, and economic equality for blacks and women. These radical, or in nineteenth-century terms ultraist, positions were held by women whose families were on the fringes of or just entering Rochester's commercial circles and who were—by virtue of family background, religious affiliations, and length of residence in Rochester—socially marginal. Yet the opinions of ultraist women were so bold and so boldly stated as to thrust members of this network into the center of local activism from the mid-1840s through the 1860s.

At any one time between 1822 and 1872, approximately 10 percent of

Rochester's adult women were active in public endeavors.[6] Rochester's first formal women's association was the Female Missionary Society, established within the First Presbyterian Church in 1818. The first civic association was that founded at the home of Mrs. Peck four years later. Sixty women joined the Rochester Female Charitable Society as charter members in 1822. The society attracted 125 to 225 women annually during its first fifteen years and by the late 1840s listed 300 to 350 women as members each year. In 1837 several CS leaders helped to found Rochester' second major benevolent enterprise, the Female Association for the Relief of Orphan and Destitute Children or the Orphan Asylum Association. Numbering 50 members in 1837, the OAA soon attracted 150 to 200 women per year. During the 1830s and 1840s several associations garnered even wider support though none lasted more than a decade. In 1835 evangelical women founded the Rochester Female Anti-Slavery Society, possibly inspired by a black women's antislavery society founded a year earlier. In 1837 some 50 perfectionist women led a campaign during which they collected over 900 of their sisters' signatures on antislavery petitions. Perfectionist women also established a Female Moral Reform Society, active between 1836 and 1845, which claimed 500 members, and a Ladies' Washingtonian Total Abstinence Society, which claimed 350 to 450 members during the mid-1840s.

By the latter date a third cluster of associations began to appear. Comprised of 30 to 70 women each, these vocal groups launched campaigns against the evils of alcohol, slavery, capital punishment, and tobacco and for the virtues of communitarianism, spiritualism, health reform, dress reform, and woman's rights. Far smaller in numbers than their benevolent or perfectionist counterparts, these ultraists were both visible and vocal. They were particularly notable for trying to forge links with their working-class and black sisters not as clients but as coworkers.

Alliances between ultraists and blacks or workers were short-lived,

[6]For example, in 1822 Rochester's population was 2,700, of which approximately 40 percent were female and 50 percent were 16 years or older. Thus the population at risk was approximately 540 women of whom 60, or 11 percent, joined the CS. In 1842 there were 5,170 white women aged 16 and over in Rochester, of whom some 400, or 7.7 percent, were active in benevolent associations alone. When figures for other women's associations are added for this period, the percentage rises well above 10 percent. Figures for other years produce similar results.

but they did heighten public recognition of working-class and black concerns. Black women had formed Rochester's first female antislavery society in 1834, though little more than its founding was recorded by local chroniclers. At mid-century, another black female abolitionist society appeared, the Union Anti-Slavery Society. The only recorded activity of this group was the holding of fairs to raise funds for Rochester's black abolitionist publisher, Frederick Douglass. It was the women of this society who joined white female abolitionists in April 1851 to manage a grand antislavery festival at Rochester's Corinthian Hall. Beyond these few formal notices of black female activism are evidences of informal interactions between black abolitionists and white ultraists. Such activity is recorded in the pages of the *Liberator,* the *National Anti-Slavery Standard,* and the *North Star;* in the autobiographies of ex-slaves and Rochester residents Frederick Douglass and Harriet Brent Jacobs; and in the private correspondence of Rochester ultraists with Philadelphia, New York City, and Boston coworkers. Ultraist ties with working-class women are less well-documented, but economic issues loomed large at the Rochester Woman's Rights Convention of August 1848 that led to the formation of a Working Women's Protective Union the same month. In 1853 working-class women made their first independent public appearance by organizing a Semptresses' Protective Union. The women involved complained of poor wages—fifty cents per day—and "public opinion won them a 25 per cent advance."[7] Seamstresses had learned quickly the advantages of collective action and soon founded Rochester's first clothing workers' union, but the recession of the mid-1850s undermined all workers' associated efforts and postponed large-scale organization until after the Civil War.[8]

As black and working-class women were entering the domain of public activism, white middle-class women were reshaping their activities and alliances. Ultraist women promoted the Working Women's Protective Union in 1848. In 1849 benevolent and perfectionist women joined in founding the Home for Friendless and Virtuous Females through which they hoped to alleviate some of the evils experienced by

[7]Blake McKelvey, *Rochester: The Water-Power City, 1812–1854* (Cambridge: Harvard University Press, 1945), p. 328. *Semptress* was the early-nineteenth-century term for seamstress.
[8]Ibid., see also Alan Gleason, "The History of Labor in Rochester, 1820–1880" (Master's thesis, University of Rochester, 1941), pp. 75–78.

"worthy and industrious females."[9] The HF annually maintained an association of 150 to 200 middle-class women reformers to house 50 to 100 working-class women. During the same period, a group of about 50 women sought to revitalize evangelical antislavery activity through the Rochester Ladies' Anti-Slavery Sewing Society, which was active through the 1860s raising funds for the antislavery cause and aiding fugitive and free blacks in Rochester, Canada, and Virginia. Just before the Civil War, a city hospital committee and an Industrial School Society brought as many as 100 more women into public activity, and the Civil War itself expanded these efforts and inspired additional women to join the Soldier's Aid Society in 1863. The late 1860s and early 1870s saw a continued high level of participation in benevolent activities though both the SAS and antislavery societies gradually disbanded as they saw many of their goals achieved. At the same time, a new coalition of antislavery and woman's rights advocates was beginning to form in support of women's suffrage. With the celebration of the CS's fiftieth anniversary in 1872 and the attempt of 40 women to register to vote the same year, one era of women's activism ended alongside the drama of a second beginning.

The women who joined benevolent, perfectionist, and ultraist organizations could be easily distinguished from their black and working-class counterparts and from each other on the basis of nativity, church membership, residence, and economic status. The economic and social changes that swept through Rochester in its first three decades crystalized these differences into three distinct activist networks. Women's experiences before settling in Rochester also helped to determine the forms of activism they pursued. In the early years, experience in church and charitable activities combined with frontier conditions to promote female benevolence. By the 1830s extralocal associations were important models for evangelical women activists, while the 1840s brought a new group of agrarian women trained in Quaker meetings to public endeavors.

The greatest testimony to the importance of previous experience and frontier conditions in fostering women's activism was the ease with which the founders of the CS defined an acceptable public domain for women within a decade of the community's settlement. The existence of a legitimate arena—the church—for women's collective activity al-

[9] HF, Minute Book, 28 March 1849, FHP.

lowed the mothers, wives, and daughters of Rochester's leading families to develop organizational and leadership skills.[10] The quickness and efficiency with which these women turned to associational activity outside church offices suggests that they also had experience with cent, mission, tract, and Bible societies and other organizations to aid the poor and destitute that dotted the eastern seaboard in the early nineteenth century.[11] Many of Rochester's pioneer women activists had lived in precisely those areas where these organizations flourished. Their ages, social status, and religious affiliations made them likely members of, or at the very least familiar with, the workings of these agencies. Even women from Maryland, wives and daughters of Rochester's founders, may have been acquainted with the Baltimore Female Humane Society, founded in 1798 across the state from the Nathaniel Rochester family's Hagerstown homestead.[12]

The CS clearly attracted the efforts of those women who had already gained local organizational experience in the charity school or Missionary Society, such as Mrs. Elizabeth Atkinson, Mrs. Elizabeth Backus, and Mrs. Josiah Bissell. At least some of their fifty-seven coworkers had also labored earlier in church, Sunday school, or charity school activity. Moreover, those first benevolent women came from families in which religious and benevolent activity was highly regarded. As members of Rochester's social, religious, political, and economic elite, these women were likely to view charitable work not as an opportunity for escaping woman's sphere but as an appropriate vehicle for carrying out the responsibilities appropriate to wives and daughters of community leaders.

For the men of these families, individualism and the work ethic were becoming the touchstones of economic success in their native New England villages. At the same time, the commercial revolution of which these ideals were a part was demanding women's increased relegation to the home and their continued subordination to men. Benevolent activity, by providing affluent women with socially accept-

---

[10]Before 1822, women were involved in the founding of First Presbyterian Church (1815), St. Luke's Episcopal Church (1818), First Methodist Church (1818), the Female Missionary Society (1818), and the charity school (1820).

[11]For a detailed discussion of the establishment of such associations, see Keith Melder, *The Beginnings of Sisterhood: The Women's Rights Movement in the United States, 1800–1840* (New York: Schocken, 1977). Cent societies were local associations of women, usually charging dues of one or several cents, that performed charitable labors or contributed to missionary efforts.

[12]On Baltimore Female Humane Society, see Melder, *Beginnings of Sisterhood*, p. 40.

able and valued labor and an autonomous identity, seems to have been one means of resolving these emerging contradictions for female members of the new community's elite. Yet in 1806 in Guilford, Connecticut, female parishioners at the Presbyterian Church failed in their attempt to form a female charity society. Their major opponent was the Reverend Mr. Elliott, whose "opinion would bear great weight with many." He believed such societies "to be ostentatious" and felt women could "find sufficient objects upon which to bestow their mite, within their own limits." Mary Stone did not entirely agree with her spiritual leader but wrote to coworshiper and coworker Mabel Ward that it was perhaps best to "omit meeting" and "gather what money we can, . . . and send it enclosed in a letter with as little noise and ostentation as possible."[13] Frontier conditions and the attendant necessity of everyone's labor apparently made women's public labors more acceptable, for in 1822 Mabel Ward became the first president of the Rochester CS.[14] Moreover, she and her coworkers received the wholehearted support of village fathers, including the leading clergymen, who preached fund-raising sermons on the CS's behalf in 1822.

For perfectionist women, the frontier was less geographical than moral. The land and animals around Rochester had been tamed, but men themselves had grown wilder, demonstrating vices too numerous to count and too lascivious to contemplate. In organizing local campaigns to rid the land of intemperance, slavery, and licentiousness, perfectionists drew on their experiences as benevolent laborers, revival agents, and small-town moral reformers and on their knowledge of activities in New York City, Philadelphia, and Boston.[15] The achievement of a perfect society demanded a nationwide effort, and the existence of the American Anti-Slavery Society in Boston and the American Female Moral Reform Society in New York City eased women's entrance into public activism in smaller communities. The initial support of evangelical clergy, including such national figures as Charles Grandison Finney, also legitimated women's efforts. Once involved in perfectionist activities, local women were spurred on by the need to send periodic reports to the parent societies and reinforced by

[13] Mary Stone to Mabel Hand Ward, 20 August 1806, Ms., Presbyterian Historical Society, Philadelphia, Pennsylvania. I thank Lori Ginzberg for bringing this letter to my attention.
[14] Mary Stone also apparently moved to Rochester, and it is probably her daughter Mary Stone (Mrs. John F. Bush) who served as a CS officer in the 1840s.
[15] These associations are explored more fully in Chapters 3 and 4.

the publication of letters and reports in national journals such as the *Liberator* and the *Advocate of Moral Reform*. Even when retreating from perfectionist labors in the 1840s, evangelical women would follow the paths set by their big-city sisters, who first moved from moral reform to the institutionalization of "friendless" women and from immediate emancipation to aid for free blacks and fugitive slaves.[16]

Ultraists, settling in Rochester later than their benevolent or perfectionist counterparts, arrived with the greatest amount of public experience. Within Quaker meetings and farming communities, women were active in the promotion of social order and community welfare. Traditions of social service—to the poor, imprisoned, and insane—and of social reform—in religious testimonies against slavery, intemperance, and war—characterized Quaker circles throughout England and America. From the 1834 founding of the Genesee Yearly Meeting, which encompassed portions of Canada, central New York and the Old Northwest as well as Rochester, the women's and men's "meetings" also voiced their disapproval of capital punishment and tobacco and their support of Indian rights, manual labor schools and woman's rights.[17] In the transition from Quaker activism to worldly activism, ultraist women, like their perfectionist counterparts, utilized the resources of national associations such as the American Anti-Slavery Society. Since they came to worldly labors in Rochester with considerably more experience than earlier female activists, however, ultraists were less dependent on extralocal models and sometimes surpassed national leaders in their vision of a free and equal society.[18]

Frontier conditions, previous experience, clerical support, and extralocal models and resources all bolstered women's entry into the public domain. On an individual basis, however, the most important factor may well have been the support of family and friends, especially of female kin and husbands. In many families both men and women responded to appeals for action from ministers, village leaders, itinerant reform agents, or their own conscience. Activist networks overlay kinship networks, which also formed the infrastructure of Rochester's business community, neighborhoods, and political leadership. These

---

[16]"Friendless" referred to women without family or friends in Rochester.

[17]Testimonies on each of these issues can be found repeatedly in the Minutes of the GYMWF, 1834–1885, HRR.

[18]Local ultraists' independence and their challenge to national leaders was particularly notable at the Rochester Woman's Rights Convention, 2 August 1848, discussed in Chapter 4.

family ties both bound together women and men of the same economic and social circles and separated them from those of other such circles. It was, moreover, these distinct circles that largely determined the moral and material resources available to various groups of women activists.

Mabel Ward rested her benevolent labors on a solid but not atypical foundation of family ties. Born Mehitable Hand in 1772, she married Levi Ward of Killingworth, Connecticut, in 1791. After bearing eight children in twice as many years, Mrs. Ward and her family moved west to the village of Bergen, New York, in 1807. Four more children were born to Levi and Mabel Ward in the next seven years, by which time two of their older sons had settled slightly to the north in the new village of Rochester. When two daughters married and also settled at Rochester, Levi, Mehitable, and the rest of the family joined them. Dr. Levi Ward soon become involved in local politics, religious and educational affairs, and temperance. His son Levi A., sons-in-law Silas O. Smith and Moses Chapin, and future sons-in-law Samuel L. Selden, Charles Lee Clarke, and Freeman Clarke joined Dr. Ward in his political and charitable activities and extended their efforts to antislavery, prison reform, and other endeavors. By 1822 Dr. Ward was well known in the village, and in that year he helped to found the Rochester Library Company.[19] The same year, his wife entered the public domain as first president of the CS. She was joined at the founding meeting by her daughters Susan Ward, Mrs. Moses Chapin, and Mrs. Silas O. Smith. Susan's future sister-in-law, Mrs. Joseph Spencer, was also a charter member. By the 1830s Levi A. Ward's wife, Harriet Kemp, and the two younger Ward daughters, Mehitable E. (Mrs. C. L. Clarke) and Henrietta (Mrs. F. Clarke), joined their female kin in benevolent efforts.[20]

Similar joint ventures were apparent in other benevolent families. Mrs. Everard Peck and her sister-in-law Emily Peck were active in the church and the CS, while Everard Peck rose to prominence in local temperance and Sabbatarian movements. William Atkinson was secretary of the Monroe County Bible Society in the early 1820s, and Josiah Bissell was the village's most prominent Bible and tract society leader

---

[19] Information on the Ward family is derived from Blake McKelvey, comp., "Letters Postmarked Rochester," Rochester Historical Society, *Publications* 21 (1943): 2–163.

[20] Eight other pairs of CS charter members shared last names; four of these pairs were definitely related, four were probably related.

during the 1820s and 1830s. Bissell and Atkinson were joined in these and other reform labors by Frederick Backus and Jacob Gould as well as Everard Peck and Levi Ward. All were married to CS charter members. In addition, at least four of the women who were single when they joined the CS in 1822 soon married local activists: Elizabeth Cuming to Thomas Rochester, Emily Peck to Thomas Kempshall, Mary Sibley to Edwin Scrantom, and Susan Ward to Samuel Selden.

Both Mrs. Ward and Mrs. Peck—Yankee, Presbyterian, and affluent—were representative of the largest sector of Rochester's leading families in the decade after settlement. Registering a counterclaim to the social, economic, and political leadership of the community were Colonel Nathaniel Rochester and Colonel William Fitzhugh—Maryland aristocrats, slaveholders, and Episcopalians—who founded Rochester in 1812 and controlled thereby a good share of its natural, and hence its political and economic, resources.[21] The Rochester and Fitzhugh families worshiped under the ministry of Francis Cuming at St. Luke's Episcopal Church. Colonel Rochester's daughter, Mrs. Anson Colman, and the Reverend Mr. Cuming's wife, Caroline, were the two leading representatives of the congregation at the founding meeting of the CS. They were joined by Cuming's sister, who was soon to marry Colonel Rochester's son, and by at least eleven other members of the St. Luke–Southern contingent. While the southern-born founding fathers battled Yankee entrepreneurs for economic and political power from the early years of settlement, their wives utilized the resources of both factions to provide "education, nourishment and consolation" for the sick and needy.[22]

One basis for women's shared labors in the CS was their shared experience of pioneer life in Rochester. At least ten of the CS's charter members had moved to the village during its first year of settlement, including the Rochester and Fitzhugh daughters and Mrs. Bissell and Mrs. Ely of the Yankee Presbyterian contingent. These CS members and the dozen or more who followed within five years lived in close proximity. They worshiped together for a time in a room over Jeheil Barnard's tailor shop; their husbands met daily to transact business and debate politics; their families attended the few village social functions, shared resources in times of crisis, and intermarried with regu-

[21]Charles Carroll was the third proprietor of the settlement, but he never played a significant role in local affairs. Colonel Rochester brought a few slaves with him to Rochester, but he freed them soon after moving to western New York.
[22]Quote from *Rochester Telegraph,* 18 February 1823.

larity. The founding of First Presbyterian Church in 1815 and St. Luke's Episcopal in 1818 meant the establishment of rival religious and social centers, yet the proximity of the two churches, which faced each other across Court House Square, and the previous shard experiences of their members assured the continued mingling of congregations. Moreover, mingling sometimes led to matrimony, to changes in church membership, and thence to a new interweaving of the two groups. CS charter member Rebecca Fitzhugh, for example, a Maryland-born Episcopalian, married Frederick Backus, a Yankee Presbyterian, in 1818 and transferred her allegiance to the First Presbyterian Church in the early 1820s. Almost simultaneously, Connecticut-born Siba Ward married Silas O. Smith and followed him from her father's pew in First Presbyterian to his in St. Luke's. In the rounds of weddings, housewarmings, and births that followed these and similar occasions, Rochester's first families became more intimately acquainted.

Within and across these families shared experiencs of courtship, marriage, and child rearing blended with those of frontier life, family, and faith to create a female web of experience and association that was thickly embroidered, dense as well as intricate.[23] Twenty-five of these women were married, eight having been wedded in Rochester during the three years before the CS's founding; fourteen bore or baptized children during the next five years. These women joined at least a dozen older women in marriage and motherhood while five young singles and five middle-aged widows formed smaller circles of shared experiences.[24]

Youth and courtship, marriage and motherhood, middle age and widowhood linked together women of different familial and religious circles. Such links were strengthened by the assumptions these women shared about the proper attributes of social and domestic life. While the primitive conditions of frontier life demanded physical labors and

[23] For the importance of these kinds of dense webs of association for present-day women's activism, see Juliet Mitchell, *Woman's Estate* (New York: Pantheon, 1971), p. 101.

[24] Household composition was impossible to verify for any significant number of the charter members, though some evidence exists of extended and complex households in census data and in Paul Johnson, *A Shopkeeper's Millennium: Society and Revivals in Rochester, New York, 1815–1837* (New York: Hill and Wang, 1978), chap. 2. The relationships between benevolent activism and family and household composition will be discussed further below. The ten unmarried women form about one fifth of the identifiable charter members. While this is a high percentage, five of these women had been married previously and the five single women would all marry within a few years.

domestic deprivations from all pioneering women, those who entered benevolent ranks sought and soon obtained the accoutrements of the settled societies from which they came. Saturday teas, weekly visiting, stone or frame houses, glass windows, store-bought clothes, a servant: the resources of benevolent women's families provided the trappings of affluence.[25] At the same time, through Sunday schools, missionary societies, and charitable societies, benevolent women transformed affluence into education and alms.

Affluence and its female applications to benevolence were products, pillars, and public signs of membership in Rochester's emerging elite. The families of benevolent leaders were the builders of Rochester's early kin-based economic and political order. Their initial leadership in land ownership, occupational status, and religious and political offices combined with education, advantageous marriages, and the perquisites of power to extend their control over local social, economic, and political domains. The men of these families could thus provide their wives, sisters, and daughters with three crucial resources for public activism: legitimacy, money and materiel, and political favors. The church and the press largely provided the first, success in business the second, and political office the third. Benevolent women were intimately connected to powerful figures in each of these domains. Everard Peck, for instance, whose three wives successively engaged in more than fifty years of benevolent activity, was a church elder and newspaper editor, a successful merchant and manufacturer, and a village trustee. He was also a leader in male Bible, missionary, and temperance societies, a Sunday school teacher, and an officer of one of Rochester's first public libraries. In full sympathy with his wives in their public projects, Peck provided them with "the means of continuing their divine administrations."[26]

While Peck was unusual in his succession of wives, and in the breadth of their combined benevolent labors, he was representative of the husbands of benevolent women in the forms and degree of aid he provided his female kin.[27] From the press and pulpit came the most

[25] On the early social and domestic life, see Johnson, *Shopkeeper's Millennium*, chap. 2; McKelvey, *Rochester*, pp. 136–48; and McKelvey, "Letters Postmarked Rochester."

[26] Everard Peck's views were publicly expressed in an editorial in the *Rochester Telegraph*, 18 February 1823.

[27] The generalizations about CS husbands and families are based on detailed analysis of the social, economic, and political fortunes of the husbands of thirty (one half of) CS charter members. The thirty charter members, nine of whom served twenty years or more in benevolent enterprises, were models and molders of local power and patronage.

widely heard public pronouncements on female benevolence. The leading spokesmen of social legitimacy in the community were Rev. Francis Cuming and Comfort Williams, the pastor of First Presbyterian Church. Both were husbands of CS charter members and in 1822 both "appeal[ed] with . . . eloquence and effect to the citizens of [the] village on behalf of the Female Charitable Society," "irresistably proving that it is the duty of the affluent to cherish the unfortunate."[28] The call of duty, which had beckoned CS charter members months earlier, now reached their male coworshipers. The First Presbyterian congregation included church elders Levi Ward, Jacob Gould, Moses Chapin, Russell Green, and Everard Peck, as well as tract and Bible society leaders Josiah Bissell, Ira West, and Frederick Backus: all were charter members' husbands. The First Church collection totaled almost forty-two dollars. The husbands of CS charter members at St. Luke's—Anson Colman, William Pitkin, and Thomas Rochester among others—donated thirty-two dollars.[29] Both the sermons and the donations they encouraged helped to legitimate women's public labors.

The press multiplied the effects of these fund-raising sermons by reporting their substance and results to the larger community. Everard Peck gave the CS its first published notice in response to a sermon by the Reverend Mr. Penney on the association's first anniversary. Edwin Scrantom and Josiah Bissell, also husbands of charter members, were editors and publishers of four local papers between 1822 and 1830. They supported women's benevolent efforts not only through laudatory editorials but also through the publication of announcements, appeals, and reports and the gratuitous printing of hundreds of copies of the same for distribution.[30] Thus, as with fund-raising sermons, social legitimacy and material support went hand-in-hand.

Historian Paul Johnson, in *A Shopkeeper's Millennium,* has described the "fraternalization of economic relationships" in Rochester during the 1820s. The kin-based business arrangements among

[28] Quoted in *Rochester Telegraph,* 18 February 1823. The third early church in Rochester was the First Methodist, whose lay leader was Abelard Reynolds, husband of a CS charter member. Annual fund-raising sermons were preached at one or more churches in the city throughout the period under study.

[29] All donations may not have come from husbands of CS members, but a large portion of the congregations were linked by kinship to the CS. Descriptions of these sermons and donations are in Amy Hanmer-Croughton, "The Rochester Female Charitable Society," Rochester Historical Society, *Publications* 9 (1930): 63–90.

[30] Colonel Rochester established the village's first newspaper in 1816, but it was defunct by 1822. Between 1822 and 1830, eight general and news papers were established in Rochester and five were the work of CS husbands.

brothers, brothers-in-law, fathers, and sons "united large segments of the business elite," creating "a federation of wealthy families and their friends."[31] Husbands of CS founders, who were members of this federation, willingly turned professional practices and business profits to the service of benevolent projects, indicating both their support of women's activities and their success in securing the local resources that formed the material base of that support. Rooms were offered rent-free to house the charity school. Merchant husbands provided bedding, clothing, and other items from their stockpiles, while bankers, lawyers, and physicians donated their skills and knowledge. Spaces in churches and public buildings were lent gratuitiously for fund-raising events and exhibitions, and stationers and booksellers printed and sold tickets to benevolent affairs.

In a boom town flooded with laborers, artisans, shopkeepers, and farmers, the husbands of charter members filled the merchant, manufacturer, and professional ranks. Some men, such as Colonel Rochester, Colonel Fitzhugh, Everard Peck, Levi Ward, and Josiah Bissell brought wealth and experience with them to Rochester and bought position and prestige with it. Others gained occupational prominence and wealth through pioneer efforts: the village's first shoemaker, boat-builder, tavern keeper, dry goods merchant, druggist, editor, physician, lawyer, and judge were all represented by female kin on the CS's 1822 roster. Some of these men combined the skills they brought with them to Rochester in the late 1810s with patronage and initiative to establish manufacturing and mercantile careers in the 1820s. Jacob Gould, for example, used his shoemaking skills to establish a thriving boot and shoe factory within a few years of settling in the city, and Ira West opened a grocery store in 1812 that he expanded into one of the town's leading dry goods stores by 1820.[32]

Rochester's social and economic order was, like that of many frontier towns, highly fluid during the first decade of settlement. Those families who arrived with the advantages of resources or skills in the 1810s or early 1820s were able to enter the new community's elite circles with relative ease. They were also able to consolidate power and thereby limit access to their ranks after the mid-1820s. By 1827, for instance, a hierarchy of occupational status was well established, and the husbands of CS charter members were well entrenched at the top.

[31] Johnson, *Shopkeeper's Millennium*, p. 27.
[32] *A Directory for the Village of Rochester* (Rochester: Elisha Ely and Everard Peck, 1827); Johnson, *Shopkeeper's Millennium*, pp. 28–32; and McKelvey, *Rochester*, pp. 236–237.

The city directory for that year listed the principal occupations of the village and the number employed in each. According to this survey, 57 percent of Rochester's nonagriculturally employed population worked as artisans, 23 percent as laborers, 6 percent as grocers or innkeepers, 5 percent as clerks, 4 percent as merchants, 3 percent as professionals, and 2 percent as millers or millwrights—this last occupation being the most lucrative in early Rochester. Of the thirty charter members' husbands who could be identified in this directory, none were laborers, grocers, inkeepers, or clerks and only three (10 percent) were artisans. Seven (23 percent) were millers or millwrights, ten (33 percent) merchants or manufacturers, and sixteen (53 percent) professionals.[33]

Shared occupational and economic status, however, was only the most visible manifestation of a tightly knit network of business and financial partnership and patronage that was closely intertwined with the female web of associated effort. The list of early millers, for example, included partners Hervey Ely and Josiah Bissell as well as William Pitkin and James L. Livingston. The first three were husbands of charter members and the last the husband of the CS's 1827 president. In 1828 Josiah Bissell was partners with both William Atkinson on the Pioneer Line, his Sabbatarian shipping venture, and Everard Peck on the *Rochester Observer*. Two other husbands of charter members, Ira West and Thomas Kempshall, formed a partnership in 1823 in the dry goods business. When West retired the following year, Kempshall took John Bush, whose wife was soon serving on the CS's executive board, as his partner. It was in this same year that Kempshall married charter member Emily Peck, Everard's sister. Kempshall was also linked to at least six charter members' husbands through the Masons, including his partner Ira West. West appears on the board of directors of Rochester's first bank, established in 1824, along with Levi Ward, William Pitkin, and Abelard Reynolds. Reynolds was a Knights Templar, as were Francis Cuming and Jacob Gould, the last of whom served with Levi Ward as a trustee of Rochester's first incorporated academy, Monroe High School. Here, as among benevolent women, the web of association was thickly woven.[34]

Moreover, this economic network had a political parallel and coun-

---

[33] Some worked more than one occupation in early Rochester, causing the numbers to add up to more than thirty and the percentage to more than 100.

[34] Information on partnerships, associational affiliations, bank boards, and school boards comes mainly from the city directory of 1827. On Bissell's partnership with Atkinson, see Johnson, *Shopkeeper's Millennium*, p. 91, and on Bissell's partnership with Peck, see McKelvey, *Rochester*, p. 192.

terpoint. The members of the boards of banks, for instance, were originally appointed by the common council, the village's main governing
body. Six husbands of charter members were elected to the council
between its 1817 establishment and the city's incorporation in 1834,
and they selected many of their peers to bank boards during that period. They were joined in political office by at least six husbands who
served as port collectors, fire wardens, assessors, or school trustees.
When the village was incorporated in 1834, the first mayor was
Jonathan Child, son-in-law of Colonel Rochester, brother-in-law of a
CS charter member, and husband of a CS officer. Further, political
power was never a matter only of officeholding. It was controlled in the
early years by two competing factions, ruled over respectively by the
Episcopalian Rochester clan and a more diverse group of Yankee Presbyterians.[35]

In sheer numbers, the female kin of the Yankee Presbyterian faction
dominated the CS. With fewer representatives of the village's southern
contingent at the founding meeting, Yankee women easily elected two
of their own as the first CS officers. Yet numerical predominance did
not exclude the Southerners from leadership. In 1823, for example,
both the president and the treasurer were from this group, and for
almost twenty years thereafter one of its members was elected to one
of the top three CS offices.[36] Women's willingness to share power may
have been a response, in part, to the realization that the CS benefited
no matter which of its representatives was linked to local power and
influence; and links to both factions assured continued support regardless of which male faction attained power in any one year.

By the late 1820s, male legitimation and resources combined with
female labor and initiative to establish a new public arena for women
that served as an indicator of, rather than a challenge to, female and
familial status.[37] The number of women in the CS and the other benevolent enterprises it spawned was impressive. The impact of their activism, however, was less a matter of numbers than of identity. The
women who formed the CS were members of Rochester's first settled

[35] On political factions, see Johnson, *Shopkeeper's Millennium,* chap. 3. Political
power of the husbands of CS charter members increased over time with four serving as
mayor during the 1830s and 1840s, three as state legislators, and one as a United States
congressman.

[36] There was one exception to this pattern between 1822 and 1859. The election of Mrs.
Rebecca Backus as president in 1823 is noted in *Union and Advertiser,* 26 February 1872.
All other information is from the CSP.

[37] This is not to deny that opposition was voiced by a few community leaders but to
indicate that the dominant pattern was one of support and aid.

and most prestigious families. As they entered public paths on errands of mercy, few fellow townsmen would accuse them of stepping outside their sphere, for Rochester's early ladies bountiful were precisely those women who were chargd with defining the proper place of their sex in community life.

For men, business and political networks based on kinship declined under economic and party pressures in the 1830s.[38] For women, the strength of associated effort prevailed. In the face of turmoils among male kin that rent the fabric of local economic and political life, benevolent women forged bonds of community that bridged differences of nativity, faith, and family. For benevolent women, who were largely removed from direct participation in productive labor and political office, commonalities of wealth and status overshadowed competition for profits and party leadership. It was in large part through these woman-based kin networks that patterns of activism were replicated and extended across time and into new organizations. Finally, these family networks, which in benevolent activity joined together women of the professional and merchant class in ameliorative efforts, would be reproduced by kinswomen of other social and economic strata in pursuit of other social goals during the 1830s, 1840s, and 1850s.[39]

The Finney-led revivals of the early 1830s, for instance, inspired large numbers of men and women to join in movements to eradicate immorality and thereby hasten the millennium. The female leaders of these perfectionist campaigns often had ties of membership and kinship to the CS, yet they represented a distinct economic and social sector. Susan Farley Porter, a CS member from her arrival in Rochester in 1835 and the wife of Mrs. Everard Peck's younger brother Samuel, was one such leader. Samuel D. Porter moved to Rochester in 1827 to clerk in Everard Peck's store. He traveled to Waldoborough, Maine, in 1835 to marry Susan Farley, and the couple returned to a comfortable life among Rochester's younger and upwardly mobile second generation of settlers.[40] While Samuel was making a tidy sum in land speculation and

[38] On decline of kinship as the basis of male business and political ventures, see Johnson, *Shopkeeper's Millennium*, chaps. 3 and 4, and McKelvey, *Rochester*, chaps. 6 and 7.

[39] For a very suggestive analysis of the role of family networks in reproducing social order, see Pierre Bourdieu, "Marriage Strategies as Strategies of Social Reproduction," in Orest Ranum and Elborg Forster, eds., *Family and Society: Selections from the Annales* (Baltimore: Johns Hopkins University Press, 1976), pp. 117–44.

[40] Generation refers partly to age since many of the settlers of the 1830s were younger members of first-settled families; but more generally, it indicates families who moved to Rochester after 1825 when the pioneer familial, economic, and political network had clearly been established.

joining antislavery, temperance, and moral reform societies, Susan was beginning a cycle of household labor, childbearing, and community work. The Porters, like the Pecks, were active in church affairs but were more closely tied to the newer evangelical congregations than to Rochester's first churches. Samuel converted under Charles Grandison Finney in 1831; Susan appears to have undergone conversion upon her arrival in Rochester. In 1836 both Samuel and Susan joined other dissenters from First and Third Presbyterian churches to form a Bethel Free Church. The "active Christianity" advocated by the Bethel founders was grounded in the perfectionist tenets of Finneyite Evangelicalism, tenets that were also reflected in perfectionist campaigns for temperance, abolition, and moral reform.[41]

The women who led these campaigns mirrored the kin networks of their benevolent counterparts, although because they were younger and more recently arrived in Rochester, the extent of their networks was more circumscribed in the early 1830s. By 1837 when the women of the Rochester Female Anti-Slavery Society circulated two massive antislavery petitions throughout Monroe County, female family groups were clearly at the center of perfectionist activism. The name of Mrs. Susan Porter was joined by those of her sisters Martha Farley Peck, Elizabeth Farley, and Delia Farley and sisters-in-law Almira, Mary Jane, and Maria G. Porter. Mrs. Chloe Bullen signed beneath her daughter, Mrs. Mary Hoyt, on the 1837 petition as she had on the FASS's 1835 constitution. Mrs. Abigail Moore, Mrs. Silas Cornell, and Mrs. Russell Green also joined daughters on the 1837 petition, while Martha Bullen, Phebe Cornell, and Mrs. Almira Galusha joined sisters-in-law. Clusters of Greens, Wests, VanHoustons, Seelyes, Allings, Allyns, Goulds, Reids, and Underhills also appeared. Though some of these names were common in Rochester, clustering suggests at least residential proximity, visiting, or shared sites of worship since those were the circumstances in which petitions were likely to circulate.[42]

Kinship ties among abolitionists extended across gender though perfectionist men and women still organized sex-segregated associations.

[41] Samuel Drummond Porter to Pastor, Washington Street Presbyterian Church, 29 September 1845, SDPFP. Detailed information of FASS and FMRS participants exists only for the leaders of the associations, thus generalizations here are based primarily on their characteristics.

[42] The local 1837 women's petition campaign contained signatures from throughout Rochester and the surrounding county of Monroe; presented 30 January 1837 and 19 September 1837, House of Representatives Document HR25A-H1.8, Library of Congress, Box 83. I thank Paul Johnson for reference to this source.

Of the seventeen women who organized the FASS, twelve had husbands who served as leaders of the men's county and city antislavery societies between 1833 and 1835[43] Mrs. Elon Galusha, directress of the FASS in 1834, was married to the first president of the Monroe County Anti-Slavery Society. The husband of the FASS's first secretary signed the call for a state antislavery society; the husband of another directress labored as an antislavery lecturer. Of an additional twenty-one married women who can be identified as antislavery activists in the years 1835 to 1837, at least thirteen shared antislavery labors with husbands.[44] In addition six single women joined fathers or brothers in the movement. Almost two-thirds of eary female abolitionists, then, emerged from identifiable antislavery families.

Many perfectionists sought the eradication of vice as well as slavery. Husband-wife teams, such as the Reverend and Mrs. Elon Galusha and the Reverend and Mrs. Roswell G. Murray, were active in this cause as were ministers' families generally. Ministers also forged important links between small-town moral reform societies and the larger Rochester association, while within Rochester, churches often provided the rooms for meetings and lectures. Bonds among evangelical sisters and brothers often served as an equivalent of kinship where blood ties were limited. The familial rhetoric employed by the female parishioners of Third Presbyterian, Bethel Free, and Second Baptist churches suggested that spiritual bonds could be as thick as blood ties. It was evangelical churches that provided for perfectionists the type of shared experiences that frontier life provided for benevolent women.

Perfectionist women's ties to evangelical churches were far stronger than those of their benevolent counterparts. Their ties to local economic and political power, however, were far weaker. The husbands of FASS leaders were as likely to be jewelers or booksellers as doctors or millers. Predominantly from New England, FASS families moved to Rochester in the late 1820s or early 1830s, after the village's earliest centers of authority and power were well established. FASS husbands

[43] A larger number of men than women were involved in early antislavery activity in Rochester so that many women not involved directly in the cause would have been familiar with it. Many women, for instance, who confined their own work to benevolence had male relatives in the antislavery and temperance movements.

[44] These women were identified through local newspapers, the national antislavery press, proceedings of antislavery conventions, and James McElroy's "Social Reform in the Burned-over District: Rochester, New York, as a Test Case, 1830–1854," (PhD. diss., State University of New York at Binghamton, 1974).

were less likely than their CS counterparts to be bank directors or city officials, and their families were less likely to live in the city's third or "Ruffled Shirt" ward. Finally, while active in church affairs, it was the atypical FASS family who attended one of the city's two most prestigious houses of worship, First Presbyterian or St. Luke's Episcopal Church.

Yet FASS women were limited in access to political and economic resources only in comparison with their CS counterparts. Within the community at large, their husbands and fathers were part of an occupational elite with access to centers of religious and political influence. Turning again to the 1827 city directory's list of occupations, the husbands of perfectionist women were seven times as likely as their neighbors to be professionals, four times as likely to be merchants and only half as likely to be artisans; none were laborers. A few perfectionist husbands served in political office, as aldermen and assessors, and at least one was a long-term bank director.[45] While only a few resided at the city's social center, most lived in comfortable circumstances along the community's major thoroughfares. In evangelical churches, FASS women and their male kin served in positions of religious leadership. Five FASS women and six FASS husbands helped to found new congregations during the 1830s and 1840s in which at least eight husbands served as elders or trustees and one as minister. FASS husbands were also active in local reform circles. Although only three are known to have joined Bible, tract, or missionary societies, at least seven labored for moral reform, ten for temperance, and fifteen for abolition. Thus FASS women, fully as much as benevolent women, emerged from activist families. These families, while not the most affluent or powerful, held political, economic, and religious positions that clearly distinguished them from most of their fellow Rochesterians.

In general, the members of moral reform societies replicated the social, economic, and political circumstances of their antislavery peers: they too were relatively recent Rochester arrivals, from New England or eastern New York, whose families were comfortable but not necessarily affluent, publicly visible but not necessarily powerful, and thoroughly evangelical. Yet a few differences are noteworthy. The Female Moral Reform Society was the first to draw at least half of its members from west of New England, and they moved to Rochester

---

[45] Statistics here are based on the same occupational listing used to determine the status of benevolent husbands above: *Directory for the Village,* 1827.

slightly later than their antislavery peers. The FMRS was the first white women's organization to contain employed women in its ranks— two schoolteachers, a boardinghouse keeper, and a dressmaker—all of whom were among a comparatively large number of single and widowed FMRS leaders. Married women of the same association, however, were actually from more affluent families than their FASS peers. Similarly, while more moral reformers than abolitionists lived on the outskirts of the city, more also lived in the Ruffled Shirt ward.

The economic and social fluidity of perfectionist ranks was clearly visible in patterns of religious, economic, and residential location during the late 1830s, but a general trend of upward mobility was apparent by 1840. For instance, antislavery perfectionists were most active between 1834 and 1838 and moral reformers between 1838 and 1845. Those women who served in both associations brought greater financial resources to the latter. Mrs. Samuel D. Porter, for instance, brought the resources of a store clerk to the FASS and those of a land agent to the FMRS; another leader's husband rose from bank clerk to head cashier between 1834 and 1838. Nor were these exceptional cases: only a single artisan's wife graced the roster of early moral reformers while five attorney's wives appeared on the list. Five bank directors and six city officials, including a city, a state, and a federal judge, had wives who were moral reformers. More female moral reformers than abolitionists lived in the third ward and more had been members of the CS before entering perfectionist ranks. Yet a seemingly significant gap still existed within the FMRS between single and widowed women, some of whom were employed, and the wives of professionals, merchants, and bankers; between those inhabiting centers of economic and political power and social prestige and those outside them; between those strongly attached to benevolent ventures and those detached from them. While most pronounced in the FMRS, these differences existed among perfectionists as a whole, and the balance between those of affluent and those of middling status shifted over time both within perfectionist associations and among them.

The dynamic character of that middle-class sector from which perfectionist women emerged assured such differences, but perfectionist associations did not contain two discrete groups facing each other across an economic chasm. Rather, many perfectionist women lived along the frequently shifting boundary between unstable affluence and solid but unostentatious comfort. Mrs. Benjamin Campbell, for instance, was the daughter of Rochester's principal tavern keeper and the wife of a merchant miller and bank director. She was a CS district visitor in the early 1830s and joined moral reform efforts in 1836, but the resources she brought to the latter were diminished by her husband's business failures at the end of the decade. He soon recovered, however, and she remained active in a number of associations. In 1842, the year Mrs. Campbell was elected a vice-president of the CS, her husband failed once again, and the family was forced to sell their third ward home. Soon after, the Campbells left Rochester, reappearing in Buffalo in 1850, where Benjamin listed himself as a merchant and Mrs. Campbell served as the matron of a residential hotel. In other families, the precariousness of middle-class comforts was made apparent in other ways. Mrs. Samuel D. Porter, for instance, was joined in her labors by her three single sisters-in-law, all of whom moved between Rochester and Philadelphia, between their parents' home and boardinghouses, and among a variety of female occupations in order to maintain an urban bourgeois lifestyle. Thus, in terms of stability and status, perfectionists lived lives of comfort but not of certainty when they entered activist ranks.

Many perfectionist women experienced economic uncertainty but not, like Mrs. Campbell, economic collapse. A small number who did not achieve financial stability severed their ties with perfectionists, either by leaving the city, ending their activist careers, or joining with the city's third activist network of ultraist men and women. The untraists' formal introduction to worldly activism in Rochester came at the founding meeting of the Western New York Anti-Slavery Society in 1842. The founding meeting was held at the Washington Street Presbyterian Church—spiritual home in the 1840s of the Porters, the Mathews, the Scovilles, and other perfectionists—and Samuel D. Porter was elected the society's first president. Yet Porter's coworkers in the association included no evangelical women and few evangelical men. The presence of Abby Kelley, whose election to the American Anti-Slavery Society executive committee in 1840 had sent evangelical chauvinists fleeing the organization, may well explain the general absence of evangelical support in Rochester.[46]

---

[46] Debates within the American Anti-Slavery Society over the role of the churches, politics, and women in the abolitionist movement resulted in the division of that society in 1840. The immediate catalyst for that split was the election of Abby Kelley, a Garrison supporter, to the executive committee. For a thorough analysis of this division, see Aileen Kraditor, *Means and Ends in American Abolitionism: Garrison and His Critics On Tactics and Strategy, 1834–1850* (New York: Pantheon, 1969).

As a Quaker and one of the leading female antislavery agents and lecturers, Kelley's presence may also explain the large turnout at the founding meeting of Hicksite Quaker men and women. It was this group that soon dominated WNYASS offices. One of the most active Quakers was Amy Post. Born in a farming community on Long Island, Amy Kirby joined Isaac Post in Scipio, New York, upon their marriage in 1828. Eight years later, Isaac and Amy along with Amy's stepdaughter, Mary, son Joseph, and sister Sarah resettled in Rochester. There Isaac gave up farming for shopkeeping, while Amy increased her activities in Quaker meetings and antislavery campaigns. She combined this work with the rearing of five children and the care of a household continually, if erratically, expanded by relatives, boarders, free black and Irish servants, fugitive slaves, and itinerant lecturers.

In 1842 both Amy and Isaac Post served in WNYASS offices. They were joined there over the next decade by daughter Mary, now Mary Hallowell, and her husband William, sister Sarah Kirby Hallowell and her husband Jeffries, and Isaac's nephew Edmund Willis (who would become Sarah's second husband). At the end of the decade, Isaac's aunt, Phebe Post Willis, would arrive from Long Island to join the antislavery circle along with cousins George and Ann Willetts. George Willett's sister Mary worked with Amy Post at antislavery fairs, while her husband, Elihu Coleman, served as a WNYASS officer. The Thayer, Anthony, and Fish families were similarly engaged in the society's activities with at least five members of the first family, eight of the second, and nine of the third actively involved.

These same families formed kin-connected communities in the first and second wards and on the city's northwest border. In the mid-1840s, the twelve Post relatives lived within a ten-block area surrounding Isaac and Amy's house on Sophia Street in the first ward. In the second ward, Benjamin and Sarah Fish and their daughters Catherine and Mary shared a double house with Sarah's sister and brother-in-law, Mary and John Braithewaite, and their daughters Ann and Catharine. Along the northwest corner of the city, Daniel, Lucy, Mary, and Susan B. Anthony inhabited an old farmhouse next door to Elias and Rhoda DeGarmo. Asa and Huldah Anthony and their family, cousins of Daniel and Lucy, lived nearby, as did another set of cousins, Lewis and Sarah Anthony Burtis. This proximity and density allowed them to maintain an agrarian Quaker enclave within the confines of an increasingly commercialized and gradually industrializing city.

Amy Post and her ultraist coworkers could be clearly demarcated from their benevolent and perfectionist counterparts. First, they were predominantly Hicksite Quakers. Second, they were predominantly from New York farming villages rather than New York or New England commercial centers. They were younger, on the average, than women who entered benevolent ranks, and they arrived in Rochester later than either benevolent or perfectionist leaders: at least thirty of the fifty ultraist women active in the 1840s did not arrive in the city until 1835 or later. When ultraist women did arrive, they lived on the outskirts of the city or in its less affluent wards. Only five ultraist women lived in the city's prestigious third ward by mid-century. Thus in terms of religious affiliation and length and place of residence, the ultraist women were clearly marginal to the ranks of fashionable society.

Their families also resided outside the ranks of local economic and political power. Yet the first half of the nineteenth century was a period of enormous economic expansion and mobility. Many ultraists had moved to central and western New York in the 1830s in search of better farmlands: those who moved on to Rochester took advantage of the opportunities afforded by the city's boom-town economy to move into the bottom ranks of the emerging bourgeoisie. Some improved their economic position by turning family farms into more commercial ventures, such as cherry or apple orchards or nurseries. A few ultraist men began manufacturing ventures—in stoves or woolens—and a few became merchants in dry goods, drugs, or clothing. Others entered professional ranks, though none were lawyers and only one a physician. New to such positions, they entered the professions at the lowest rungs, as itinerant ministers, reform agents, or antislavery lecturers, while one took on the singular occupation of a "philosophical machinist."[47] A number of ultraist women were married to artisans—jewelers, tailors, butchers, and stone cutters—who defied the general trend toward economic decline among that class of workers. Instead, they used artisanal skills to aid them in the transition from agrarian to commercial pursuits, such as clerking or shopkeeping. Ultraists also improved their economic, if not their social, status through women's employment. Eleven of the fifteen single or widowed women in ultraist circles were

---

[47]Daniel Pickard was listed as such in the *Daily American Directory of the City of Rochester, for 1851–1852* (Rochester: Lee and Mann, 1850). He was listed as both a machinist and a minister at other times and was, perhaps, a deist in the Thomas Paine mold. For other ultraists' attachment to Paine's ideology, see Chapter 7.

employed; most were in such female occupations as teaching or dress-making, but at least two were antislavery lecturers.

Ultraists, then, were gathering at the lower rungs of the new urban bourgeoisie. Their resources were limited relative to those of benevolent or perfectionist families but were increasing in absolute terms. Similarly, their political resources, while limited in comparison with those of their activist counterparts, increased over time. Not a single ultraist woman's husband or father held a local, state, or national political office; only one could even claim a prominent role in third-party politics. Yet ultraists agitated political issues, such as emancipation and woman's rights, which were increasingly the focus of national political debate, by forging ties with sympathetic agitators in Boston, Philadelphia, and New York City. Socially, economically, and politically marginal to Rochester's rising bourgeoisie, ultraist women sought only limited support within the city. Their strongest ties were to family, friends, and fellow reformers throughout the Northeast and the Old Northwest.

At the point of both their emergence and their public articulations, women activists drew upon shared experiences of kin and class as frequently as the shared experiences of gender. By virtue of their links with local power, their family backgrounds, and their length of residence in the city, Mrs. Ward and her coworkers emerged from the apex of the middle class in the 1820s and never relinquished their position as the female voice of the dominant sector of local business and politics. They were joined in the 1830s and 1840s, in the context of an expanding urban bourgeoisie, by their perfectionist sisters. Beginning in slightly less favorable economic circumstances and entering the local arena later than benevolent women, perfectionists such as Mrs. Porter were still bound to their benevolent counterparts by ties of kinship, religion, and patronage. They were not so bound to Amy Post and other ultraist women, who lacked both the initial economic and social standing of benevolent women and the connections that perfectionist women had to that standing. Marginal to Rochester's dominant middle-class sector, ultraist women and their families nonetheless sought to permeate the social conscience and thereby shape the economic and political power of that sector. Thus, while all three groups of women activists were members of Rochester's emerging bourgeoisie in its broadest outlines, they vied with each other for the determining voice in shaping social order and social value.

The differences that were apparent as women entered the public domain were extended and crystalized by the rapid social and economic changes of the early nineteenth century. Commercialization, population growth, occupational and residential segregation, religious revivalism, the rise of domesticity, and changes in transportation and communication: these forces by the mid-1840s led to the establishment of a segmented society in Rochester. While the clearest differences were between rich and poor, native-born and immigrant, and whites and blacks, the emerging middle classes were also increasingly fragmented. The fragments from which benevolent, perfectionist, and ultraist women emerged varied in material resources and fostered different social visions, leading bourgeois women to pursue three increasingly distinct forms and styles of activism during the first two decades of public labor.

The Erie Canal was only one of many forces that shaped female activism in divergent ways. As noted above, the canal opening in 1822 was a propitious moment for local entrepreneurs; the CS was founded the same year. Five years later, the city directory claimed that the city's board of trustees held all the powers "necessary to secure and enforce neatness, regularity, good order, and safety" and "to restrain whatever may be offensive or detrimental to decency, good morals, or religion." Yet it simultaneously noted the expansion of the CS's labors among "sick and distressed families."[48] The women of the CS—Mrs. Child, Mrs. Norton, Mrs. Bissell, Mrs. Ely, Mrs. Livingston, Mrs. Kempshall, and others—were joined in their ameliorative efforts by male temperance advocates and by members, both male and female, of Bible, tract, and missionary societies. Such labors were considered essential to assure order among the casual laborers and immigrants, in taverns and shacks that flourished along the canal. In the 1820s private charities were the only means of providing the required social services, and the profits of millers and merchants, such as the Messrs. Childs, Norton, Bissell, Ely, Livingston, and Kempshall, were the primary means of funding those charities.

The economic boom following the canal's completion expanded entrepreneurial opportunities in Rochester and allowed newer and upwardly mobile settlers to dream of canal-based fortunes. Grocer George Avery, clerk Samuel D. Porter, young lawyer Selah Mathews, and forwarding merchant Walter Griffiths were among those who

---

[48] *Directory for the Village,* 1827, pp. 98, 105.

sought to use the canal as a path to material success. Yet the path was fraught with dangers—sons enticed by the free-flowing liquor of the dockside bars, daughters enraptured by some cold-hearted adventurer, materialism running rampant over morality, and a sense of community lost to competition.[49] The religious revivals of 1830–1831 were one means of reasserting community and morality; but by the end of the decade those who strove for economic success were again voicing concern over the "hundreds of transients and the great number of more or less unsettled residents who crowded the 'tenements' and boarding houses" and who "were forced to seek diversion in public places."[50]

George Avery and his fellow entrepreneurs formed temperance and moral reform societies, but their voluntary efforts were limited by the demands of business. It was their wives, then, who took charge of uncovering and controlling those who "sustain vice, in its most degrading and loathsome forms."[51] While the canal encouraged the spread of licentiousness, it simultaneously supplied the resources for its control. Many of those who built new fortunes on the canal were willing to use some portion of those profits to dispense religion and bourgeois values along the canal's path. In addition, the canal supplied local perfectionists with copies of national journals, such as the *Advocate of Moral Reform* and the *Liberator,* and provided transportation to semiannual moral reform meetings in Utica and for traveling ministers and lecturers seeking audiences in upstate New York. These latter services were more important for perfectionists than for their benevolent counterparts since the former were more strongly tied to extralocal models of organization.

For ultraists, whose primary bonds were to New York City, Boston, Philadelphia, and central New York, the canal was essential. The canal trade allowed some Quakers to expand from subsistence to commercial

[49]Tales of such tragedies appeared regularly in the *Advocate of Moral Reform* (New York City), which was circulated among Rochester moral reformers. For stories sent by Rochester subscribers, see issues of 1 July 1838 and 1 March 1840.

[50]McKelvey, *Rochester,* p. 142. The *Directory* of 1827 lists Rochester's population in 1822 as 2,700 permanent residents and 3,130 persons including laborers on the public works. Thus casual laborers and other itinerants constituted approximately one-seventh of the village population. "Public places" here refers to taverns, boardinghouses, and the theatre, all of which were considered to have bad moral effects when visited solely for the purpose of amusement.

[51]*Advocate of Moral Reform,* 1 October 1843. This issue contained the proceedings of the semiannual meeting of the American Female Moral Reform Society held in Rochester. The first Rochester men's moral reform society was established in 1833 and resurrected in August 1836. Both disbanded in less than one year.

agriculture, but the canal's greatest importance for ultraists was not the fortunes it provided but the lifeline to other activist centers. Goods for antislavery fairs, bundles of the *Liberator* and the *National Anti-Slavery Standard,* and agents of the American Anti-Slavery Society, including Abby Kelley, William C. Nell, and Frederick Douglass, all arrived via canal. Douglass arrived in Rochester in 1847 on a speaking tour of western New York and returned a year later to publish his *North Star* in the booming village. Even with an increasingly vocal circle of local coworkers, ultraist women traveled extensively to promote their causes, attend meetings and lectures, raise funds, gather signatures on petitions, and lecture themselves. The canal eased and speeded their sojourns.

The Erie Canal changed Rochester from a prosperous village to a thriving city, and thus exacerbated the economic differences in the bases of female activism by accelerating the spread of cosmopolitan culture, religious revivalism, and political doctrines through western New York. As printed sermons and pamphlets, women's magazines, and romantic novels were unloaded at the port of Rochester so too was the cult of domesticity they proclaimed. The women of the new urban middle classes were the primary consumers of this literature in which women of all classes were portrayed as one entity—pious, pure, domestic, and submissive.[52] All of Rochester's women's associations adopted some of the rhetoric of domesticity and all claimed a desire for universal cooperation, which should flow easily from woman's universal nature and which would repudiate the individualistic and competitive ethos of the male-dominated world.[53]

Yet the domesticity rendered as a universal ideal in the popular literature in practice separated women from each other. In Rochester the material accoutrements of the new domestic culture were most readily available to the most affluent women, those who ran benevolent societies, while the privatization of the family and companionate marriage were more easily initiated by their younger perfectionist counterparts. Ultraist families, less urban and less affluent, continued to rely

[52] See Welter, "Cult of True Womanhood," and Douglas, *Feminization of American Culture.*

[53] The differences among activist women concerning woman's nature and woman's role are discussed in detail in Chapters 4 and 7. Ultraists believed that differences between men and women were largely products of socialization rather than of nature but that women's character should nonetheless be the standard of virtue for both men and women.

on both female labor and complex households to sustain themselves economically while adopting some of the artifacts and attitudes of urban domesticity.

When transferring domestic culture from private households to public arenas, the differences among female activists were even more sharply drawn. Benevolent women transferred their roles as household superintendents to public institutions and utilized surplus or worn household goods, such as bedding and clothing, as alms for the poor. For perfectionist women, the transferrence of familial values and the conversion of individuals to an ethic of moderation and cooperation were more important than the transferrence of material goods. Ultraist women, finally, converted domestic labor itself into public resources— by sewing garments and baking food for sale at antislavery fairs, for instance, or by taking in fugitive slaves as domestic servants.[54] Ultraist women's contributions were, moreover, augmented by those of men and children, the former supplying produce for sale at fairs and the latter supplying labor. Where benevolent women emphasized the segregation of men's and women's labor in both private and public spheres, perfectionists emphasized commonalities of values, and ultraists, the commonalities of both labor and values. Where the first assumed superintendence over working-class clients, the last two groups of women performed most of the mundane chores of activism themselves, with ultraist women being the most dependent on their own productive labor to advance the cause of change. Varied patterns of private domesticity thus helped to shape varied patterns of public activism. All were grounded in the virtue of female domesticity, but the private and public forms of that domesticity were mediated by material resources.

Whether fostered by economic stratification, the rise of domesticity, or religious heterodoxy, the differentiation of activist networks and their programs for social change were entrenched by the 1840s. The patterns that arose, initially only dimly perceived products of social experience, were crystalized in the heat of rapid economic and cultural change and by the second half of the nineteenth century provided

---

[54]The use of fugitive slaves as servants or laborers was largely discontinued after passage of the Fugitive Slave Act in 1850 because most fugitive slaves sought to go directly to Canada. Harriet Brent Jacobs, who worked for Isaac and Amy Post in 1849 and 1850, was the best known ex-slave to hold a job in Rochester.

women with clearly alternative forms of public labor. In the process of becoming clearly defined alternatives, patterns of female activism also became clearly embedded in the public domain.

Establishing female-run institutions of public welfare, providing an acceptable framework for women's public labors, and introducing new topics of public discourse, women activists changed the material and moral landscape of the community. In turn, women themselves were socialized into existing and developing economic, political, and social relations. They served as both agents and objects of social change, as reproducers and reshapers of social order and social value. The internal dynamics of women's associations and institutions did not respond only to the formation and fragmentation of the emerging middle classes but were elaborated and molded in the context of a female world of work. Women's activism created identities for middle-class women that combined features of voluntarism, domesticity, and labor. These identities, structured within organizations and institutions, then provided a relatively autonomous framework within which women could locate themselves, either as new members of the community or as members of new social or economic groups within the community. Finally, once publicly recognized as symbolizing a certain social and economic standing, women's associations served as channels to or assertions of public status for women and for their families.

Women's activism in Rochester emerged and operated at the intersections of public and private, male and female, affluent and poor, and local and extralocal worlds. At moments, female activists reached across class, ethnic, and racial divisions to touch the lives of other women while they simultaneously reproduced patterns of work, family, and social life that were distinctively bound to their own class and lineage. The relations among groups and the location of the crossroads at which they operated changed through the course of the nineteenth century. Women's participation in these changes expanded as they reshaped the terms of public discourse and solidified as they responded to larger economic, political, and social forces. By the 1870s, the profusion of pathways carved out by women in the 1830s, 1840s, and 1850s were well worn, providing entrance into new realms of community welfare and politics. When women first struck out on those paths in 1822, however, they envisioned a necessary but nonetheless narrow role for themselves and their followers.

[3]

From Amelioration to Perfection

Women's labors were strikingly visible in the early life of Rochester. Rochester's pioneers, few in number and drawing only limited distinctions between private and public domains, applauded women's spiritual, educational, medical, and domestic efforts. Yet the contours of the public sphere and women's access to it changed rapidly within a decade of settlement as male ministers, teachers, and physicians established institutions and practices that left women, especially affluent women, with few essential tasks outside the domestic circle. If the ladies of the village were to maintain their public presence, they would have to extend and formalize their public roles.

The Female Missionary Society (1818) was the first sign of this extension and formalization, though its members limited their efforts to raising funds for male missionaries rather than missionizing themselves. In 1821 a few women participated in a mission closer to home, opening a school for "orphans or those whose parents are in such indigent circumstances that they are totally unable to defray the expense of their children's tuition."[1] The effort was supported by the village fathers, with Josiah Bissell donating a room for the school until 1824 when it was moved to a lot given by Colonel William Fitzhugh.[2] The school was superintended by Mrs. Elizabeth Atkinson, wife of flour miller William Atkinson, and Huldah Strong, sister-in-law of

[1] Amy Hanmer-Croughton, "The Rochester Female Charitable Society," Rochester Historical Society, *Publications* 9 (1930): 68.
[2] The charity school remained in its second location until it was closed and its work was taken over by the public school system in the 1840s.

Abelard Reynolds, the village's first postmaster, saddler, and tavern keeper. Along with providing free education, these women and their coworkers took it upon themselves to "visit the homes of the children," "care for the sick and cloth the ragged."[3] It was "these educational wants of the poor, together with other destitutions consequent upon sickness in a new country" that "prompted for the purpose of more efficient action" the formation of the Female Charitable Society on 26 February 1822.[4]

The CS soon became the primary vehicle for pioneer women's public labors. The constitution stated the society's objects as "the relief of indigent sick persons, and the establishment of a Charity School."[5] Since the latter was already in operation, CS founders concentrated on devising a systematic method for effecting the former. The plan proposed was district visiting, the adaptation of a customary form of female sociability to public service. The city was divided into fifteen districts with a visitor assigned to each according to "their proximity to the district of which they are to have charge." It was the "duty of each Visitor to visit her district, at least once a month and oftener if necessary; to ascertain and relieve the wants of the sick poor; to notify them of her place of residence;" and "to make an annual report of the number of persons assisted, amount of money expended," and similar information.[6]

CS members paid annual dues of twenty-five cents and pledged themselves "to solicit money, provisions, clothing, and bedding from the community to be used in works of charity."[7] Initially, all "articles of clothing, bedding, etc., belonging to the Society" were to be "*loaned* by the Visitors," who were then responsible for retrieving them "in due season."[8] Here, as with district visiting, charitable women extended their resources by applying customary forms of female neighborliness, forms particularly necessary in a frontier setting, to communitywide concerns. The application of these techniques to benevolent labors was made easier in the early years of Rochester's development because the

[3] Hanmer-Croughton, "Rochester Female Charitable Society," p. 67.
[4] CS, *Charter, Constitution, By-Laws, and Officers of the Rochester Female Charitable Society (for the Relief of the Sick Poor), Together with Its History and Annual Reports for the Year 1860* (Rochester: D. C. Tracy, 1860), p. 3.
[5] CS, *Charter*, p. 9.
[6] Ibid., pp. 10–11.
[7] Hanmer-Croughton, "Rochester Female Charitable Society," p. 70.
[8] CS, *Charter*, p. 10.

homes of the almsgivers and the needy were interspersed throughout the village and because the almsgivers could frequently loan articles from their own large and fluid households.

By 1827 the CS had more than doubled in size, and its members for the first time selected a board of managers to transact daily business. The success of the association was attested to not only by membership statistics but also by the paeans of praise flowing from press and pulpit. The fund-raising sermons of the Reverends Comfort Williams and Francis Cuming, preached in 1822, supplied seventy-five dollars for the society's coffers. The following year, the charity sermon preached by Rev. Joseph Penney at First Presbyterian Church gained forty dollars and fifty cents and the approbation of the *Rochester Telegraph*. Editor Everard Peck claimed that on "no former occasion have we heard the claims of the poor urged with more ability." The Reverend Mr. Penney "irresistibly" proved that "it is the duty of the affluent to cherish the unfortunate," and that the CS was the proper agency to fulfill that duty. "It would be an offense against God and humanity," Peck concluded, "to withhold from these almoners of Heaven who are carrying education, nourishment and consolation into the retreats of ignorance, sickness and misery, the means of continuing their divine administrations."[9] All the congregations in the young community apparently agreed as the ministers of the First Baptist and First Methodist churches offered their appeals in 1824 and 1825, respectively.

The suspicions of female societies expressed by the Reverend Mr. Elliott in 1806 were certainly not shared by his Rochester counterparts in the 1820s. The approval of the latter was due not only to frontier conditions but also to a shift during the previous decade toward a more rationalistic religious tone, most forcefully articulated by Ashael Nettleton, Lyman Beecher, and Nathaniel Taylor. Known as the New Haven theology, it was a response, in part, to the transition to a commercial, market-oriented economy. It encouraged individual efforts to order and control society and emphasized man's active role in his spiritual and social well-being, asserting that man was "a free, rational, moral creative cause." Taylor insisted that "no man becomes depraved but by his own act. . . ."[10] Beecher, focusing on the positive side of this theology, linked man's moral agency to his duty to promote charity,

[9] *Rochester Telegraph*, 4 March 1823.
[10] Sidney E. Ahlstrom, *A Religious History of the American People*, 2 vols. (Garden City, N.Y.: Doubleday, 1975), 1: 509 and chap. 26 *passim*.

temperance, and virtue. Women formed a majority of the congregations in which powerful preaching brought the message of free moral agency to man and inquiry meetings fostered small-scale revivals. Few New England preachers, however, actually offered women the wider roles that the New Haven theology suggested for man. Nettleton, for instance, considered the "praying of females in the presence of males as the greatest evil to be apprehended," while Beecher sought to channel women's religious impulses into maternal associations and child nuture.[11]

Still, the sense of social duty contained in New Haven doctrines encouraged women to initiate charitable ventures. In Rochester, with its primitive social institutions and needy population, female benevolence was more easily acknowledged as an important component of the establishment of community order than it had been in turn-of-the-century Connecticut. Both men and women of the founding families believed in "our Savior's admonition 'the poor ye have always with you'."[12] Now they also accepted women's role in publicly and collectively "softening the pangs of grief, soothing the despair of affliction, assuaging the pains of sickness, wiping the widow's eyes and warming and educating her orphans."[13]

When CS women entered the streets on their errands of mercy, they continually crossed paths with coworshipers and kin as well as the sick poor. First Presbyterian and St. Luke's churches, both on South Fitzhugh Street, were important extradomestic meeting places for business and benevolent as well as spiritual interchanges. The more secular institutions of the city—banks, businesses, and shops—were also in close proximity to the homes of the charitable, and CS women visited the offices of bankers, merchants, attorneys, and manufacturers with regularity to solicit financial and legal advice and donations. They also visited the County and City Physicians and the Overseer of the Poor, the only city official designated to minister to the needy, to obtain free medical care for destitute families. At times, they even traveled to the common council chambers to petition for tax relief or a parcel of land.[14]

The success of CS members in obtaining the resources of benevo-

---

[11] John Frost to Charles G. Finney, 21 April 1827, Microfilm, Roll 1, CGFP.
[12] CS, *Charter*, p. 5.
[13] *Rochester Telegraph*, 4 March 1823.
[14] There is no evidence of CS members actually speaking before the common council. Rather, they sent letters or petitions or spoke with men privately, who then presented their positions to the council.

lence aided them in retaining their praiseworthiness since they were not forced to compromise their moral principles for material rewards. In 1828, for instance, the CS board considered the "proferred benefit by the Manager of the Theatre" and resolved to decline the offer as "the Theatre has a demoralizing effect on the morals and principles of this community" and was thus an enterprise the society did not wish "even indirectly to patronise." Turning from their normal path of unobtrusive activity, the CS published their resolution in the daily papers and added, "respectfully," that "an opportunity will be given to contribute in aid of its funds at the annual sermon."[15] Additional funds could be raised, in emergency situations, from the congregations of First Church, which "number[ed] among its members a large portion of the wealth, talent, and influence of [the] village," and St. Luke's, which could be similarly characterized.[16]

The women who led the CS had their needs publicly voiced by clergy, editors, and councilmen, many of whom they could solicit at home as well as in their public offices. They asserted themselves sufficiently to gather in a regular meeting but only to pursue more effectively missionary and charitable labors. Benevolent women shared a strong sense of spiritual and social duty, and by employing instruction, visitation, and similar unostentatious means to spread their moral influence, they could maintain the full support of male kith and kin. For CS women, then, spiritual concerns were well integrated with family interests and civic duty.

In November 1830 Charles Grandison Finney stepped to the pulpit of Rochester's Third Presbyterian Church and declared the primacy of spiritual concerns.[17] According to one parishioner, "Finney stared down from the pulpit and said flatly that if Christians united and dedicated their lives to the task, they could convert the world and bring on the millennium in three months.[18] The tenets of millennial perfectionism announced by Finney redefined both family interests and civic duties, momentarily at least making spiritual concerns the focus of both private individuals and public servants. Rochesterians had

---

[15] CS, Minute Book, 8 January 1828, CSP.

[16] James K. Livingston to Charles G. Finney, 7 December 1832, Roll 3, CGFP. Mrs. James K. Livingston served as president of the CS in 1827 and in numerous other offices during the following thirty-five years.

[17] Paul Johnson, *A Shopkeeper's Millennium: Society and Revivals in Rochester, New York, 1815–1837* (New York: Hill and Wang, 1978), p. 3.

[18] Bradford King, quoted in ibid., p. 4.

pleaded with Finney to come to their city for at least a year before his arrival. Those pleas suggested that benevolent attempts to ameliorate social ills, even with the support of village elites, were insufficient to guarantee community order in the midst of rapid economic and social change.

The first individuals to promulgate revivalism as the antidote to disorder were men such as Josiah Bissell. Bissell supported his wife's benevolent activities until his economic resources were drained by his investments in Sabbatarian campaigns. An elder of Third Presbyterian Church, Bissell wrote Finney of "'the large budget of evils rolling through our land & among us', dwelling on the moral dangers of canal life" and concluded with an invitation for Finney to preach in Rochester.[19] In this endeavor, Bissell was ultimately successful, and Finney's arrival unleashed precisely the revivalistic enthusiasm that he and like-minded men sought.

While it was churchmen and businessmen who requested Finney's services, after Finney's arrival it was women who became the primary agents of personal and community salvation. Revivals first intensified the spiritual commitments of church members, the majority of whom were women, and then spread to unregenerate family members, friends, and neighbors.[20] It was female Finneyites like Melania Smith, Mrs. Selah Mathews, Artemissia Perkins, Mrs. David Scoville, and Mrs. Hobart Ford who focused their kin's, coworshipers' and community's attention on the floodtides of revivalism. Finney's own recollections of his work in Rochester are laced with stories of women's prominent roles as converts and agents of conversion. "The wife of a prominent lawyer . . . was one of the first converts": her experience, as described by Finney himself, provides insight into women's general significance in the 1830–1831 revivals. A "Christian woman" had "persuaded [Mrs. M——] to come and see me," Finney recalled. She "had been a gay, worldly woman, and very fond of society. She afterward told me that when I first came there, she greatly regretted it, and feared there would be a revival; and a revival would greatly interfere with the pleasures and amusements that she had promised herself that winter." Finney detected, however, that "the Lord was indeed dealing with her in an unsparing manner," and that she was "bowed down with great

[19] Josiah Bissell to Charles G. Finney, 15 September 1829, quoted in ibid., p. 94.
[20] Ibid., p. 98. I have used women's names here as they appear in the documents, including conversion narratives and private correspondence.

conviction of sin." After "considerable conversation" and prayer, her "heart broke down," and she "settled into a joyous faith. . . . From that moment, she was out-spoken in her religious convictions, and zealous for the conversion of her friends." Her lawyer husband also soon converted, and to Finney's delight the entire ordeal "produced much excitement among that class of people to which she belonged."[21]

Brought to Finney by an already converted woman friend, Mrs. M—— challenged the revivalist by virtue of both her social standing and her lack of religious conviction. As a result of only a few hours' labor, however, Finney not only converted Mrs. M—— but also thereby provided a role model for male kin and for other affluent women. Mrs. M—— and her converted sisters gave revivalism an entree into the homes of some of Rochester's most influential citizens, and Finney utilized women's seemingly greater susceptibility to his preaching to orchestrate the revivals. For example, he introduced the "anxious seat" in Rochester to bring members of the higher "classes" out from the mass of the ungodly, to a public renunciation of their sinful ways, and a public committal of themselves to God." When Finney made his first call for the anxious to come forward, a "prominent lady, and several others of her acquaintance, and belonging to the same circle of society, responded. This increased the interest among that class of people," wrote Finney. His meetings "soon became thronged with that class. The lawyers, physicians, merchants, and indeed all the most intelligent people, became more and more interested and more and more easily influenced."[22]

As wives, mothers, mothers-in-laws, daughters, and daughters-in-law, Rochester women spread evangelical tenets within family circles in dramatic and enduring ways. When Mrs. Everard Peck died in January 1831, in the midst of Finney's labors, her last wish was to see her unregenerate father converted.[23] A "godly woman" of Third Presbyterian Church was very anxious for her son-in-law's soul and spent "much time in prayer for him." As soon as "he declared his conversion to her, and from his countenance she saw that it was really so, it overcame her, and she swooned away, and fell dead."[24] Melania Smith wrote to Finney that she prayed all day for her husband's conversion;

[21] Charles Grandison Finney, *The Memoirs of Rev. Charles G. Finney, Written by Himself* (New York: F. H. Revell, [1876]), pp. 287–288.
[22] Ibid., p. 289.
[23] Johnson, *Shopkeeper's Millennium*, p. 98.
[24] Finney, *Memoirs*, p. 292.

she survived his decision to join her as a member of Brick Presbyterian Church. Artemissia Perkins "prayed with her fiancé in Brick Church. Suddenly her voice rose above the others, and over and over she prayed, 'Blessed be the name of Jesus,' while her future husband, her neighbors, and people who never again could be strangers watched and participated in the awsome work."[25]

Finney preached an active Christianity, one involving public display and public commitment. In accordance with his sentiments, Brick Church soon rewrote its convenant, demanding of its parishioners not only "that they renounc[e] all ungodliness and every worldly lust" and "live as an humble Christian," but also that they "promise to make it the great business of . . . life to glorify God and build up the Redeemer's Kingdom in this fallen world."[26] As neighbors, friends, and teachers, evangelical women followed these dictates and extended their spiritual concerns from the family to the larger community. The concern seemed intrusive to some, as when the converted Mrs. M—— denounced Mrs. Levi Ward's daughter Susan for marrying "an almost infidel" and wondered how she could "ask the Lord to smile upon their union." Generally, however, the currents of revivalism flowed through more constructive channels. Mrs. Scoville visited New York City in the spring of 1831 "for no other object but to endeavor to be useful to the souls of her friends there who are unconverted."[27] Sarah T. Seward, principal of a female seminary, gave up her own soul to Christ and then fostered conversions among a number of her scholars.[28] Miss A——, a teacher at the coeducational Rochester high school, invited Finney to visit the school and a "revival took tremendous hold." A few years later, Miss A—— informed Finney that "more than forty persons that were then converted in that school, had become ministers."[29]

Finney and his followers were not unopposed in Rochester. In January 1831 a local meeting to disclaim "King-craft and Priest-craft" attracted a large crowd, numbering six to seven hundred persons. The sponsors, which included several leading citizens, hoped to awaken the public to the dangers of religious societies that were amassing wealth

[25] Johnson, *Shopkeeper's Millennium*, p. 101.

[26] Second (Brick) Presbyterian Church, Session Minutes, December 1825 and June 1831, Presbyterian Historical Society, Philadelphia, Pennsylvania.

[27] Mary S. Mathews to Mrs. Charles G. Finney, 1 August 1831 and 24 April 1831, Roll 3, CGFP.

[28] Sarah T. Seward to Charles and Lydia Finney, 9 March 1835, Roll 3, CGFP. In this letter, Seward recounts conversion experiences from 1831.

[29] Finney, *Memoirs*, p. 293.

and power and, through the press, voluntary associations, and legislation, were promoting a "self-styled Orthodoxy."[30] Nor did all religious
leaders agree with Finney's revivalistic techniques. The Reverend Mr.
Hotchkiss, an Old School Presbyterian, was apparently "horrified because women were allowed to lead in prayer at some of the meetings,"
particularly as the "minister 'not only allowed but encouraged' them to
do so."[31] The Rochester *Observer,* the voice of the city's most zealous
Evangelicals, reported in early 1831 that a few conservative elders
were roused to public criticism of several women who "ventured to
speak out in weekly testimonial meetings." Other religious groups,
primarily the Quakers, saw nothing wrong with the roles accorded to
women but disapproved of the " 'fanatical' measures" employed by
evangelical preachers.[32]

In addition, many people who were swept into the fires of revivalism
by Finney's presence cooled considerably in his absence. Merchant-
miller Hervey Ely was forced to write to Finney within weeks of his
departure that the community had not kept up "the pecuniary side" of
their bargain with the revivalist.[33] By spring 1831 a Finney convert was
writing to Mrs. Finney that "coldness" had already set in. The village
was "a disgrace to religion," she lamented: tell Mr. Finney "his children are starving here."[34] Yet not all converts were guilty of backslid-
ing, and many female Finneyites became more self-conscious of their
special role in achieving the millennium as they noted the ungodly
defections around them.

While Finney claimed to have attracted the highest classes of society, those who remained most active in seeking the millennium were
those who sought entry into, rather than emerged from, Rochester's
most affluent sector. Josiah Bissell was in the throes of bankruptcy by
the time of Finney's arrival and died shortly after Finney's departure;
his wife remained an active evangelical for many years. Samuel D.
Porter was in a healthier economic and physical state in 1831, but he
was just beginning to climb to a comfortable position, and his parents
and sisters continued to struggle to maintain even a moderately com-

[30] *Proceedings of the Friends of Liberal Principles and Equal Rights* (Rochester: H. S. Salisbury, 1831), pp. 1–4.
[31] Alma C. Ruch, "Rochester Revivals," TS, n.d., Rochester Public Library.
[32] Blake McKelvey, *Rochester: The Water Power City, 1812–1854* (Cambridge: Harvard University Press, 1945), pp. 193, 134.
[33] Hervey Ely to Charles G. Finney, 5 March 1831, Roll 2, CGFP.
[34] Mary S. Mathews to Mrs. Charles G. Finney, 24 April 1831, Roll 3, CGFP.

fortable lifestyle. The husbands of Mrs. M—— and Melania Smith, a lawyer and a physician, respectively, were also just beginning their careers. Another active Evangelical, Mrs. Elizabeth Eaton, had entered Rochester as a member of the well-to-do Selden family and then married attorney Joseph Spencer. But she, too, found herself in precarious economic circumstances by the time Finney reached Rochester. Her first husband had died in 1823, and when she remarried in 1831 it was to Amos Eaton, an army supply officer who traveled extensively to maintain an adequate income for his family. It was at this time that Mrs. Eaton joined the Finney-led Third Presbyterian Church. In general, it was those people tied to new commercial ventures—including forwarding merchants and lawyers—or those just below affluence—master craftsmen and small merchants—who were the most willing converts.[35] The men in these occupations were dependent to a large degree on the canal traffic and on the population, property, construction, and crime boom that it engendered. Their families would have been particularly concerned about the uncertainties, immediate and eternal, of rapid economic and social change. Within these families, it was women who had the time and now the inspiration and justification to pursue community stability through new evangelical forms of public activism.[36]

Across the North and in Rochester in particular, female Finneyites voiced new ideas and pursued new activities under the banner of millennial perfectionism. Some women came to view the criticism of unregenerate men and "cold" ministers as part of their mission, though initially they reserved their diatribes for private conversation and correspondence. In May 1831 Mrs. Mathews, the Mrs. M—— of Finney's *Memoirs,* claimed that only two of the male church elders at Third Presbyterian evidenced sincere concern for the community's spiritual state and that Josiah W. Bissell, whose father had called Finney to Rochester, was "as hardened as ever." She condemned the husband of an evangelical sister as "entirely thoughtless," that is, entirely without religious feeling. She bemoaned the "deplorable state" of religion in the village and described a minister being considered for the Third Church

[35] Johnson, *Shopkeeper's Millennium,* pp. 102–108. Finney had begun his career as a lawyer and appealed to that class specifically in Rochester as elsewhere.

[36] For similar interpretations of this process, see Mary P. Ryan, *The Cradle of the Middle-Class: The Family in Oneida County, New York, 1780–1865* (Cambridge: Cambridge University Press, 1981); Carroll Smith-Rosenberg, "Sex as Symbol in Victorian Purity: An Ethnological Analysis," in John Demos and Sarene Spence Boocock, eds., *Turning Points: Historical and Sociological Essays on the Family* (Chicago: University of Chicago Press, 1978), pp. 212–247.

pulpit as "a lovely spirit" but "lack[ing] energy."[37] Mrs. Mathews's concerns were echoed by Mrs. Eaton. In 1831 the latter complained to her husband that Judge Ashley Sampson, chosen as a Third Church elder, "*never* had the holy ghost, instead of being filled with it as the deacons of the primitive church were." She was particularly concerned about Sampson's and others' rejection of Finney's idea of sanctification and, with no apparent consideration of women's "inferior" intellect, devised "a way of getting at the subject among old stupid professors." By taking "them on their own ground *& language* with *their own terms,*" she argued, they could be shown "the necessity of striving for a *deeper work of grace.*" The following year, Mrs. Eaton wrote to Amos of a new religious " 'circle' " about which there were "many falsehoods afloat . . . & much misunderstanding." But the condemnations did not deter her, for she found her "own faith" was "strengthened and confirmed."[38]

There were many religious circles formed in the aftermath of Finney's revivals as evangelical women channeled their energies into religiously directed and sanctioned activities. Believing that "the sin of unbelief [is] truly the 'Parent of all other sins,'" female converts formed prayer circles to strengthen their own faith and encourage each other.[39] Convert Charlotte Bloss, for instance, wrote to Finney a year after his departure that she and the Third Church had slipped somewhat in his absence, "but I try with Mrs. Mathews to raise myself up."[40] When Mrs. Atkinson's husband "entirely failed" in business, she accepted it as a true Christian with the help of Mrs. Mathews and "two or three others" whom she met with "every Saturday for prayer."[41] Mrs. Ely had written to Mrs. Finney just previously that the female prayer meetings at Third Church were well attended: "we have four weekly in our church—the old established ones, the young ladies, and the young married ladies." In addition, the female parishioners were running a "charity infant school" that was "flourishing."[42]

Finney converts also formed maternal and Sunday school societies,

[37] Mary S. Mathews to Mrs. Charles Finney, 9 March 1835, 1 August 1831, 16 May 1831, and 1 August 1831, Roll 3, CGFP.

[38] Elizabeth Seldon Eaton to Amos Eaton, 20 April 1833, 16 April 1833, and 22 February 1834, in Blake McKelvey, comp., "Letters Postmarked Rochester," Rochester Historical Society, *Publications* 21 (1943): 45–47. On this religious circle and community responses to it, see McKelvey, *Rochester,* p. 193.

[39] Catharine A. [Mrs. Hervey] Ely to Mrs. Charles Finney, 3 May 1831, Roll 3, CGFP.

[40] Charlotte M. Bloss to Charles G. Finney, 22 October 1832, Roll 3, CGFP.

[41] Mary S. Mathews to Mrs. Charles Finney, 20 October 1832, Roll 3, CGFP.

[42] Catharine A. Ely to Mrs. Charles Finney, 20 June 1832, Roll 3, CGFP.

again with Third Church apparently leading the way. In summer 1831 Mrs. Mathews lamented that maternal societies had not yet been started at any of the other churches and that attendance at Third Church's was limited by "so much sickness among the children."[43] A few years later a women's Sunday school society required aid from Mrs. Finney in finding teachers to send west, all expenses paid.[44] Foreign missions also gained local evangelicals' attention; one in the Sandwich Islands attracted the labor of several Rochesterians. In fall 1832 Mrs. Mathews reported to the Finneys that her husband, Selah, was contemplating a missionary career: "it would be delightful," she claimed, "to spend my life in teaching the heathen."

Mrs. Mathews admitted, however, "I think of the toils and hardships and privations of a missionary life" and "my heart fails me."[45] Selah himself soon gave up the idea of missionizing among heathens and, very successfully, refocused his attention on his law practice, banking ventures, and political career. He was able to combine successes in these fields with social concerns by joining other evangelical men in a temperance society that sought the legal prohibition of the liquor traffic. His wife and her evangelical sisters truggled far longer to find appropriate and effective vehicles for eradicating vice from the world.

Evangelical women's boldness in private correspondence and their innovativeness within church walls was not at first paralleled in more public arenas. While the centers of revivalism—Brick and Third Presbyterian churches, First Baptist, and the newly formed Free Presbyterian and Second Baptist congregations—did not replace First Presbyterian or St. Luke's as centers of female benevolence, they did supply the CS with newly active women. At the same time, at least seven long-active CS leaders shifted their membership from First to Brick or Third Presbyterian Church. There, as agents of Rochester's only formal female civic association, they attracted at least thirty-three new members to their organization. A new Episcopal congregation, St. Paul's, was founded in the late 1820s. It attracted evangelically oriented Episcopalians, including CS charter member Mrs. Elizabeth Atkinson, who by 1832 brought eight sister communicants into the

[43] Mary S. Mathews to Mrs. Charles Finney, 1 August 1831, Roll 3, CGFP.
[44] Susan W. Selden (secretary, Women's Infant School Society) to Mrs. Charles Finney, 11 June 1834, Roll 3, CGFP.
[45] Mary S. Mathews to Mrs. Charles Finney, 20 October 1832, Roll 3, CGFP.

CS.[46] Yet benevolent labors did not satisfy evangelical women's drive for personal and social perfection. Once again, Mrs. Mathews captured the anxieties of her perfectionist sisters. "It is my delight," she wrote to Mrs. Finney, "to visit the poor, to converse with them and watch by their sick bed—but after all I find so many unholy motives and such unsanctified feelings rise up while performing these external Christian duties."[47]

As revival enthusiasm waned, it was clearer than ever that conversions alone could not stem the tide of disorders rolling along the canal's path. Rochester's second city directory, published in 1834, revealed increasing residential segregation by class, a proliferation of taverns and groceries along the canal and river, growing numbers of immigrants, and an astounding rate of mobility into and out of the city. Criminal convictions had also increased, reaching a new but soon surpassed high of sixty-three in 1834, including two for bawdy houses.[48] Nor was Rochester alone in this sorry state. The pages of big-city newspapers were filled with tales of licentiousness and crime, while reform journals made the evils of slavery increasingly visible to Northern dwellers. For women, only the CS and prayer circles existed to combat such sins. Finally, after years of seeking church-based means of perfecting the world or relying on previously established benevolent societies, female perfectionists stepped into the gap between affluent almsgivers and their destitute recipients, between northern humanitarians and southern slaves. They were armed not only with religious zeal but also with petitions, pledges, and moral tracts.

Though licentiousness and crime attracted greater attention from Rochester's chroniclers, slavery became the first focus of perfectionists' organizational efforts. Whether influenced by the intense involvement of male kin or shamed by the abolitionist activities of black female neighbors, perfectionist women established the Rochester Female Anti-Slavery Society in 1835. Evangelical women were probably not the first white women in the city to join in collective condemnations of slavery. The Society of Friends had established a meetinghouse on

---

[46]On the evangelical tendencies of St. Paul's founders, see Johnson, *Shopkeeper's Millennium*, pp. 91–92, and McKelvey, *Rochester*, pp. 132–133. On "Presbyterianisms" at St. Luke's Church, see Johnson, *Shopkeeper's Millennium*, pp. 97–98, and McKelvey, *Rochester*, pp. 129–131.

[47]Mary S. Mathews to Mrs. Charles Finney, 16 May 1831, Roll 3, CGFP.

[48]Johnson, *Shopkeeper's Millennium*, pp. 48–55; McKelvey, *Rochester*, pp. 165, 229, 252–253.

Fitzhugh Street in 1822. After 1828 both the Orthodox and the Hicksite branches of the Friends maintained local meetings, and leaders in both played prominent roles in the establishment of the first Rochester men's abolitionist societies. Since women generally joined men in signing Quaker testimonies against slavery, it is likely that they were the first of Rochester's white women to denounce the institution publicly.[49] By 1835, at the first anniversary session of the Genesee Yearly Meeting of (Hicksite) Friends, Hicksite women and men united in "consideration of the subject of Slavery," producing a minute of advice to subordinate meetings, such as the Rochester Monthly Meeting, and a memorial to Congress.[50]

Both black women and Hicksite women, for different reasons, had difficulties making their voices heard on the slave's behalf.[51] Evangelical women, with the support of clergy and reform-minded male kin, were more audible, though it is unclear precisely how or by whom the FASS was organized. A longhand copy of the society's proposed constitution was apparently circulated throughout the city for signatures; the only extant copy, however, contains only five signatures, all in pencil.[52] On 24 September 1835, the organization of the FASS was announced by the publication of the constitution and a list of the FASS officers in the *Daily Democrat*. The first directress of the association, Mrs. David Scoville, was the wife of a bank clerk and a member of Third Presbyterian Church. Among the original seventeen officers were at least five other Third Church and two Brick Church members along with two Orthodox Quakers and four Baptists. All four Baptists had been founders in 1834 of Second Baptist Church, the first local congregation to allow blacks to be seated in the main body of pews.[53] Two ministers, both Baptists, had female kin in FASS offices, but most of the society's leaders were wedded to members of the city's dynamic

[49] The Society of Friends divided into Orthodox and Hicksite meetings in 1828; the Hicksites generally contained the more agrarian-based and reform-minded members. At this time, there were about six hundred Quakers in the county and three hundred in the village, the largest number of which joined the Hicksite Meeting.

[50] GYMWF, Minutes, 1834–1885, HRR. Quote from Minutes, June 1835. Memorials to Congress on the subject of slavery were acceptable if sent from a regular meeting of the Society of Friends but joint Quaker and non-Quaker petitions were generally frowned upon.

[51] There were fewer than three hundred free blacks in Rochester at this time, and they were ignored by a large portion of the community. The Quakers were more numerous and vocal but at this point discussed slavery primarily within Quaker meetings, and their published testimonies were not widely circulated.

[52] FASS, Constitution, [1835], SDPFP.

[53] McKelvey, *Rochester*, p. 279.

commercial sector: their husbands included a forwarding merchant, surveyor, commercial farmer, land agent, painter, carpenter, printer, saddler, bank clerk, and grocer.

Some early abolitionists had brought experiences from the CS into the FASS. Mrs. Scoville, for instance, had served the CS intermittently as a district visitor, school committee member, and directress. The third FASS directress, Mrs. Selah Mathews, was a CS directress before the FASS's founding, while the secretary of the new organization had been a district visitor and directress in the older society. Though not significant numerically, these three former CS officers held important posts in the FASS and may have been instrumental in providing associational experience and models of organization.

Most antislavery women had worked only briefly or not at all in benevolent ventures before entering the FASS. Whereas the CS's greatest resource had been its link to local financial and political power, the FASS's was its evangelical zeal. "Believing that in this as in similar cases we can act more efficiently by way of organized effort, therefore in obedience to our Saviour's golden rule 'all things whatsoever ye would that men should do unto you do ye even so to them,' " evangelical abolitionists agreed to "form [them]selves into a Society." Having entered the field of abolition, they claimed the boldest positions as their own: the "fundamental principles of this Society are that slaveholding is sin and that immediate emancipation without the condition of expatriation is the duty of the master and the right of the slave." They justified their public endeavors by "the law of God" of which slavery was "a gross violation" and by the directive of God that "made it the duty of all, of every sex, class and condition to do what they can to remove this sin."[54]

Yet in specifying the actual forms of their involvement, the FASS articulated a more modest stance: the society would "do what it [could] by moral and religious means." It would "aim to improve the character and condition of the people of colour by encouraging their intellectual, moral and religious improvement and by correcting prevailing and unchristian prejudices." But FASS members assured their fellow citizens that they would "never countenance the oppressed in vindicating their rights by resorting to physical force."[55] A year after the FASS's founding, its leaders still seemed uncertain how to proceed. "Our Anti-

[54] FASS, Constitution, SDPFP.
[55] Ibid.

Slavery Society does pretty well," wrote Mrs. Mathews to Mrs. Finney in the summer of 1836. "We have pledged ourselves to raise $200 the present year—and think we shall succeed." However, "[we] have the most trouble in rendering our meetings sufficiently interesting to induce ladies to attend," and Mrs. Mathews wished that the "Secretary of your Moral Reform and Anti-Slavery Societies would write to us— perhaps it will give us a new impulse."[56]

Uncertainty was only one of the obstacles lining the new public path forged by perfectionist women. In May 1835, before the official announcement of the FASS's founding, a group of antislavery women circulated a request for "assistance with regard to procuring a petition to our national Legislature from the Ladies of Rochester for the immediate Abolition of slavery in the District of Columbia." Mrs. Jonathan Child, a CS officer and daughter of the city's founder, declined to assist them. She wrote, "I greatly respect your principles and motives," and "I concede & claim for our sex the right and priviledge [*sic*] at all times to express our views and sentiments on this, & every moral, religious, & political subject." Yet she "doubt[ed] whether the influence of females can be exerted with propriety or efficiency, by any *combined public* effort or co-operation." Particularly as "political considerations are involved," she concluded, "I deem the measure you contemplate more properly the business of those who by the constitution of our government are entrusted with the management and direction of its political affairs."[57]

Apparently Mrs. Child did not view CS work, effected through personal donation and private visitation, as combined public effort. She did, however, at least grant respect for abolitionist women's principles. A few months later, Mrs. Child's brother, Thomas Rochester, and the husbands of several CS officers held a meeting at the court house to announce their opposition to immediate emancipation. Though they claimed to believe that slavery should be abolished, they wished any decision on the matter to be left to the individual states. The announcement of this meeting appeared on 24 September in the column next to that containing the FASS's constitution.[58] No other mention of the FASS's activities ever appeared in the local press, suggesting the muteness that could be imposed when women sought to speak too boldly.

[56] Mary S. Mathews to Mrs. Charles Finney, 22 June 1836, Roll 3, CGFP.
[57] Sophia E. [Mrs. Jonathan] Child to Sarah D. Fish, 14 May 1835, BFFP.
[58] *Daily Democrat* (Rochester), 24 September 1835.

In the winter of 1836 evangelical women joined forces with their male kin and counterparts to petition for the abolition of slavery in the nation's capital. While perfectionists established sex-segregated societies and even sex-segregated sections on their petitions, they shared aversion to slavery. Evangelical women's agreement with male kin on principles and their difficulty in forging alliances with benevolent ladies led to the joint petition of 1,559 citizens of Monroe County.[59] It read like a roster of Rochester's evangelical families accompanied, especially in the agricultural hinterland, by smaller circles of Orthodox and Hicksite Quakers. The last group comprised only a small part of the total signers, yet their signatures were the first local evidence of Quaker interest in working for abolition outside their own religious meetings.[60]

The flush of success felt by perfectionists after the 1836 petition campaign was offset some months later by the reception accorded lecturer Theodore Weld in the very heart of Rochester's evangelical community—Third Presbyterian Church. Weld was no stranger to the city. At Finney's behest he had delivered a four-hour temperance lecture at First Presbyterian Church, ringing in New Year's 1831 with violent denounciations of the sins of alcohol. His views, dramatized by sweeping gestures and firebrand depictions of the hell awaiting even the moderate tippler, stunned the packed house into silence and led to the formation of an interdenominational pact in favor of total abstinence.[61] When Weld returned in 1835, however, to make a similar plea on behalf of abolition, the response was less universally positive. Indeed, his visit may have contributed to the calling of the anti–immediate emancipation meeting at the court house that fall.[62] By 1836 Weld was no longer entirely welcome even within the Third Church. As Mrs. Mathews reported to Mrs. Finney: "We had a small riot in the old Third Church. If it had been any other lecturer, and in any other house, I could have borne it, but to see a crowd in that house, where every association is sacred hissing and insulting Mr. *Weld* who came next to Mr. Finney in my affections, it was more than I could endure."[63]

[59] Anti-Slavery Petition from the Men and Women of Rochester, New York, 27 February 1836, House of Representatives, LC74, Library of Congress, Washington, D.C. I thank Judith Wellman for reference to this source.

[60] Debates erupted within the Hicksite meeting at this time over the propriety of members working for reform in "worldly," that is, non-Quaker, associations. Only Hicksite Sarah D. Fish seems to have been active in such associations before 1836. See n. 57 above.

[61] Johnson, *Shopkeeper's Millenium*, pp. 113–114.

[62] McKelvey, *Rochester*, p. 285.

[63] Mary S. Mathews to Mrs. Charles Finney, 22 June 1836, Roll 3, CGFP.

The Mathewses did endure, however, with Selah in particular turning away from perfectionist doctrines to become a "shrine of orthodoxy" within the congregation.[64] Mrs. Mathews, meanwhile, redirected part of her attention, not away from perfectionism but away from abolition and toward moral reform. In the same letter in which she bemoaned Weld's treatment, she noted more hopefully, "We have at length organized a Moral Reform Society here, about 60 members. I believe you will be glad to hear this." Beginning in 1834, evangelical ministers had helped to focus perfectionist women's attention on moral reform issues. The Reverend William Wisner, called to Brick Church in 1831, denounced the double standard of morality three years later. His sermon, printed in pamphlet form, was distributed throughout the city. The Baptists also encouraged their female parishioners to consider the issue by recommending the *Advocate of Moral Reform* "to the patronage of the community." In the same report, the Monroe Baptist Association resolved "that as a proper division of labor is desireable [*sic*], we affectionately recommend to sisters in all our churches (aided by their pastors,) to undertake the monthly distribution of *Tracts*, . . . to bear against the sins of the age. . . ."[65] A member of the Monroe Association, Rev. Elon Galusha of Rochester's Second Baptist Church, circulated the *Advocate* among his flock with the aid of his wife, who was active in the newly formed Rochester Female Moral Reform Society.

The Third Presbyterian Church pastor must have been less forthcoming with advice, for Mrs. Mathews appealed to Mrs. Finney for counsel on suitable and interesting topics for FMRS meetings. "Do you approve of discussing subjects in the meetings?" she inquired. Specifically, she wondered whether they should consider "such a question as 'Ought licentious men be exposed,' " appointing "committees to report on each side."[66] The queries may have been rhetorical, however, since a report from the FMRS in favor of exposing licentious men appeared in the *Advocate of Moral Reform* one month later, on 15 July 1836. The report reveals that FMRS members, like their FASS counterparts, relied on evangelical injunctions to perfect the world and on

[64] Waldo G. Wildes, Elder, "History of Third Church," TS, n.d., Presbyterian Historical Society, Philadelphia, Pennsylvania.

[65] Monroe Baptist Association, *Proceedings of the Monroe Baptist Association* (Rochester: Shepard and Strong, 1835).

[66] Mary S. Mathews to Charles Finney, 22 June 1836, Roll 3, CGFP.

biblical claims for equality, at least of sin, to justify entrance into new public endeavors.

Men whose sin was "trifling" should only "be slightly censured," according to the report, "but if it be heinous, soul-destroying, abhorrent in the sight of God and man, and to our sex most ruinous, let us beware how we tolerate it." The committee of the Rochester FMRS "on the treatment of licentious men" noted God's use of the sin of lewdness to represent all "the abominations and idolatries of his people." Moreover, in opposition to what "public sentiment has long been teaching," God does not claim that this "sin is less criminal in the other sex than in our own," they argued: "Lev. 20:10 'The adulterer and the adulteress shall both be put to death.'" As the licentious man is equally guilty with the licentious woman, he too should be ostracized from society. Evangelical women, by virtue of their virtue, had a special role to play—"a work which we alone can do"—"to refuse to put vice on an equal footing with virtue" and "to cease to greet as a companion and equal, the fell destroyer of our sex."[67] While equally guilty with man once she had fallen, the pure woman could be the savior of both sexes. The husbands and brothers of FMRS leaders attempted to share the burden of purity, forming a new male Moral Reform Society and charging themselves to discountenance vice "by regarding licentious men as equally guilty with licentious women."[68] Within six months, however, the interest of many of the men lagged, while others became zealous in expelling their less pure brethren, depleting the association of members. By 1837 the men's society was defunct, and women were clearly in charge of eradicating vice in Rochester.[69]

Evangelical women had now formalized their quest for perfection through the FASS and the FMRS. Simultaneously, they had increased their participation in benevolent works by infiltrating the membership, though not the leadership, of the CS. A year after Finney left Rochester, the evangelical churches supplied more than a quarter of all CS members and by 1836 more than one third.[70] In each of those years,

---

[67] *Advocate of Moral Reform* (New York City), 15 July 1836.

[68] [Male] Moral Reform Society, Minute Book, 1836–1837, preface, Rochester Public Library.

[69] On the men's Moral Reform Society, see McKelvey, *Rochester*, p. 283, and James McElroy, "Social Reform in the Burned-over District: Rochester, New York as a Test Case, 1830–1854" (Ph.D. diss., State University of New York at Binghamton, 1974).

[70] The number of perfectionists may be underestimated since those for whom no religious affiliation was listed were not likely to be from First Presbyterian or St. Luke's Episcopal churches. In 1836 the CS contained 230 members, of which 86 were from

however, evangelical women filled but two (13 percent) of fifteen major offices—president, vice-president, secretary, treasurer, or directress. Those evangelical women who held benevolent offices were generally in the more minor positions of church collectors and district visitors. Only with the founding of the Orphan Asylum Association in 1837 did perfectionist and benevolent women truly attempt to share labors.

In January 1837 the inquiries of several ladies revealed "upwards of twenty orphan children, dependent on private charity, and exposed to all the evils consequent upon a loss of Parental care." There were others, children of "poor widows" or of parents who were "extremely poor and addicted to every vice," who also cried for aid."[71] "In view of all these circumstances the Ladies felt that something should be done immediately—and submitted the question to a committee of gentlemen (without whose cooperation and influence they felt that nothing could be done & that the project must be abandon'd)."[72] At a meeting at Mrs. Atkinson's, a discussion of the subject and a favorable reply from the gentlemen induced the ladies to form an association. Drawing on their experiences in the Charitable, Anti-Slavery, and Moral Reform societies, the founders of the OAA quickly adopted a constitution and bylaws, rented and furnished a house, selected a matron, and solicited operating expenses. On April 13, less than two months after its formation, the OAA held its first meeting at the asylum.

The establishment of the OAA followed immediately on a new wave of revivalism and drew at least half of its first eighteen officers from those Presbyterian and Baptist congregations most affected. While attracting many CS leaders, the OAA was clearly evangelical in style in its early years. In 1830 Finney had assured his Rochester parishioners that "genuine faith is always accompanied by good works. . . ."[73] To foster faith and works through conversion, Finney had introduced new revivalistic techniques, including door-to-door canvassing for potential converts, inquiry meetings, intensified family devotions, prayer meetings, and the "anxious seat" for the about-to-be converted. Religious

---

evangelical churches, 71 from Episcopal churches, 64 from First Presbyterian, and 9 from unidentifiable churches.

[71] OAA, *History of the Rochester Female Association for the Relief of Orphan and Destitute Children, Together with Its Organization, By-Laws, &c.* (Rochester: Shepard and Strong, 1839), pp. 3–4.

[72] OAA, Minute Book, preface [1837], HCCP.

[73] Quoted in McKelvey, *Rochester*, p. 190. See also, Johnson, *Shopkeeper's Millennium*, chap. 5.

conversion was to proceed from private soul-searching, discussion, and instruction to a public admission of "anxiety" and a public pronouncement of conversion. The OAA founders followed a similar course: they first discussed the proposition privately, then canvassed the city for orphans and destitute children, and finally inquired among themselves and in conference with local gentlemen whether this was "the proper time for an effort in behalf of the Orphan." Thus "after much deliberation and painful anxiety, but with reliance on him" who is the "Father of the fatherless," the OAA was formed.[74]

Nonetheless, half of the first OAA officers were not from newly formed evangelical congregations but from Rochester's first Presbyterian and Episcopal congregations. Four CS charter members were among these officers—Mrs. Elizabeth Atkinson, Mrs. Thomas Rochester, Mrs. Silas O. Smith, and Mrs. Ira West. Other CS charter members—Mrs. Levi Ward and her daughter, Mrs. Samuel Selden, and Mrs. Edwin Scrantom—joined the OAA in its founding year, while Mrs. James K. Livingston, former president of the CS, served as a directress of both the CS and OAA in 1837. In addition, Everard Peck's second wife served as first treasurer of the OAA, as his first wife had served the CS. While Mrs. Atkinson, though Episcopalian, was zealous in her support of revivalism, most of the CS leaders were more orthodox in their religious tendencies. By virtue of their social status and long years of public service, they wielded considerable influence within the OAA.

Benevolent and perfectionist women, by merging their efforts in the OAA, produced a new form of female association in Rochester. The OAA was the first female association to establish an asylum for its charges, making women's combined public efforts visible in brick and board.[75] Yet OAA leaders also made visible their submission to male authority, having been willing to abandon their plans entirely if the village's gentlemen leaders disapproved. The OAA was more hierarchically structured than other perfectionist associations, following the CS's model of administration in the selection of officers and the scheduling of meetings. At the same time, within this structure, the OAA was more religiously oriented than the CS, emphasizing religious

[74]OAA, *History*, p. 4; OAA, 1839 Annual Report, Scrapbook, HCCP.
[75]The development of institutions to care for a variety of social problems is best analyzed in David Rothman, *The Discovery of the Asylum: Social Order and Disorder in the New Republic* (Boston: Little, Brown, 1971).

instruction for orphans and among themselves as one of the primary tasks of charitable work. Orphans received copies of the Testaments upon entering the asylum and Bibles when leaving; they attended religious services with the matron and weekly Sunday school classes. Monthly meetings of the OAA were opened by readings from the Scriptures, and a local clergyman was invited to offer prayer at the annual meeting.[76] The OAA, unlike the CS, the FASS, or the FMRS, not only sought to "interest the whole community" in its work but actually formed an executive board in which, they claimed, "all the different religious societies of the city were represented."[77] Despite the absence of Catholic, Quaker, German Lutheran, and African Methodist board members, the OAA was the most ecumenical association in Rochester in 1837.[78]

One of the leading organizers of the OAA was Mrs. Samuel D. Porter. In the winter of 1837 Mrs. Porter dedicated what would have been her leisure time to two door-to-door canvasses of the city: one to raise funds for the orphan asylum and the other to obtain signatures on a massive antislavery petition. While for the former she solicited donations from men as eagerly as from women, for the latter she was dependent on her sisters' cooperation alone. Six hundred seventeen female residents of the city responded to the appeal of Mrs. Porter and the FASS, "earnestly entreat[ing]" Congress "to pass without delay such laws, as to your widsom may seem right and proper for the entire abolition of slavery and the slave trade in the District of Columbia."[79] After the submission of the petition to Congress on 30 January, Mrs. Porter and at least a dozen of her coworkers devoted their attention to the asylum.

Then in May, a month after the asylum opened, a momentous event in the history of women's activism occurred: the country's most prominent female abolitionists met at the first Anti-Slavery Convention of American Women in New York City. The Grimkés, Lucretia Mott,

[76]These features may not seem unusual in the context of Rochester's revivals, but the CS does not record similar rituals at its meetings.

[77]OAA, Minute Book, preface [1837], HCCP.

[78]Evangelical women dominated the first OAA board since women from Second and Third Presbyterian, First and Second Baptist, First Methodist, Saint Paul's Episcopal, and Bethel Free Church were all evangelicals, while only First Presbyterian and St. Luke's women represented orthodox views.

[79]Anti-Slavery Petition from the Women of Western New York, 30 January 1837, House of Representatives Document HR 25A-H1.8, Box 83, Library of Congress, Washington, D.C. I thank Paul Johnson for a copy of this document.

Lydia Maria Child, Maria Weston Chapman, Abby Kelley, Mary Grew, and others debated procedures and techniques and raised fundamental questions about women's roles in social activism. One of the most controversial resolutions to arise in the convention claimed that "as certain rights and duties are common to all moral beings, the time has come for women to move in that enlarged sphere which Providence has assigned her, and no longer remained satisfied in the circumscribed limits which corrupt customs and a perverted application of the Scripture have encircled her."[80] The measure was finally approved, though not unanimously, and appeared in the published proceedings.

Before those proceedings reached Rochester, Mrs. Porter received a letter from Julianna Tappan. The daughter of abolitionist and Finney convert Lewis Tappan and a founder of the New York City Female Anti-Slavery Society, Julianna Tappan was one of those appointed to execute the project agreed upon at the May convention—a highly organized petition campaign to send one million female signatures to Congress.[81] The plan involved delegating at least one woman from each town and village to be responsible for circulating petitions. Cities were to be divided into districts, with antislavery women to "visit *every house* and present to *every female* over sixteen years of age, a petition for her signature."[82] Each antislavery society was to return the petitions by October along with a financial contribution to defray expenses.

On 19 September 1837 the petition of the women of Rochester, New York, was presented to the House of Representatives.[83] It contained the names of eight hundred women opposed to the annexation of Texas, the extension of slavery into new territories, and the continuation of slavery and the slave trade in the nation's capital. Despite the growing antiabolitionist sentiment evidenced in Rochester in 1836, the FASS was able to produce its greatest triumph the very next year with its two massive antislavery petitions. Their success was due in part to the strong support given antislavery women by members of Second Baptist, Brick, and Bethel Presbyterian churches. Bethel Church, founded in July 1836, "had its origins in a spirit of Christian progress

[80] Quoted in Keith Melder, *The Beginnings of Sisterhood: The Woman's Rights Movement in the United States, 1800–1840* (New York: Schocken, 1977), p. 75.

[81] Ibid.

[82] Julianna Tappan to Mrs. Samuel D. Porter, 20 May 1837, SDPFP.

[83] Since the "gag rule" that tabled all antislavery petitions was in effect from 1836 to 1844, these petitions were never read into the *Congressional Record*.

and reform" and nearly all of its members were of that "despised sect called *Abolitionists*."[84] The views of the Bethel congregation and other abolitionist Presbyterians triumphed over those of their more conservative brothers and sisters when the Presbytery of the Genesee and the Association of Western New York passed a series of antislavery resolutions in spring 1837.[85] While the Monroe Baptist Association tabled an antislavery resolution in 1835 because it did not receive the unanimous endorsement of the delegates, at least a majority supported its passage, including Rev. Elon Galusha and other members of Rochester's Second Baptist Church.[86]

Other religious and community groups also aided women's antislavery efforts. Both the Orthodox and Hicksite Friends continued to denounce slavery, the local Orthodox meeting publishing its testimony in the *Liberator* on 27 January 1837, signed by clerks Lindley M. and Abigail L. Moore.[87] Nor was the local press entirely hostile to abolitionist efforts. Though there were no reports of FASS activities in 1837, the *Rochester Democrat* did respond to a spate of antiabolitionist riots in that year by chiding those "Senators and Congressmen" who "have headed mobs, prevented free discussion, and muzzled and *destroyed* the Press." The "doctrines" of the *'fanatics'* and *'agitators,'* " the editor concluded, "are taking deeper and deeper root, and becoming more and more extended."[88] That extension was revealed in the June 1837 issue of the *Liberator*. The journal listed the men's Rochester Anti-Slavery Society, with seven hundred members, as the second largest in the country and the FASS, with four hundred members, as the thirteenth largest overall and the largest female society. Thus it was no surprise to *Liberator* readers to see that eight hundred Rochester women and an equal number from surrounding towns submitted their antislavery pleas to Congress.[89]

Clearly, the appeal of FASS women had reached large numbers of local women. Even if one considers the signing of a petition a minimal

[84] Samuel D. Porter to the Pastor and Sessions of the Washington Street [formerly Bethel] Presbyterian Church, 29 September 1845, SDPFP. The inspiration to form a Bethel Church came partly from Theodore Weld's ill-treatment at Third Presbyterian Church in 1836 (see n. 64 above).

[85] Reported in the *Liberator* (Boston), 31 March 1837.

[86] Monroe Baptist Association, *Proceedings* (Rochester: Ansel Warren, 1835).

[87] Lindley M. Moore was active in founding men's city and county antislavery societies in the early 1830s; Abigail Moore was a founder of the FASS.

[88] Reported in the *Liberator*, 28 January 1837.

[89] Ibid., 23 June 1837, and 30 September 1837.

act, it was an innovative one for many women, especially when performed by so many over such a short span of time. Yet the circle who led perfectionist antislavery activities remained small and rarely extended outside the evangelical churches. Few benevolent leaders, for example, signed either 1837 petition: of fifty-four women serving as CS officers in the previous decade, only five joined perfectionist petitioners. While half of the OAA's founding officers signed, four of these had begun their public careers in the FASS rather than in benevolent enterprises. The Orthodox Quakers were relatively well represented on the petitions, led by Abigail Moore and her daughter Ann and by Mrs. Silas, Anna, and Almira Cornell. While this Quaker group had been active in the FASS from its founding, Hicksite Quaker women were still rare in worldly antislavery ranks. They were represented on the 1837 petition by Amy Post, her daughter Mary, and Mary Dale, a free black resident of the Post household, and by a few other members of newly arrived farm families. The bulk of the petition, however, was formed by perfectionist parishioners of Baptist and Presbyterian congregations, clustered in twos or threes by kinship, and overall uniting large segments of Rochester's upwardly mobile commercial and professional circles.

A few months before Amy Post affixed her signature to the 1837 petition, she received a letter from Phebe Post Willis of Long Island. "How is it," queried Aunt Phebe, "that you tell us nothing about abolition movements in Rochester. I should scarcely suppose you were members of that society by your silence on the subject."[90] The Posts, along with the Fishes, DeGarmos, and Thayers, were still focusing their attention on matters internal to the Society of Friends. A resolution asking that "the discipline be so alter'd that men & women shall stand on the same footing in all matters internal in which they are equally interested" was introduced at the Genesee Yearly Meeting in June 1837. Though supported by the Posts and their Rochester friends, the "meeting" as a whole found the "way not open" to alter the *Rules of Discipline* and postponed any changes to the following year, and for several years thereafter.[91] Whether or not such postponements led directly to Amy Post's decision to sign a non-Quaker petition that fall, her entrance into worldly activism in Rochester clearly coincided with

[90] Phebe Post Willis to Isaac and Amy Post, 5 April 1837, IAPFP.
[91] GYMWF, Minutes, June 1837, HRR.

increasing frustration over the remaining limits on women's roles within Quaker "meetings."

The women who led perfectionist compaigns had gradually extended their roles within the church and the community since the Finney-led revival of 1830–1831 and by 1837 counted hundreds of evangelical sisters as supporters. Female perfectionists still trod lightly in their published statements, calling themselves "weak instruments" and constantly seeking the approval of evangelical clergy, male kin, and the agents of extralocal associations.[92] Yet their actions were increasingly bold as they moved from private concerns and condemnations to a public and collective campaign against slavery. They also campaigned against vice, but these efforts were less successful initially. In the same year that hundreds of women appended their names to antislavery petitions, a local moral reformer wrote that she "circulated" the *Advocate* "to some exent, but [it] is now and then handed back to me by those who say 'Exposure on this subject only increases crime.'" In a report to the *Advocate* covering the FMRS's activities for the last half of 1837, the secretary criticized the "want of zeal on the part of the members" but claimed it was due to "uncertainty as to the means best calculated to do good" and "the want of entire consecration to the work."[93]

It was easier for women anxious over assuming any public role to consecrate themselves to the work of the OAA, the labors of which were certainly well calculated. Having achieved public visibility, a fund of $1,650, a charter membership of fifty women, and the asylum itself in a matter of two months, the OAA provided a ready field of labor for evangelical women. The association was perfectionist in only a very limited sense, however: individual children, if brought to the asylum soon enough, could be educated and converted, saving them from lives of privation and the community from their future depredations. Half of the OAA leadership did not even advocate perfection but instead held amelioration as their ultimate goal. Nor did all OAA board members share the abolitionist sentiments of the perfectionists; in the founding year a lengthy debate ensued over the admission of "colored orphans" to the asylum. While the final decision was to accept free black children, the presence of several FASS leaders on the asylum

[92] Quote from FMRS report published in *Advocate of Moral Reform*, 15 July 1836.
[93] Ibid., 1 May 1837, and 15 June 1838.

board of managers suggests substantial resistance from other, benevolent, board members.[94]

Nevertheless, the asylum was a more hospitable home for perfectionist, and particularly antislavery, women than the CS. The CS charter members included the wives and daughters of the city's founders, who had arrived in western New York with slaves in tow. They had long since emancipated their blacks, but the men of the Rochester family and others linked to CS leaders were still leading antiemancipation meetings in the mid-1830s. Only seven of the FASS's approximately sixty charter members were on the CS's membership roster by 1834. Perhaps the most important bond between the CS and the FASS was the experience gained by six members of the latter as district visitors in the former. In this office, abolitionist women may have come in contact with Rochester's small free-black population, and they certainly learned the door-to-door techniques necessary to canvas the city effectively on behalf of the slave.[95] Female moral reformers were even more strongly tied to the CS's district visiting plan. At least eleven of the twenty-eight most active early moral reformers had served previously as CS visitors, although five of these women along with seven others may have also gained canvassing experience in the FASS. The FMRS applied the CS's model directly to their own endeavors. To discover and aid the victims of vice, the founders claimed that district visitation was required among the "abandoned of our sex" to "ascertain something as to their number and place of residence" and to "circulate appropriate tracts" among them.[96]

The CS, even with only the limited participation of perfectionist leaders, continued to be viewed by many as Rochester's premier female association. In revival years, CS leaders asked evangelical ministers, such as Rev. Joel Parker of Third Presbyterian Church, to preach the annual fund-raising sermon and were obliged. First Presbyterian

[94] OAA, "History of the Asylum," [186–], MS, HCCP.

[95] Approximately three hundred free blacks lived in Rochester in the early 1830s. Some district visitors of the CS would have come in contact with these families since the entire city was divided into districts. A peculiarly high proportion of perfectionist women, including those involved in moral reform and temperance as well as abolition, served as district visitors in the 1820s and 1830s. The prevalence of CS district visitors among perfectionists in Rochester suggests that, as Carroll Smith-Rosenberg found for New York City, close contact with the problems of the poor and destitute through house-to-house visiting could lead to the redirection and expansion of women's voluntary efforts. See Smith-Rosenberg, *Religion and the Rise of the City: The New York City Mission Movement, 1812–1870* (Ithaca: Cornell University Press, 1971), chap. 9.

[96] *Advocate of Moral Reform*, 1 May 1837.

and St. Luke's Episcopal, which remained healthy and wealthy despite the emergence of new congregations, continued as the mainstays of CS membership and leadership. Simultaneously, increasing numbers of evangelical women, many of whom played minimal roles in perfectionist associations, swelled CS membership to 230 women. The winter campaigns of 1837 to collect abolitionist signatures and asylum donations absorbed the labor of many activist women but still did not interfere with CS business. The *Daily Deomcrat* regularly announced and reported the activities of the benevolent women. In a single week in February 1837 the paper reported that the Young Ladies' Benevolent Society of First Presbyterian received $73 from a fair at the music hall, announced that a sermon "for the benefit of the Poor" would be preached at First Presbyterian, and printed a "Card of Thanks" from the CS for the receipt of $149 from that annual sermon.[97]

Increasingly from the mid-1830s and most dramatically in 1837, Rochester's public women competed for the community's attention and resources. Even though overlaps existed between benevolent and perfectionist associations, two distinct networks of female activism were established that emphasized different justifications, techniques, and goals. While benevolent women maintained their position as the most acceptable, applauded, and affluent public servants of their sex, that dominance was seriously challenged in 1837 by the upsurge of antislavery sentiment among women petitioners and OAA board members. Then, in the following five years the growth of moral reform efforts and the initiation of temperance campaigns along with the return of Finney and revivalism to Rochester suggested that perfectionist women might gain the apex of female activism.

[97] *Daily Democrat,* 9, 11, and 14 February 1837.

[4]

Moral Crusades and
Ultraist Alternatives

On 30 January 1838 Mrs. Thomas Kempshall ended her affiliation
with the Rochester Female Charitable Society. Mrs. Kempshall, a CS
charter member, was an active participant in the society's affairs and a
district visitor in the 1830s. When notified in 1837 of her appointment
as a directress, however, she not only declined the office but also
tendered her resignation. With "deference always, to those Ladies,
who may differ in opinion from me," she began, "I look upon the *funds*
of your society, however judiciously distributed, among the destitute
sick of our city, as being wholly inadequate to meet their necessities."[1]
Yet the resources of the CS had by no means diminished during Mrs.
Kempshall's tenure. In 1822 about half of the charter members had
been married to leading merchants, manufacturers, or professionals;
by 1838 nearly 90 percent of CS leaders were wedded to such wealth.[2]
In the latter year at least a third of the city's physicians and three-
quarters of the attorneys had wives in the CS. Bank directors, newspaper editors, clergymen, and village politicians, all of whom were
represented on the CS board, continued to sustain benevolent ladies'
efforts. And, indeed, when asked to explain herself at length, Mrs.
Kempshall admited, "It is neither the Fund of the society that I would
enlarge, or its constitution that I would change if I could. It is only the
situation of the recipients of your bounty, that I would alter if I might."[3]

[1] E[mily] G. (Mrs. Thomas) Kempshall to president of CS, 30 January 1838, CSP.
[2] In 1838, 86 percent of CS leaders were married to merchants, manufacturers, or
professionals; by 1849 the figure was over 90 percent. Despite major changes in the city's
economic structure in this period, benevolent women's families remained in the most
lucrative occupations and positions.
[3] Kempshall to president of CS, 30 January 1838, CSP.

The antidote to that situation seemed to lie in the expansion not of charitable resources but of perfectionist campaigns.

Although primarily concerned with the condition of the recipient of alms, Mrs. Kempshall in her resignation letter first noted the problems that confronted the almsgiver. There were "whole Districts appointed to females as visitors," she contended, "where no decent female should go" because of "their vile and degraded inhabitants. . . ." One such district was that along the canal's towpath. In 1836 Mrs. Kempshall was "a *frequent* and for weeks, almost *daily* visitor" to "8 or 10 families crowded . . . into two small frame houses" in that district. "I *gave* them food, clothes and medicine, *loaned* them Bedding, etc., from my own house." The last "my husband would not suffer me to *borrow* back . . . lest these people should resent the affront by burning our house." Her own fears did not blind her to the dreadful conditions of her clients. A "drunken and cruel mother" had "torn and destroyed" a "good strong suit of woolen clothes" given her eight-year-old son and then locked this "worse than orphan child . . . out doors to sleep." A family of eight to ten children were abandoned by the father while "the mother [went] with a young infant in her arms into the Grocery near by—for whiskey." The family from whom she feared retrieving her "Bedstead etc." wished, in the opinion of the neighbors, "to sell them for whiskey."

Mrs. Kempshall reminded those board members who had not recently served as visitors that "while your Banner . . . has been held up as a beacon of hope" to the destitute sick, "it is painful to tell them to read the other side where want of funds has written Despair. . . ." The only long-term solution, she thought, was the establishment of a workhouse "where idle drunken fathers and mothers *must* go and *work*." Since "the Legislature of our State *has not yet* 'granted power' to erect a Work House," Mrs. Kempshall argued, the "dear Ladies" of the CS should go "as a body of Females" to the "City Council Men, praying them immediately to give this city a work-House."

The vile and degraded inhabitants of the canal district, their idleness, drunkenness, and affronts to decency, were the concern not only of Mrs. Kempshall but also of the city's perfectionist leaders. One of these leaders, Maria G. Poter, resided with the Kempshalls in 1836 and may have encouraged her hostess's transition from benevolent visitor to perfectionist publicist. Mrs. Porter did not, however, convince Mrs. Kempshall to join her in the antislavery petition campaigns of 1836 and 1837 or in the moral reform or temperance work of the following years.

Instead, the ex-CS visitor decided to labor alongside perfectionists in the orphan asylum. She may have chosen this type of work in part because an illness that had plagued her for several years had left her an invalid by 1838: though she could not canvass door to door, she "gave very liberally from her abundant means and her pen was ever ready and active" in the orphan's behalf.[4] The paths followed by Maria G. Porter and Mrs. Kempshall were replicated by many perfectionists and a considerable number of benevolent women. Through the OAA, CS members expanded and institutionalized their charitable efforts in company with perfectionists. Perfectionists, in turn, gradually shifted the focus and forms of their labor in the decade after the OAA's founding. The petition campaigns of that same year were the culmination of perfectionist women's antislavery efforts, after which temperance and moral reform absorbed most perfectionists' energies. Then, in the mid-1840s, a combination of forces shifted evangelical women's attention from perfection to amelioration and made the OAA the perfect home for them.

In the revivals of the early 1830s the signing of a temperance pledge had become the most widely acknowledged symbol of spiritual rebirth, a virtual prerequisite for salvation.[5] Men's temperance societies flourished in the following years, while women organized prayer circles and maternal associations and fought slavery and licentiousness. Temperance became a women's issue in Rochester in the late 1830s, when female abolitionists, seeking to escape the dissension in antislavery ranks, combined with moral reformers who increasingly defined intemperance as the primary source of all vice. A new wave of revivals in the same period infused the women's temperance enterprise with evangelical zeal and encouraged perfectionists to believe that the eradication of alcohol and of vice were obtainable goals.

Since 1839 Rochester had been poised for the "refreshing showers" of God's grace.[6] Revivals at First Baptist Church and the rapid growth of the Methodists foreshadowed a more all-embracing religious floodtide in the early 1840s. The greatest barrier seemed to be the disputatious Presbyterians, as Old and New School ministers debated doctrine

[4] Mrs. Gilman H. Perkins, "Orphan Asylum Notes," n.d., HCCP. Mr. Kempshall was the largest contributor to the asylum building fund.

[5] See Paul Johnson, *A Shopkeeper's Millennium: Society and Revivals in Rochester, New York, 1815–1837* (New York: Hill and Wang, 1978), pp. 113–114.

[6] Blake McKelvey, *Rochester: The Water-Power City, 1812–1854* (Cambridge: Harvard University Press, 1945), p. 279.

while male parishioners battled over the church's stand on slavery. Under the leadership of Tryon Edwards, First Presbyterian had once again become a bastion of orthodoxy; but so, too, had Finney's first home, Third Presbyterian. The latter, led by Albert G. Hall, made its second stone edifice a bulwark of conservative Calvinism. Even Bethel struggled to sustain its evangelical and abolitionist zeal, and a number of communicants fled the congregation in 1841 to reassert their millennial vision within First Congregational Church.[7] Still, Mrs. Eaton wrote to her husband on Thanksgiving Day 1839 that there "seems much more feeling upon the subject of religion in most of the churches than for a long time." Two days later she hosted a "neighborhood meeting," one of many held in the city to discuss the evidences of a renewal of religion.

On 13 December 1839 "all the churches (except the Episcopal) in the city" declared a day of fasting. The fast was a response not only to the hopes for a revival but also to the fears of a recession. Rochester was now feeling the aftershocks of the Panic of 1837: the "complaint of hard times is on all sides & more universal . . . than ever before," reported Mrs. Eaton. "*Every one* is in debt, & none can get their dues."[8] By 1842 a few of the city's leading businessmen faced bankruptcy, including Benjamin Campbell and Hervey Ely. The latter's Greek Revival mansion in the third ward was sacrificed to debts, along with the homes of James K. Livingston and Selah Mathews, two of his endorsers.[9] While the number of bankruptcies remained small, the fear they engendered spread rapidly.

When Abelard Reynold's fortunes declined, forcing him to sell off large tracts of land, he was certain that his failings were punishment for placing temporal concerns above spiritual, and he struggled to "expiate" his "delinquencies" in the latter.[10] He had ample opportunity and company in the winter and spring of 1842 with Finney's return to Rochester. As Finney appeared in the Bethel pulpit, Rev. Jedidiah Burchard was called to Brick Church, and a great revival took hold.

[7] Ibid., pp. 277–278. First Congregational Church attracted Third Presbyterian and Bethel Church communicants and at least one evangelical Episcopalian, Mrs. Elizabeth Atkinson.

[8] Elizabeth Selden Eaton to Amos Eaton, 28 November 1839, 12 December 1839, and 17 February 1839, in Blake McKelvey, comp., "Letters Postmarked Rochester," Rochester Historical Society, *Publications* 21 (1943), pp. 66, 67, 72.

[9] McKelvey, *Rochester,* p. 220. Livingston and Mathews recovered quickly; only Campbell appears to have continued to suffer serious financial difficulties.

[10] Ibid., p. 279.

While First Presbyterian remained largely aloof from the excitement, the rest of the city, including the Episcopalians, were aroused to a fever pitch by protracted meetings and an outpouring of conversions across all classes.[11] As in previous decades, revivalism and women's activism prospered together.

As early as 1839, members of a local women's temperance society advocated total abstinence with such ardor that Monroe County residents were twice as likely to have signed a temperance pledge that year as the average citizen of the state.[12] The women's "temperance enterprise" was still going "extremely well" in December 1841 when the Vigilance Committee reported that "they had . . . obtained (in about 4 weeks) in all 1000 signers to the pledge!" The following month Mrs. Eaton informed her husband: "We have now recorded 1350 names of females, & probably at least 500 more have been obtained but not yet reported."[13]

Combining district visiting and the signing of pledges in the midst of renewed revivals, female temperance advocates outdistanced even their antislavery sisters of 1837 in attracting community support. In January 1842, just before Finney's return to the city, Mrs. Eaton wrote to her husband: "Our temperance enterprize seems to be pro[s]pered, & blessed. . . . I have no doubt that the great & universal disposition & effort to forsake this vice is a distinct harbinger of the millenium [*sic*]." Mrs. Eaton voiced the feelings of her perfectionist sisters when she reminded her spouse that "christians cannot expect the blessing of God in these times who do not do whatsoever their hands find to do to rid the world of this vice."[14] Revival enthusiasm also induced the OAA board to seek several thousand dollars for a new asylum despite "the pecuniary pressures" that "rested like an incubus upon all the interest of our country. . . ." The following year the board reported that, indeed, "God smiled upon our efforts": the "new Orphan Asylum, now nearly completed . . . speaks in tones most eloquent of the benevolence

[11] Finney generally led revivals among the professional, merchant, and manufacturing families and those seeking entry to such ranks, while Burchard focused on working-class revivals.

[12] McKelvey, *Rochester*, p. 283.

[13] Elizabeth Selden Eaton to Amos Eaton, 31 December 1841 and 25 January 1842, in McKelvey, "Letters," p. 73, 74–75. The Vigilance Committee had divided the city into thirty-six districts, the same number recorded by the CS in these years. Since several temperance workers were also CS visitors, they probably employed the same district blueprint.

[14] Elizabeth Selden Eaton to Amos Eaton, 11 January 1842, in McKelvey, "Letters," p. 73.

of the inhabitants of Rochester."[15] At least for the advocates of temperance and the protectors of orphans, revivalism and recession were boons to women's activism.

Not all of Rochester's female public servants found the city's residents so generous. The labors of the perfectionist FASS and FMRS declined, the CS membership roster was depleted of all but its most ardent supporters, and ultraists struggled to assume the antislavery labors forfeited by their evangelical sisters. The difficulties of the ultraists can be traced to their small numbers, limited resources, and radical doctrines and those of the CS to the business failures of the period.[16] The diminished labors of evangelical abolitionists and moral reformers rested on more complex grounds.

Mrs. Bishop, secretary of the local FMRS in 1838, reported to the parent society that "some interest" had been "excited" in the cause but the work had "failed to awaken deep feeling, or to elicit new plans of operation."[17] Throughout the next four years the society struggled to survive, sending only a single representative to a single meeting of the American Female Moral Reform Society. In the same period, auxiliaries from many of the small-town and rural communities of western New York—Bloomfield, Clarkson, Sweden, Ogden, Brockport, Greece, and Lima—were more active than their urban counterpart. A few individuals, including Mrs. Mathews and Mrs. George Avery, wrote letters to the *Advocate* and sent one-dollar donations, but the general malaise of the FMRS was better indicated by the paucity of their appearance in the journal's pages and the society's financial reports.

The Rochester group was hopeful of its future in 1839, however. Community concern over the rising number of female criminals led the grand jury to suggest that special cells be set aside in the jail to house women, and arrests for various licentious acts were increasing as were attempts to close one or another "disorderly house."[18] A meeting of tract distributors revealed that "through visitation, prayers, tracts & conversation . . . some of the criminals confined in the jail have been

[15]OAA, Annual Report, 1842, 1843, Scrapbook, HCCP.

[16]CS membership leveled off at 230 women in the late 1830s, then dipped to 150 in 1840, 138 in 1841, 118 in 1842, and finally fell below 100 dues-paying members in 1843. After 1843 a resurgence occurred and in the mid-1840s the CS reached its largest size ever.

[17]*Advocate of Moral Reform* (New York City), 15 June 1838.

[18]McKelvey, *Rochester*, p. 254.

hopefully converted."[19] Believing that both community and churches were ready to act on this issue, the FMRS reasserted itself and sent Sarah C. Owen to the parent association's semiannual meeting in Utica that fall. The resolutions put forth by her were extensively reported in the *Advocate* the following month along with the notice of a twenty-nine-dollar contribution from the Rochester society.[20]

Owen's performance at the Utica meeting revealed the renewed zeal of the FMRS, but it also pointed to the renewed hostility of some of its Rochester neighbors. The *Advocate* noted two resolutions "offered and sustained" by Owen, both of which focused on women's proper role in moral reform. The first claimed that in pursuing this cause, women were "not leaving [their] own proper sphere, or usurping the prerogative of the other sex; but acting strictly in accordance with the dictates of reason and the word of God." The second argued that such activity did not "degrade the character or blunt the sensibilities of women—but, on the contrary, exert[ed] a softening, enobling [*sic*], and purifying influence. . . ."[21]

These resolutions, for which a majority of all those present at the meeting voted, had a local impetus. The previous June, Brick Church had hosted a meeting of the FMRS that was well attended, engendering some optimism on the part of the association's officers. The editor of the *Daily Sun,* however, charged that clergy "generally *look sheepish*" when reading notices of such meetings, and rightly so since the church "should not be prostituted by such unholy purposes. Neither," he continued, "should ladies having any pretensions of decency, congregate, or in any other way have meetings to *converse about, consider and talk over the debauchery and licentiousness* of our city." The *Daily Sun*'s editor accepted the need to resist "moral depravity" but questioned whether "ladies of respectable standing" were "the proper persons to correct the evil." His answer was a resounding "No!"[22]

Female abolitionists came under a similar if more subtle attack. Responding to a call for civil rights for free blacks, the editor of the *Daily Advertiser* suggested that "manly virtue" would oppose such measures

[19]Elizabeth Selden Eaton to Amos Eaton, 27 October 1839, in McKelvey, "Letters," p. 65.
[20]*Advocate of Moral Reform,* 15 October 1839.
[21]Ibid.
[22]*Daily Sun* (Rochester), 27 June 1839. While some evangelical ministers still supported women's moral reform efforts, they emphasized moral training within the home. See report on the lecture of Rev. Albert G. Hall of Third Presbyterian Church in *Advocate of Moral Reform,* 1 January 1842.

in order to protect womanly purity, for the right to a trial by jury might lead "the rank and curly pated negro to associate with your wives and mothers—to marry your sons and daughters—your mothers and sisters." Since that did not sufficiently deter female abolitionists, the editor next turned to sarcasm. Pointing to dissension in antislavery ranks over the role of women, he opined that "the *women* are determined not to be *abolished* whatever may be the fate of slavery" and suggested that "the Ladies" might be "much better employed . . . in superintending their own households, if married, and, if not, in making up their minds who they will bless by a bestowal of heart and hand. . . ."[23] The founders of the FASS had attempted to respond to such criticisms even before they were voiced by stating in their constitution that the society would avail itself of "appropriate means for the correction of public sentiment in its own immediate sphere of action."[24] The early successes of the FASS suggested that the society and the community were in general agreement on those means, but extralocal events soon impinged on community perceptions.

At the moment of the FASS's most successful campaign, members of the American Anti-Slavery Society began debating the best means to obtain the end of slavery. By May 1840 the war of words escalated into full-scale battle, and the society divided. Those who remained within the American Anti-Slavery Society criticized churches' collaboration with slaveholders, advocated moral suasion as the primary means of social change, and supported the full and equal participation of women in antislavery agitation. Those who abandoned the society emphasized, instead, evangelical faith, political action, and the separate and subordinate role of women.[25] This turn of events posed a serious problem for such auxiliary associations as the FASS whose members were female Evangelicals without formal access to the political sphere. The extent of the problem was clarified that summer by Rev. Elon Galusha at the World's Anti-Slavery Convention in London. The husband of a FASS founder, Galusha assured the London leaders, who refused to seat female delegates at the convention, that among his "exceedingly numerous constituency in America" the "ladies took no part in the

[23] *Daily Advertiser* (Rochester), 16 October 1839 and 15 June 1840.
[24] FASS, Constitution, [1835], SDPFP.
[25] For a detailed discussion of this division, see Aileen Kraditor, *Means and Ends in American Abolitionism: Garrison and His Critics on Tactics and Strategy, 1834–1850* (New York: Pantheon, 1969). This division was not as clear-cut in western New York as elsewhere; see below, Chapters 5 and 6.

business of societies." He admitted that "a very small minority" had "allowed the innovation," but assured his British colleagues that "it ought not to be acted upon" here.[26]

Whether or not Rochester's evangelical women were in total agreement with male kin and clergy, the members of the FASS virtually disappeared from public antislavery labors after 1840. Some may have continued to voice antislavery sentiments from within church walls, joining the First Congregational Church in 1841 or the First Unitarian Society in 1842, both congregations being founded on the basis of strong abolitionist commitments. Yet by April 1842, not a single perfectionist woman was willing to add her name to an antislavery petition even though the document's prime concern was freedom for the "Children Born of Slave Mothers." The men who signed the petition included Samuel D. Porter, Ashbel Riley, David Hoyt, and Silas Cornell, all husbands of FASS founders; only the wife of the Quaker Cornell appeared among the female signers.[27]

One of the most notable leaders of the antislavery cause and a national organizer of the 1837 petition campaign was Abby Kelley. An active agent of the American Anti-Slavery Society, it was Kelley's election to the executive committee in 1840 that precipitated the association's division. Twice in 1842 she toured western New York, and her appearance in Rochester, though welcomed by ultraists, called forth condemnations from evangelical churchmen and the press. On the occasion of her first visit, in August, the trustees of Third Presbyterian Church "object[ed] to a 'female' Abby Kelley addressing a convention which had taken possession of the church without permission. . . ."[28] Before Kelley's return in the fall, Samuel D. Porter attempted to limit Evangelicals' attacks on her by suggesting that she "prevent the *inference* . . . that Garrison and the Garrison school are opposed either to the church, the clergy or christianity." Claiming that he only wished to avoid *"false inference,"* Porter wanted to reassure

[26]Quoted in *Liberator*, 24 July 1840. Of the fifteen FASS husbands who were active abolitionists, at least nine sided with those who abandoned the American Anti-Slavery Society and its stand for woman's rights; the decisions of the other six are unknown.

[27]Anti-Slavery Petition from the Men and Women of Monroe County, New York, 1 April 1842, House of Representatives, Document HR 27A-H1.7, National Archives, Washington, D.C. I thank Judith Wellman for this reference. Most of the 63 women who signed this petition did not sign earlier petitions. All 30 of the signers who could be positively identified were Hicksite or Orthodox Quakers.

[28]Third Presbyterian Church, Trustees Book, 24 August 1842, Presbyterian Historical Society, Philadelphia.

"the witnesses of our debates" that abolitionists had been unjustly "styled agrarians, disorganizers, infidels, & fanatics." Porter concluded by noting that "in a community where nine tenths of the people recognize the divine institution of the Sabbath as still binding," it would be "wise and prudent" to rest on that day and "avoid the scandal and hinder the reproach which now rests in consequence of your neglecting this prudential consideration both upon the *Abolition Cause* and yourself."[29] In November, Kelley, who now shared the stage with William Lloyd Garrison, did schedule her meetings for mid-week, although that did not save her entirely from condemnation. The press was not unkind to Garrison or the Garrison school, focusing their attacks instead on Kelley herself. The editor of the *Rochester Citizen,* for instance, characterized Garrison's speech as "straight-forward, forcible, and useful" but described his female coworker's as "full of words and sounds, tedious and *boaring,* [sic], to the extermination of the larger part of the audience."[30]

Porter's faith in Kelly was still unshaken, however. The November meetings were held at Porter's spiritual home, Bethel Church, and Porter and several coworshipers felt free to express their support of third-party politics and antislavery churches. The convention as a whole, though comprised mostly of ultraist Quakers, "disclaim[ed] any intention of impeaching the anti-slavery fidelity of those abolitionists who deem it better to organize a distinct political party . . . and regard them as sincere coworkers in the same great cause."[31] When the participants agreed to form themselves into the Western New York Anti-Slavery Society, Porter was elected president of the new association. Yet his personal popularity could not stem the tide of local support for the American Anti-Slavery Society's brand of moral suasion abolition or attract the support of many Evangelicals. John Kedzie, one of the few other evangelical converts to join Porter as a WNYASS officer, had been excommunicated from Brick Presbyterian Church two weeks earlier on the basis of his antislavery, anticlerical pronouncements. Another "Brick Church perfectionist," Abigail Bush, the only evangel-

[29] Samuel D. Porter to Abby Kelley, 16 September 1842, AKFP. It is interesting that Porter, who was employed in commercial ventures, would note the use of agrarians as synonymous with infidels and fanatics.
[30] Quoted in *Liberator,* 3 February 1843. Former Rochesterian James M. Schermerhorn, no advocate of woman's rights, heard Kelley's speech and wrote to his wife that she was "rather an Eloquent Speaker" though "rather out of her proper sphere." See James M. Schermerhorn to Mrs. Schermerhorn, 29 August 1842, in McKelvey, "Letters," p. 78.
[31] *Liberator,* 6 January 1843.

ical woman known to have participated actively in the meetings, withdrew from the congregation about the same time.[32]

The roster of convention participants and WNYASS officers repeated the names of those Hicksite Quakers who had signed the 1842
antislavery petition—the Posts, Hallowells, Burtises, and Fishes. This
group's support of Porter's leadership may have been owing, in part, to
their own tenuous position as Quaker members of a "popular," that is,
non-Quaker, reform association. By 1840 the yearly meeting to which
they belonged was the arena for wide-ranging debates over the nature
of authority, religious leadership, and sex roles. The 1837 resolution
that would have placed women and men on an equal footing within the
meeting had been tabled for three consecutive years.[33] By that time, the
women's meeting proposed another significant alteration in the administration of church offices. Quakers sought to minimize church hierarchy by eliminating both a formal ministry and a board of elders, but
most meetings came to depend on a core of leaders, known as the
Meeting of Ministers and Elders, to determine and implement major
decisions. The women wanted to limit the authority of the ministers
and elders by allowing "all members of our religious Society . . . the
privileges of sitting with them in a meeting capacity."[34] Once again, a
decision to alter the discipline was postponed.

Simultaneously, debates over Quaker participation in "popular" assemblies and associations erupted among Hicksites in Philadelphia,
New York City, western New York, and Michigan.[35] Rochester
Quakers, such as Daniel and Lucy Anthony and the Posts, began to
hold "numerous little abolition meetings" in their homes and to consider the organization of an antislavery society made up predominantly
of Hicksites.[36] Yet by 1841 Isaac and Amy Post wondered why they
should "exclude all who do not happen to be included within the pale of

[32] Second (Brick) Presbyterian Church, Session Minutes, 31 October 1842, Presbyterian Historical Society; William Channing Gannett, Speech for the Fiftieth Anniversary
of the Rochester Woman's Rights Convention, 1898, Unitarian Society of Rochester
Records, University of Rochester.

[33] GYMWF, Minutes, June 1837, June 1838, June 1839, and June 1840, HRR.

[34] Ibid., June 1840. These minutes note the concurrence of some members of the men's
meeting. The Meeting of Ministers and Elders held greater power in the Orthodox meeting but was gradually gaining authority in the Hicksite meeting. Some Hicksites saw this
as a shift toward churchly forms.

[35] These debates also found their way into major reform journals. The *Liberator* became one of the main arenas in which Quakers debated religious as well as reform
strategies.

[36] Ida Husted Harper, *The Life and Work of Susan B. Anthony*, 3 vols. (Indianapolis:
Bowen-Merrill, 1899), 1: 48.

our religious faith" from antislavery associations. A Hicksite friend from Long Island wrote to the Posts that he concurred with their "sentiment that our light (if we have any) would be more likely to shine where it would do good by uniting with all without distinction of Sect or creed. . . ."[37]

Speaking tours through western New York by antislavery agents, especially those by Quakers Lucretia Mott and Abby Kelley, fueled dissension in Hicksite meetings and the desire of some for a wider sphere of activity. Whereas a large number of Rochesterians could be reached by public speeches, testimonies within Hicksite meetings did not reach even the full membership of that sect. Thus when Kelley and other agents of the American Anti-Slavery Society held their November 1842 meeting in Rochester, a large body of Hicksites were in attendance and at least twenty were among the first thirty-four officers of the "popular" antislavery society founded there.

According to the WNYASS constitution, "any person, by signing this Constitution, shall be constituted a member of the Society," thereby allowing women to join as full and equal members.[38] Kelley was the primary female participant at the founding convention as well as the only woman to serve as an officer of the convention itself.[39] In the selection of officers for the society, however, nine western New York women, including Sarah Fish, Sarah Hallowell, and Sarah Burtis, won posts along with twenty-five men. Perhaps most important, the forms of action emphasized by the convention allowed for women's extensive involvement in the actual work of the association. Despite reassurances to third-party advocates, the WNYASS members accentuated moral suasion tactics. They resolved that "our only hope is in the regeneration of the public sentiment of the free States." The specific measures adopted for that regeneration included the "living speaker," the distribution of "periodicals and publications," petitions to state and national legislatures, and the application of antislavery principles "in all . . . social, political and religious relations."[40] Hicksite women's pursuit of these measures under WNYASS auspices would

[37] John Ketcham to Isaac and Amy Post, 11 March 1841, IAPFP.

[38] *Liberator*, 6 January 1843.

[39] Abby Kelley was the most important role model for Rochester's ultraist women in terms of antislavery activity, while Lucretia Mott was the person they sought to emulate in Quaker meetings, though Mott was also praised for her antislavery and woman's rights pronouncements.

[40] *Liberator*, 6 January 1843.

soon carry them the final step from Quaker testimony to worldly activism just at the moment that perfectionist women accepted their abolition from the antislavery cause.

Perfectionist women, however, did not wholly retreat from worldly
activism. Indeed, 1843 was a felicitous year for both moral reformers
and temperance advocates, with the former hosting the semiannual
meeting of the American Female Moral Reform Society in September
and the latter establishing a Ladies' Washingtonian Total Abstinence
Society in December. Benefiting from economic recovery and the
afterglow of evangelical zeal, female perfectionists entered the mid-
1840s with renewed hope of achieving the millennium. The support of
clergy and kin once again offset the criticism of more conservative
community leaders, while the addition of former abolitionist leaders'
skills and labor to female moral reform and temperance movements
boosted the latter's morale and efficiency. Temperance remained the
most acceptable form of female activism, with clergy, councilmen,
editors, extralocal reform agents, and benevolent ladies all reinforcing
perfectionists' efforts. Female moral reformers, while less universally
applauded, received strong commendations from a number of evangelical clergy, from rural and small-town auxiliaries, and from several of
the city's leading lawyers and politicians.

In July 1843 the *Advocate of Moral Reform* announced that the
semiannual meeting would be held in Rochester. In appointing the site,
"there was a trembling solicitude on the part of some, lest it should not
be well sustained." When the meeting was called to order on September 6 at the Washington Street (formerly the Bethel) Church, however,
"the body of the church was well filled." The Reverend Mr. Bassett,
speaking from his own pulpit, said that "he felt himself surrounded by a
stimulating moral atmosphere," and lawyer Joseph D. Husbands noted
that "judging from the size and character of the audience before him,
he should infer that "the cause] was anything but *unpopular*." Frederick Starr, a former state legislator, suggested that the trembling was all
on the side of the perpetrators of vice: "those who may sneer at your
convening in this city to-day, are quaking with fear, in view of the
effect this meeting may have upon Rochester."[41]

Two hundred fifty women from some five dozen communities were
officially enrolled as delegates at the meeting. Mrs. Hawkins, president

---

[41] *Advocate of Moral Reform*, 1 October 1843.

of the parent society, opened the meeting with selections from the Scriptures and a prayer. Mrs. Selah Mathews and Mrs. Eliza West of the Rochester society were appointed to the business committee along with representatives from nearby Ogden and Arcade. The Reverend Pharcellus Church of the First Baptist Church was appointed chair of the meeting; he was aided in his labors by Baptist Rev. Elon Galusha, Unitarian Rev. Frederick Holland, Methodist Rev. John Parker, and Mr. Bassett of the host church. One-hour prayer sessions were held each morning of the three-day meeting, where "the presence of the Saviour was peculiarly manifest," and the ladies' meeting affirmed that "the finger of God" could be "clearly discerned" in their labors.[42]

While clerical kudos and God's blessing were important justifications for women's moral reform efforts, religion alone was insufficient "in closing up the rushing fountains of human misery."[43] Even "in the city of R[ochester], noted as it was for religion and morality, a police officer had remarked . . . that there were probably 1000 profligate men, and 500 women of the same character, who found a home in their midst." Nor was the evil "confined to the openly vicious; startling developments" showed "that it existed among the more refined circles, and even in the Church of God." The reasons for such rampant debauchery went far beyond simple impiety: "wrong training (physical and moral), want of employment, oppression, love of dress, a false standard of duty, . . . laxity of the laws, and the countenance and reward given to vice" were equally culpable. The ladies, with the support of former antislavery leaders, also pointed their finger at slavery, remembering "the poor slave woman, our sister of a darker hue, who has no protection for her virtue."[44]

While female moral reformers listed economic and legal factors among the causes of vice, they suggested remedies that emphasized women's maternal and spiritual role. In resolutions and discussions, the ladies' meeting focused the greatest attention on "the influence of woman, as mother, wife, or sister," on "parental faithfulness," the elevation of standards of virtue, and the removal of temptations. They did consider the establishment of a house of industry as a necessary precondition for the rehabilitation of the "abandoned of both sexes," but such an institution's utility lay primarily in preventing idleness

---

[42] Ibid.
[43] *Daily Democrat* (Rochester), 13 September 1843.
[44] *Advocate of Moral Reform*, 1 October 1843.

rather than providing income or marketable skills.[45] In pursuing these particular measures, they were assured of male support. Joseph D. Husbands maintained "that to whatever good work virtuous and intelligent *wives* set their hearts and minds, *husbands,* as a matter of course, would unite in carrying forward."[46]

Unity seemed to characterize women's moral reform efforts for the next two years. Letters and reports from the local society to the *Advocate* increased significantly after the Rochester meeting. The FMRS claimed five hundred members by summer of 1845, though it is unlikely that nearly that many attended regular meetings since they were held at the home of Mrs. Mathews. The society did attract the active participation of some well-known women in this period: FASS founders Mrs. Galusha and Mrs. Porter; Mrs. Jonah Brown, who as Huldah Strong had superintended the first charity school; CS charter members Mrs. Eliza West and Mrs. Josiah Bissell; and Mrs. Abner Wakelee and Mrs. Erastus Cook, who had combined CS and antislavery labors before turning to moral reform. The city directory listed the FMRS among the local benevolent institutions in its 1845–1846 edition, allowing the society to publicize its resources and needs. By that date the FMRS no longer defined the eradication of vice but rather assistance to its victims as the society's primary concern. Their own moral and spiritual development, under male tutelage, was a significant if secondary consideration. Even with ties to a larger number of women and to well-known activists, the FMRS claimed that its funds were "limited, yet it afford[ed] aid to such of the unfortunate, as are disposed to return to habits of rectitude and virtue." Exposure of male perpetrators to the community had apparently been replaced by exposure of female victims to "appropriate tracts, etc., which are freely circulated among that class, whose condition, spiritual and temporal, [the Society] seek to ameliorate." Monthly meetings were often devoted to self-improvement: "Brief addresses on the subject of Moral Reform" were "delivered before the Society . . . by gentlemen appointed for that purpose." Perfection was slowly losing out to assistance, amelioration, and elevation.[47]

Female temperance workers simultaneously shifted their efforts

[45] Ibid. Legal prohibitions were also considered as an option, perhaps introduced by Joseph D. Husbands and other male kin, several of whom were lawyers.

[46] *Daily Democrat,* 13 September 1843.

[47] *Canfield and Warren's Directory of the City of Rochester, for 1845–1846, with a Map* (Rochester: John Canfield and Ansel Warren, 1845), p. 9.

from eradication to amelioration. In the early 1840s evangelical clergy and itinerant agents of the Washingtonian Society, an association of reformed drunkards with headquarters in the nation's capital, aroused Rochesterians to expand their antialcohol campaign. Temperance societies once again flourished with politicians and benevolent ladies joining in the labors. In January 1843 the CS donated several dozen shirts to the temperance association and appointed Mrs. Goodman and Miss Porter "to confer with the [men's] Washingtonian Society, & to suggest a plan of co-operation for the distribution of soup among the poor."[48] Throughout the Northeast, pious women who wished to assist the Washingtonians formed ladies' auxiliaries; by March 1844 the local LWTAS claimed upwards of three hundred members. The association's purpose was to aid the families of "poor and destitute *reformed drunkards*," and in the 1844 city directory the LWTAS reported having "rendered assistance to several destitute families," listing the number of garments distributed during the year.[49]

The LWTAS replicated the revivalistic appeals, prayer meetings, and district visiting of their moral reform counterparts and shared the FMRS's ties to both perfectionist and benevolent predecessors. Three CS district visitors were among the LWTAS's first slate of eleven officers along with the wife of moral reform spokesman Joseph D. Husbands, perfectionist Mrs. Eaton, and early abolitionist Mrs. Amos Enos. A "committee of Vigilance consisting of eighteen Ladies" was appointed to visit needy families and distribute material and spiritual resources. Replenishing its own resources through twenty-five-cent membership dues and community donations, the society "was said to be in a highly prosperous condition" by its first anniversary. Church-based and men's temperance associations also aided the LWTAS, and lectures, such as that presented *"to the ladies"* by the Reverend Mr. Graves of Washington Street Church, renewed zeal for the cause.[50]

Both female temperance advocates and moral reformers responded to urban problems with the support of small-town and rural auxiliaries. The belief that the country was purer than the city and that young women from the country were most likely to be seduced in the city led to strong bonds of sympathy and cooperation between urban and rural

[48] CS, Minute Book, 3 January 1843, CSP.
[49] *A Directory and Gazateer of the City of Rochester, for 1844* (Rochester: James Elwood and Dellon M. Dewey, 1844), p. 28.
[50] *Daily Advertiser,* 27 November 1844 and 8 June 1844.

women. Journals such as the *Advocate* spread news to the smallest rural hamlets, and itinerant ministers and reform agents carried tales of seduction and salvation from town to town, knitting a far-reaching network among women who rarely left their own home fires. The Lady Washingtonians also formed a web of auxiliaries across the Northeast, while letters to the *Advocate* and delegates to moral reform conventions arrived from dozens of New York's smaller agricultural and commercial centers. In western New York, women from the villages of Ogden, Henrietta, Irondequoit, Rush, Brockport, Brighton, and Greece—all successful agricultural communities bound into Rochester's milling and shipping network—appeared alongside their urban sisters in meetings, conventions, reports, and correspondence.

In 1846 fourteen hundred women from Monroe County "bemoan[ed] their lack of the ballot" and "petitioned voters to safeguard their welfare at the polls" by voting for candidates opposed to the liquor traffic.[51] In the number of signatures gathered, the temperance petitioners of 1846 exceeded the success of antislavery petitioners a decade earlier. Yet at the same moment, a shift in strategies by the national, male-directed temperance associations encouraged female coworkers to follow the same path out of the public domain earlier tread by female abolitionists. As male temperance advocates followed their antislavery counterparts' pursuit of political and legislative change, women's role was gradually but irrevocably diminished. Still, in 1846, perfectionist women appeared to dominate local female activism.

The successes of moral reform and temperance-minded perfectionists were more dramatic than the activities of benevolent and ultraist peers, but all three groups expanded their efforts in the postpanic period. The CS in particular benefited from the return of prosperity. Nearly every Protestant congregation increased its representation in the CS, including the new liberal Protestant stronghold, First Unitarian. In 1846 the 128 members from St. Luke's alone exceeded the total membership of four years earlier; First Presbyterian added 100 more women. The CS treasury and its charitable ventures increased accordingly. Annual fund-raising sermons once again demonstrated the strength of clerical and business support for female benevolence, and the services provided by local editors and merchants, once gratefully received as favors, were now considered rights.

[51] Quoted in McKelvey, *Rochester*, p. 284.

During the mid-1840s husbands of CS leaders not only recovered their former fortunes but took the lead in new financial enterprises. Four CS husbands served as bank presidents in the 1840s; two dozen others served on bank boards. During the same period iron foundries, woolen mills, machine shops, boot and shoe factories, and other industrial investments began to replace flour mills as Rochester's chief source of wealth, and the husbands of benevolent women successfully transferred profits from the former to the latter. Such transfers were often aided by political intervention, and here, too, benevolent families maintained disproportionate representation among village trustees, aldermen, and judges.

CS women, alone or in conjuction with the OAA board, utilized their ties to economic and political leaders to expand the benevolent network. In 1844 a joint petition of the CS and OAA was presented to the common council for the establishment of a workhouse; in 1845 the CS formed a hospital committee, which lead to the incorporation of Rochester City Hospital two years later. Neither of these projects resulted in the actual building of the requested institutions until after mid-century, suggesting that benevolent women's visions surpassed male kin's financial subsidies. Yet, as in the 1820s and 1830s, such requests indicated that connections and initiative were on the side of female benevolence.

The joint petition of 1844 was only one sign of the cross-fertilization between the CS and the OAA in these years. The *Orphan's Souvenir,* a gift book sold as part of the 1843 building-fund campaign, placed the care of orphans squarely within the benevolent tradition. The introduction to the volume by the Honorable Frederick Whittlesey, declared that "the absolutely destitute can claim the bare necessaries of life from those who are more prosperous." He noted, however, that the "promptings of humanity" are often admitted grudgingly from the belief that "abject want" is a punishment for "vicious or criminal habits." In "the case of the helpless orphan," however, "justice itself relaxes the severity of her frown, and permits all the gushing sympathies of our nature to pour forth unrepressed."[52] Ministers, teachers, lawyers, and benevolent ladies followed Whittlesey in asserting the peculiar and unfettered claims of the orphan on the affluent.

The OAA board had not completely lost its early evangelical charac-

[52]*Orphan's Souvenir: A Rochester Book, in Aid of the Rochester Orphan Asylum* (Rochester: William Alling, 1843), introduction.

ter, but the moral reform and temperance campaigns of the 1840s were directing perfectionists' attention elsewhere while CS laborers cautiously extended their benevolent hand to the orphan. By 1843 one third of OAA members, 34 of 104, had begun their activist careers in the CS. Fifteen of these women had held major offices in the older society and at least nine, minor ones.[53] Meanwhile, the evangelical churches that supplied many of the OAA's first workers, particularly Third Presbyterian and St. Paul's Episcopal, were no longer so firmly committed to perfectionist doctrines. Nor was the OAA so firmly committed to ecumenical representation on its board of managers. On its tenth anniversary, the OAA members elected nine First Presbyterian and six St. Luke's communicants to fill fifteen of the association's top nineteen offices.[54] Once the OAA achieved stability, its members reciprocated by utilizing skills learned in the younger association to aid the older. After 1842 women who entered public careers in the OAA became more frequent candidates for CS offices. Simultaneously, the OAA ended its door-to-door canvass for orphans or donations and developed more regularized forms of fund raising, including annual sermons in selected churches, exhibitions at the asylum, and public performances by orphans.[55]

As OAA leaders leaned further toward religious and secular orthodoxy, ultraist leaders announced their heterodox spiritual and social views more boldly. In the mid-1840s, debates within the Genesee Yearly Meeting came to a head, while those who were dismissed or withdrew from the Hicksite circle appeared with greater frequency as public advocates of abolition, communitarian experiments, and free religious meetings. The Genesee meeting continued to publish testimonies regarding Indian rights, slavery, capital punishment, and education, but the members could not agree on matters of discipline and authority. Simultaneously, "popular" antislavery labors brought at least a dozen Rochester Friends under review. The Rochester Monthly

[53] The dates 1837 to 1843 are used here because OAA membership lists are not broken down by the year for this period. Major officers in the CS, as in other associations, constituted the executive committee: president, vice-president, secretary, treasurer, directress, and manager. Minor officers—visitors, collectors, certain committee members, and so on—were more active than simple members but were generally concerned with only one aspect of an association's work.

[54] The other positions were filled by members from Second Presbyterian, First Baptist, First Methodist, and First Unitarian churches.

[55] For descriptions of fund-raising events, see OAA, Annual Reports for 1842, 1843, 1845, and 1846, Scrapbook, HCCP.

Meeting noticed, for instance, when Amy Post "left her home for the purpose . . . of Antislavery work" and appointed a committee to advise her "in regard to her duty toward her family" and "her attitude [in] working with the 'world's people.' "[56] Amy Post made her contempt for such proceedings clear in a letter to Abby Kelley. Penning her thoughts on a sheet of stationery embossed with an antislavery logo, she wrote, "the overseers [of the monthly meeting] have taken no further notice of my case, but I expect they will have a fresh charge against me soon, as I yesterday transcribed some Epistles for the Preparative meetings on such paper as this, and have but little doubt but that imploring image [of a slave in chains] will disturb their quiet."[57] Amy, her husband Isaac, and daughter Mary Hallowell, along with Lewis Burtis and other abolitionists were "released" from the Genesee Yearly Meeting one by one in the mid-1840s. Those members who avoided censure at that time did not necessarily relish their continuance. Hicksite activist Nathanial Potter of Buffalo, for instance, wrote to Isaac Post upon the latter's dismissal: "you have been more faithful in the cause of the downtrodden slave than I" so "I have yet to suffer in society. . . . Blessed are they that are persecuted for righteousness's sake," he concluded, "for theirs is the kingdom of Heaven."[58]

Perhaps in the spirit of sexual equality, Hicksites released female activists as readily as male ones; and ultraist women as readily made themselves candidates for expulsion by their visible and vocal roles in worldly societies. At the founding meeting of the WNYASS, five women, including Abby Kelley and Amy Post, were appointed a committee "to draft and present an address to the abolitionists of Western New York, setting forth the benefits of fairs and recommending some definite plan of action for the various sewing circles to adopt."[59] Rochester's ultraist women did more than plan for action: they set about organizing an antislavery fair for the following winter. The event was set for 22 February, "as it would be a day easily remembered by the people. The birth day of the great, good, pious, immortal, slaveholding Washington!"[60] The western New York workers sought

[56] Lucy N. Coleman, *Reminiscences* (Buffalo, H. L. Green, 1891), p. 84.
[57] Amy Post to Abby Kelley, 4 December 1843, AKFP.
[58] N[athaniel] P[otter] to Isaac Post, 18 September 1845, IAPFP. "Society" here refers to the Society of Friends.
[59] *Liberator*, 6 January 1843. Fund-raising through antislavery fairs was designated as women's work within virtually all abolitionist groups. For a comparison of the forms and contents of fairs organized by various activist women, see Chapter 7.
[60] E[lizabeth] McClintock to Abby Kelley, 10 January 1843, AKFP.

aid from local women as well as contributions left over from the Boston fair, upon which they modeled their own efforts. They planned to sell handsewn items, farm produce, and antislavery almanacs and to collect cash and pledges to fund lecturers and publications. On 2 February, an announcement of the fair appeared in the *National Anti-Slavery Standard*. Sarah Burtis and Amy Post of Rochester together with Mary Ann McClintock of Waterloo, Phebe Hathaway of Farmington, and Abby Kelley signed the call, requesting aid in the form of goods, labor, and attendance. They noted in their plea for assistance that some abolitionists objected to fund-raising fairs as too closely connected in the public mind with church and charitable enterprises. The WNYASS women argued that for precisely this reason a fair "takes captive the strong-holds of prejudice unawares, . . . a kindly feeling is kindled up in the community, and many, before indifferent or cold-hearted, ... become softened in their prejudices."[61]

Despite the optimistic tone of their public pronouncements, the fair organizers faced numerous difficulties in their first fund-raising attempt. Sarah Burtis, one of the chief managers, unexpectedly limited her labors because of the death of her "precious bird" who had "flown back to the arms of *Love,* their [*sic*] to bask and nestle in the sunshine of never ending bliss." When she returned to the antislavery circle, the bereaved mother was freshly aggrieved by news that some women "had left us on account of our admitting colored persons to our society." In relating this to Abby Kelley, Burtis assured her friend that "we do not sacrifice principles to numbers, neither will colored people be rejected, yet it is very proving. . . ." In addition, the WNYASS women reported so much competition from "the Orphan Asylum as well as all the different Church sewing societies that our claims meet with much indifference and opposition."[62] The opposition was fired no doubt by ultraist women's refusal to mitigate what they perceived as the horrors of slavery by employing the usual rhetorical indirection of female benevolent and perfectionist leaders. Rather, they thoroughly detailed "the wailings of kidnapped infants, the shriek of the agonized mother, the dumb anguish, and black despair of outraged daughters, and the deep groans of spirit-broken and imbruted mothers."[63]

Notwithstanding personal tragedies, internal dissension, competi-

[61] *National Anti-Slavery Standard* (New York City), 2 February 1843.
[62] Sarah Anthony Burtis to Abby Kelley, 17 January 1843, AKFP.
[63] *National Anti-Slavery Standard*, 2 February 1843.

tion, and opposition, the 1843 antislavery fair was a success. "Considering the shortness of the time to prepare in, and the dreadful dull and 'hard times,' it was quite a magnificent af-*fair,*" wrote a visitor from Farmington.[64] Though the Rochester "women were entirely unacquainted with the detail of Fairs," and thus "fell into some mistakes," they collected "over three hundred dollars, a sum by no means contemptible in . . . hard times, and in a city so small as Rochester, and at an Anti-Slavery Sale."[65] A month after the fair, the organizers recorded sales of $312 in the *Liberator,* thanking their Boston sisters for the contribution of "so rare a display of rich and elegant articles." More important than their pecuniary value, asserted the fair's organizers, was the cooperative effort these articles signified, "which strengthens our hands . . . and thereby prepares us for persevering in every work of reform."[66]

The western New York ultraists not only persevered, they even extended their exertions. In the summer of 1843 ex-slave Frederick Douglass's appearance in the city led to the organization of a three-day convention "characterized by a large degree of talent, eloquence, and mutual good feeling." In the fall a half dozen WNYASS members initiated a "cooperative community" at Skaneatelas in central New York, and the following year several ultraist families settled in the Fourierist Phalanx at Sodus Bay, thirty miles east of Rochester.[67] Asa and Huldah Anthony, the Fishes, and the Braithewaites were apparently still there in 1846 when Catharine Fish and Giles Stebbins, a lecturer for the American Anti-Slavery Society, celebrated their nuptials at the community. Rev. Roswell G. Murray and his wife, Laura, agents of moral reform societies in the 1830s, also moved to Sodus Bay in the 1840s and there became enmeshed in the ultraist network. Having withdrawn from other reform activities, these utopian communalists believed with Benjamin Fish that they were "engaged in a reform which if properly carried out will strike at the root of *all Slavery*. . . ."[68]

Slavery in its various forms was not to be so easily abolished, however, and most Sodus Bay residents gradually returned to Rochester.

[64] J[oseph] C. Hathaway to Abby Kelley, 26 February 1843, AKFP.
[65] E. I. Neall to Abby Kelley, 12 March 1843, AKFP.
[66] *Liberator,* 24 March 1843.
[67] Ibid., 25 August 1843 (quoting from *Daily Democrat* [Rochester]) 30 September 1843. Fourierist Phalanxes were utopian communities organized on principles set forth by the French socialist Charles Fourier. A combination of physical and intellectual labor, a simple lifestyle, and the participation of all members in decision making were the primary features of these communities.
[68] Benjamin Fish to Isaac Post, [184–], IAPFP.

There they united in the "free meetings" established by urban ultraists "for mutual improvement and the free interchange of thought on any of the great subjects of the day." Some of these meetings, exclusively for women, considered "subjects of Social and Pecuniary interest."[69] In most, however, men and women joined in "discussions upon a great variety of subjects without limitation, as to the matter or manner."[70] In addition, ultraists continued to fight prejudice and other evils within their own families, by housing, hiding, and hiring fugitive slaves, hosting antislavery lecturers and agents, mingling socially with all classes and races, and prohibiting the use of alcohol and tobacco.[71]

In the midst of these myriad concerns, ultraist women continued to focus their greatest energies on the antislavery movement and the fund-raising fairs that supported it. They held fairs annually throughout the 1840s, the proceeds of which were crucial in sustaining lecturers and publications.[72] Even after their successful 1843 venture, however, the women of the WNYASS faced many obstacles, including their own lack of experience and confidence. The absence of only one or two members of the sewing society, which rarely numbered more than two dozen active laborers, slowed the work considerably. The intimacy of the circle was due in large part to ultraists' failure to attract perfectionist coworkers. Initially, "not one person belonging to a professed Church" had "given her name as a member, not even Porter's wife." After a visit from Sarah Burtis, Mrs. Porter "readily payd [sic] her membership fee," but she did not attend the meetings.[73] Thus ultraists failed to benefit from the experience of their evangelical sisters. While preparing for their second fair, Amy Post admitted that the sewing circle's inexperience was a financial and psychological drain. She wrote to Abby Kelley that the women had to buy almost all of their own materials as they made "a poor hand at beging [sic]. We had hoped," she wearily noted, "that we should have some of thy company and assistance this winter to learn us and give us a fresh start."[74]

One week after Amy Post's plea, Kelley arrived in the city for the

---

[69] Notice of a free meeting, n.d., IAPFP.

[70] *The Circumstance* (Rochester), 20 December 1845. The editor of this paper was ultraist Eliab Capron, a primary supporter of free meetings and abolition.

[71] Amy Post, for example, though she did not join a temperance association, was anxious to instill teetotal habits in her twelve-year-old son, Joseph, sending him a temperance pledge for his signature while he was in school on Long Island. See Amy Post to Joseph W. Post, 11 April 1845, IAPFP.

[72] For detailed reports of some of these fairs, see *Liberator*, 24 March 1843; *National Anti-Slavery Standard*, 2 February 1843; *North Star*, 3 December 1847.

[73] Sarah Anthony Burtis to Abby Kelley, 17 January 1843, AKFP.

[74] Amy Post to Abby Kelley, 4 December 1843, AKFP.

first annual meeting of the WNYASS. Bethel Church again provided the site and Samuel D. Porter presided. The meeting was characterized by heated debates between third-party advocates led by Porter and moral suasionists led by Abby Kelley. Before the meeting, the Posts had feared that Porter would not attend because of Kelley's recent condemnations of political abolitionists. Yet despite fears and dissension, the WNYASS survived its first year and Porter was reelected president of the association. At least in Rochester, Liberty party and Garrisonian advocates sought to work together harmoniously. We "repudiate with indignation," they proclaimed, "every sectarian, political, or other test, that may be forced upon us as abolitionists; but though we may be of every form of religious and political opinions, Christian and Infidel, war men and peace men, voters and non-resistants, we unite for mutual co-operation to effect the one great object of converting the entire public to abolitionism. . . ."[75]

It was soon apparent, however, that the breech between perfectionist politicians and ultraist moral suasionists ran far deeper than resolutions could heal. Perfectionist women had never played a role in the WNYASS and simultaneous with its rise had retreated from antislavery activity entirely. Within two years perfectionist men had lost their leadership roles within the WNYASS, and they soon withdrew from the society. Samuel D. Porter and George Avery served on the resolutions committee at the second anniversary meeting; their arena, however, was no longer Bethel Church but Talman Hall, and their coagitators were now overwhelmingly ultraist.[76] Debates between Liberty party and moral suasion factions were more contentious than those of the previous year, and not a single member of the former group was elected to WNYASS office. By 1846 neither Porter nor any of his evangelical coworkers served as WNYASS functionaries.

Their places were filled by ultraist women who appeared in increasing numbers in WNYASS offices. In spring 1844 Amy Post was selected as the society's delegate to the American Anti-Slavery Society's annual meeting in New York City. By 1845 women formed half of the "counsellors," the WNYASS's version of an executive committee, and the first meeting of the group found Sarah Burtis as secretary and Rhoda DeGarmo as chair. The women continued to hold antislavery fairs and lost some of their uncertainty as they gained experience. By

[75] *Liberator*, 5 January 1844.
[76] For proceedings of this meeting, see *National Anti-Slavery Standard*, 6 March 184).

New Year's Day 1846, at a meeting of the counselors, a "majority of the Ladies' Sewing Circle being present, they resolved to hold a Fair . . . during the holydays [*sic*], a year from this time." The committee as a whole appeared to be more determined "to do something, than at any preceding meeting, especially . . . the females," who were now "determined that their Fair shall be second to none, save the great Boston Fair."[77]

While ultraists, especially ultraist women, did not generally gain the support of their evangelical counterparts, three Brick Church perfectionists and the wife of an itinerant evangelical minister shared WNYASS labors in the mid-1840s. By that time all four—Abigail Bush, Lemira Kedzie, Sarah C. Owen, and Laura Murray—had severed their bonds to Evangelicalism. Abigail Bush, born Abigail Norton, had been raised in a relatively affluent household and attended First Presbyterian Church as a child. In her twenties she transferred to Brick Church and became a CS member. Then in 1833 she married Henry Bush, a stove manufacturer and radical abolitionist, and her life changed drastically. Within five years her name was missing from both Brick Church and CS ranks, and within a decade she was the most prominent ex-Evangelical in ultraist circles.

Lemira Kedzie joined Brick Church in 1834 and perfectionist petitioners in 1836 and 1837. By 1840, however, as evangelical women were retreating from abolitionist campaigns, Lemira Kedzie and her husband, John, became vocal critics of the church's collaboration with slaveholders. In that year Brick Church elders admonished the Kedzies for "openly and publicly declareing [*sic*]" that "they were under no obligation to submit to the authority [of] the church with which they are commuted." The Kedzies replied that their criticism was by no means "intended for this church alone but was made with reference to all the Churches of different Sects." When "kindly admonished" to reflect on their sins, the Kedzies proclaimed themselves "at liberty to absolve . . . their covenant obligations" and follow "the direction of the Apostle 'to withdraw from those that walk disorderly.' "[78] They were immediately suspended from church membership, and within a year both were serving as WNYASS counselors.

[77] Ibid., 22 January 1846.
[78] Second (Brick) Presbyterian Church, Session Minutes, 2 November and 30 November 1840. The Kedzies' formal excommunication was recorded on 31 October 1842, Presbyterian Historical Society.

Just before the Kedzies' dismissal, Sarah C. Owen joined Brick Church. Active in moral reform efforts in western New York, Owen attended the Utica meeting of the American Female Moral Reform Society as the Rochester delegate in 1839. Several years later she was apparently involved in antislavery labors for Brick Church elders accused her of un-Christian conduct on this account. In December 1845, having refused to offer "evidence of repentance or reformation" and having been elected to WNYASS office, Sarah Owen was excommunicated.[79] Only one other FMRS member, Laura Murray, is known to have entered WNYASS ranks. Following the various ministerial callings of her husband, Laura Murray served in moral reform societies in Griffin Mills and Henrietta, New York, before her arrival in Rochester. In 1837 she served with Lemira Kedzie as an antislavery petitioner and in 1839 joined Sarah Owen at FMRS meetings. In the early 1840s the Murrays lived in the Sodus Bay Phalanx and traveled into the city to attend WNYASS meetings. For the remainder of the Murrays' stay in western New York, they shared labors with ultraists rather than Evangelicals.

It is unclear why these particular perfectionists linked their visions to ultraist means while their evangelical sisters retreated. Abigail Bush, Lemira Kedzie, and Laura Murray all married active abolitionists who differed from the majority of evangelical men by remaining within the American Anti-Slavery Society after 1840. Laura Murray and Sarah Owen shared the uncertainty of geographical mobility—Murray following her husband's itinerant ministry and Owen her family's calls for aid. Murray traveled throughout New York State before reaching western New York, while Owen journeyed as far west as Michigan and more frequently to LeRoy and other points in New York's southern tier. At least Owen and Bush shared economic uncertainty: Sarah supported herself through needlework and nursing; Abigail struggled through her husband Henry's financial misfortunes as well as six births and two infant deaths between 1834 and 1846. The combination of forces that led these women to follow the radical implications of Finneyite perfectionism was not sufficient to attract large numbers of Evangelicals. It was only the existence of a network of Quaker ultraists that allowed these ostracized Evangelicals to remain part of a collective endeavor to re-form the world.

[79]Ibid., 8 December 1845.

The common choice of female perfectionists who confronted community and clerical censure was retreat—to domesticity or benevolent enterprises—or a transfer of labor from antislavery to moral reform and temperance associations. Ironically, perfectionists' retreat was due in large part to their success, which renewed questions about the boundaries of women's public role and engendered ambivalence on the part of perfectionists themselves as to their assigned sphere. This pattern was first apparent among antislavery perfectionists but soon affected the efforts of moral reformers and temperance advocates as well. For many perfectionists, success and its attendant conflicts coincided with three other factors that redirected their activities: the achievement of economic stability and social position, increased conflict within extralocal parent societies, and the decline of revivalistic zeal simultaneous with a shift toward ameliorative goals. The American Anti-Slavery Society's division in 1840 clearly signaled the demise of evangelical women's antislavery activities, and the renewal of revivals in the early 1840s was insufficient to reactivate women in the slave's cause. Finney himself was only a half-hearted abolitionist by this time and an ardent opponent of women's work in that particular field. Moreover, the religious zeal of the early 1840s barely outlasted the economic recovery of the mid-1840s. Simultaneously, male Evangelicals began fighting slavery, vice, and intemperance primarily within the confines of electoral politics, leaving women to auxiliary and ameliorative efforts. Legal prohibition and individual rehabilitation rather than social perfection was the goal of Rochester's newly established bourgeoisie.

For many perfectionist women, there was a silver lining to their acceptance of secondary and circumscribed social roles. Mrs. Eaton's husband, Amos, for example, accumulated sufficient rank and resources in the army's service that by the late 1840s he could settle his family in a permanent residence in New York City. There Elizabeth Eaton returned to the financial security of her youth and to more privatized and institutionalized moral salvation efforts. Mary and Selah Mathews gradually moved into the ranks of middle-class comfort and security within Rochester. Despite a brief crisis in 1842–1843, Selah developed a lucrative law practice and gained political clout as a city recorder and federal judge. He combined these successes with seats on the Commercial Bank's board of directors and the Third Presbyterian Church's board of elders. He directed these manifold ventures from his new residence in the Ruffled Shirt ward from which his wife ventured forth to lead moral reform efforts and rejoin benevolent enterprises. Her return to the latter was fully attested to in the late 1840s when she was elected to CS office. In the same period Samuel D. Porter rose from store clerk to printer to land agent. He served as a Presbyterian Church elder as well, and though his abolitionist stance kept him out of local political office, he was a leader in statewide third-party efforts. While less affluent and powerful than Selah Mathews, Porter was able to establish his family in a third ward home where Mrs. Porter divided her time among the OAA, the FMRS, and child bearing and rearing. Sarah Seward, who had been led to Christ by Charles Grandison Finney in 1831, was led to the altar by Jacob Gould a decade later. A shoemaker by trade, Gould had established the Rochester Boot and Shoe Factory in the early 1820s. The first Mrs. Gould had been a CS charter member, an appropriate role for the wife of a prosperous merchant, First Church elder, bank director and pioneer politician. When Sarah Seward became Jacob's second wife, she too joined First Presbyterian Church, the offices of the CS, and the affluent circles of the third ward.

The new Mrs. Gould could look about her and feel justified in her new life as she saw Mary Mathews, Susan Porter, Elizabeth Eaton, and other evangelical sisters also settling into more comfortable circumstances and circumscribed roles. Their transition to the stability and subordination of bourgeois womanhood was eased not only by its collective character but also by the individual though oft repeated experience of total submission to God through conversion. While condemning unregenerate men and organizing activist campaigns, evangelical women had simultaneously expressed their subjection to and humiliation before God and his clerical representatives. Sarah Seward, for instance, nurtured numerous conversions among her seminary students but wrote to Finney that her successes depended on her *"soul & body"* sacrifice to her heavenly "Master."[80] Before Mrs. Mathews was converted, Finney prayed with her, repeating the text "Except ye be converted and become as little children, ye shall no wise enter into the Kingdom of Heaven." When she finally accepted God as her savior, "her sensibility gushed forth, and . . . she was indeed a little

---

[80] Sarah T. Seward to Mr. and Mrs. Charles Finney, 9 March 1835, Microfilm, Roll 3, CGFP.

child."[81] As Mrs. Mathews began her perfectionist pursuits, she claimed her "own wicked heart" as her gravest concern and wished only to be "an instrument" in Christ's hands. Increasingly active in prayer circles, maternal associations, and public societies, she reported to Mrs. Finney, "I have been led to see more and more my utter weakness—and my utter dependence on Christ."[82] Elizabeth Eaton echoed the same sentiments in 1833. Writing to her husband, she begged him "to be much in prayer. What the Lord will have us do . . . I do now know—but everywhere to do his work we must be wholly his."[83]

In pursuing antislavery and moral reform efforts, perfectionist women claimed that the Lord "often employs the feeblest instruments."[84] By such words, women asserted their own subordination even as they assumed public roles. Nor did success in those public roles necessarily diminish women's sense of dependency and humiliation. After a decade of public leadership, Mrs. Porter expressed women's subordination to a higher authority in the starkest of terms. Mrs. Lester, a friend and fellow activist, lost her baby girl "after only one or two breaths." In the face of this tragedy, Mrs. Porter reflected, the "ways of Providence sometime seem mysterious to us who are but shortsighted worms of the dust. . . . 'we have but to bow the head in silence when God calls back the things we love,' " she concluded.[85] The uncertainties of life, especially of maternity and infancy, had long heightened women's dependence on spiritual reassurances. In seeking worldly perfection, women carried some of the same uncertainties into the public domain, making them vulnerable to ministerial and male censure long after they had seemingly broken the bonds of traditional womanhood. In Rochester as elsewhere, evangelical women, who had initially emphasized the liberating aspects of revivalism, finally chose to accept the economic, social, and psychological rewards of reassuming some of those bonds.

Problems within the extralocal associations upon which perfectionist

[81] Charles Grandison Finney, *The Memoirs of Rev. Charles G. Finney, Written by Himself* (New York: F. H. Revell, [1876]), pp. 287–288.

[82] Mary S. Mathews to Mrs. Charles Finney, 16 May and 19 December 1831, 20 October 1832, Roll 3, CGFP.

[83] Elizabeth Selden Eaton to Amos Eaton, 16 April 1833, in McKelvey, "Letters," p. 45.

[84] *Advocate of Moral Reform*, 15 July 1836.

[85] Mrs. Samuel D. Porter to Mrs. Charles Finney, 20 September 1845, Roll 4, CGFP.

women relied for models and support may have increased their willingness to subject themselves to the new limits of a postrevival bourgeois order. The division of the American Anti-Slavery Society and the gradual withdrawal of evangelical men from the WNYASS sealed evangelical women's exit from abolitionism by 1842. The following year several of these ex-abolitionists could be found at the moral reform meetings held in Rochester where the participants condemned slavery as an institutionalized violation of women's virtue. By 1844, however, moral reformers began to distance themselves from the taint of abolitionist politics. Several central New York auxiliaries protested the introduction of antislavery issues into their conventions. Asserting that they "regard[ed] all the great moral causes of the day as 'sisters of charity,'" they nonetheless concluded "that in the present state of things, more will be accomplished by preserving [the] distinctive character" of each.[86] The *Advocate* refused to print the report of some moral reform meetings, affirming that they continued to consider the problems of slave women as victims of vice but were not willing to "exert their *whole* influence for the *overthrow* of *slavery.* . . ."[87]

Having survived the influx of antislavery workers with only minor disruptions, moral reformers soon battled each other over matters of policy and priorities. In 1845 the leaders of the American Female Moral Reform Society claimed that their initial goal, the purification of American society, was nearly achieved.[88] A majority of the society's board wanted to redirect their resources toward prevention and rehabilitation through houses of industry, homes for unemployed women and their children, and employment agencies. The Rochester society assured the board that they had absolute "confidence in the integrity of the majority. . . ."[89] One of the FMRS's members wrote to the *Advocate* that "much tribulation" seemed necessary to success, and that if we "do not faint in the time of adversity . . . 'God may be glorified, and the enemy be discomfited [*sic*].'"[90] Yet in the same year Mrs. Porter

[86]*Advocate of Moral Reform*, 1 February 1844. This citation is from the Oneida County Female Moral Reform Society some fifty miles east of Rochester. Items in the *Advocate* indicate that conflicts erupted between ultraist abolitionists and moral reformers in central and western New York throughout this period. On such conflicts in Rochester, see Mrs. Samuel D. Porter to Mrs. Charles Finney, 20 September 1845, Roll 4, CGFP.

[87]*Advocate of Moral Reform*, 1 February 1844.

[88]Carroll Smith-Rosenberg, *Religion and the Rise of the City: The New York City Mission Movement, 1812–1870* (Ithaca: Cornell University Press, 1971), pp. 214–15.

[89]Mary S. Mathews to Mrs. Bissell, published in the *Advocate of Moral Reform*, 1 October 1845.

[90]*Advocate of Moral Reform*, 1 November 1845.

alleged that there was "blame . . . on both sides" and discontinued her service with the FMRS.[91] By 1846 Mrs. Eaton was assuring her husband that though she was "going to a moral Reform meeting," she "hardly mentioned the subject" any more even to friends and relatives.[92]

In times of tribulation, perfectionist women could no longer rely on either external support or evangelical zeal. After 1842 Rochester was devoid of revivals for twelve years. During this period liberal Protestant congregations such as the Unitarians provided new workers for reform, but their numbers were limited. Third Presbyterian had long ago retreated from its most progressive positions, but in the mid-1840s even many of the Bethel congregation lost their earlier enthusiasm. As Samuel and Susan Porter changed religious affiliations again, they lamented "the spiritual bareness" of Bethel and "its striking and retrograde movement . . . upon the subject of slavery."[93] Thus, as other factors made the pursuit of the millennium more difficult for women, the very notion of the millennium lost its power.

As perfectionist women's public labors declined, those of benevolent ladies and ultraists expanded. Neither of the latter groups depended on millennial doctrines to justify their worldly work; neither experienced significant changes in economic or social status; and neither faced new and disruptive demands from extralocal associations. Benevolent women rested their continued success on the same foundation of orthodox religion, affluence, and localized efforts upon which they originally constructed their associations. Ultraist women, never having been dependent on evangelical clergy or affluent husbands, were less affected by the economic and religious transformations of the 1840s, while their ties to extralocal associations provided assistance rather than contention in this period. Moreover, both benevolent and ultraist activists gained from perfectionism's decline. The CS and OAA benefited the most, but the WNYASS also garnered new members while facing less competition for community resources.

The CS and OAA retained high levels of membership through the late 1840s, and their fund-raising appeals received "prompt attention

---

[91] Mrs. Samuel D. Porter to Mrs. Charles Finney, 20 September 1845, Roll 4, CGFP.

[92] Elizabeth Selden Eaton to Amos Eaton, 26 August 1846, in McKelvey, "Letters," p. 103.

[93] Samuel D. Porter to Pastor and Sessions of the Washington [formerly Bethel Free] Presbyterian Church, 29 September 1845, SDPFP.

. . . from the friends of [these] 'noble' " charities.[94] The three hundred dollars that WNYASS women considered a bountiful return on their fair labors in 1843 was multiplied tenfold when the requests emanated from the CS and OAA. As a result the number of orphans cared for yearly increased from seventy in 1843 to over one hundred five years later, while the CS added eight new districts and a dozen visitors in the same period. The CS's successes were simply an extension of the society's perennial strength; the OAA's depended on its continuing transition from perfectionist enthusiasm to benevolent stability. Dependent on perfectionists' zeal for its establishment, the OAA was the only evangelically based association to survive the 1840s intact. Its attraction and acceptance of benevolent leaders and models from its earliest years provided the basis for that survival. By 1848 the OAA board acknowledged the routinization of its affairs and the stability it fostered by apologizing in self-satisfied tones that its annual report was forced to "repeat an oft told tale" of unostentatious but effective labors.

In that same year ultraists offered the community a new tale, a "history of repeated injuries and usurpations on the part of man toward woman."[95] Not routinization but innovation characterized ultraists' efforts in the hallmark year of 1848. In the previous year abolitionism, this time the ultraist variety, had captured the attention though not the applause of the community. Frederick Douglass had moved to the city to begin publication of the *North Star,* reinforcing the city's position as a center of moral suasion abolition. Douglass's enrollment of his daughter in a previously all-white girls' seminary initially aroused more antiabolitionist hostility than his newspaper. The *Daily Advertiser* and the *Daily American* provided local Southern sympathizer Horatio G. Warner with platforms for his attacks on Douglass and for his more general racist appeals. At least indirectly the papers supported his claims with editorials denouncing immediate emancipation, though they did not advocate slavery.[96] The fruits of such sentiments were manifested by Rochesterians who could not "leave off entirely the use of eggs as arguments" against Abby Kelley when she appeared in the city that winter.[97]

[94] OAA, Annual Report, 1846, Scrapbook, HCCP.

[95] *Report of the Woman's Rights Convention, Held at Seneca Falls, N.Y., 19 and 20 July 1848* (Rochester: John Dick, North Star Office, 1848).

[96] On the positions of Rochester newspapers on the antislavery movement in this period, see Adelaide Elizabeth Dorn, "A History of the Anti-Slavery Movement in Rochester and Vicinity" (thesis, University of Buffalo, 1932), pp. 70–76.

[97] Mary Robbins Post to Amy Post, 9 February 1847, IAPFP.

Hostility from the community did not diminish WNYASS labors, however. Rather, it stirred members "to greater exertion" and led them to rebuke "the *northern* slaveholders with the greatest plainness and faithfulness."[98] Unlike their moral reform counterparts, ultraist women refused to isolate one cause from another in order to retain respectability. As Lucretia Mott observed after the Seneca Falls and Rochester woman's rights conventions, "all these subjects of reform are kindred in their nature and giving to each its proper consideration, will tend to strengthen and nerve the mind for all—so that the abolitionist . . . will not love the slave less, in loving universal humanity more."[99] Ultraist women followed Mott's dictate even when it engendered conflict with coworkers. Recognizing that woman's role in abolitionism was cause for concern and criticism on the part of even moderate antislavery men, ultraist women sold Samuel J. May's "Sermon on the Rights of Women" at their 1846 fair. Ultraist women also knew, from the early division of the sewing society, that social mingling with blacks might offend some abolitionists and would certainly outrage the larger community. Yet they proceeded to announce that in the "various relations of life . . . too little attention has been paid to our identity with our coloured citizens," and they continued to include them in their meetings, associations, and fairs.[100] Even in their fund-raising efforts, ultraist women emphasized agitation over financial success, inviting speakers, encouraging participants, and selling literature that was sure to offend.

Whether for its financial rewards or its publication of antislavery views, the antislavery fair and its female organizers garnered the approbation of William C. Nell, Douglass's first partner at the *North Star*. He proclaimed that the "cause [did] not owe" its success "to a single influence more than to the self-denying, self-devoted exertions of Woman." Ultraist women objected to the "language of flattering compliment," even when "indulged in" by ultraist men, that portrayed the female sex as more denying or devoted than the male.[101] But they eagerly accepted "evidences of improvement" among their male coworkers, such as the demand with which Nell completed his proclamation, that "women be free to carry forward the great work of regenerating public sentiment. . . . Impose upon her no restrictions,"

[98] *North Star,* 29 December 1848.
[99] *Liberator,* 6 October 1848.
[100] *North Star,* 14 January 1848.
[101] Ibid., 7 January 1848; Rochester Woman's Rights Convention (hereafter WRC), 2 August 1848, PPWP.

he pleaded, "Clip not the wings of her lofty aspiration for liberty."[102] By 1847 women of the WNYASS had tested those wings not only in fund raising but also in executive committee meetings, as correspondents to antislavery papers, as delegates to the American Anti-Slavery Society anniversary meetings in New York City, and as antislavery lecturers. They were not yet the equals of men in office holding, debating, or public speaking, but they had advanced their position in antislavery ranks considerably while in no way diminishing their demand for full equality.

It was in 1848 that ultraists' demands for sexual as well as religious and racial equality—their version of social perfection—were most forcibly asserted. In June the Genesee Yearly Meeting finally rejected the possibility of significant reform by deciding to "discontinue the Michigan Quarterly Meeting" on account of its "disregard [of] the injunctions of the discipline and the authority of the church."[103] In response, a number of Rochester Hicksites withdrew from the yearly meeting, and, along with already disowned brethren and sisters, pursued public campaigns with more vigor. The first step in that pursuit was the Seneca Falls Woman's Rights Convention of July 1848, followed by the Rochester Woman's Rights Convention in August. A Working Women's Protective Union was a direct outgrowth of the latter, and a wide range of ultraist concerns were articulated at the founding of the Yearly Meeting of Congregational Friends in October. The year ended with the fifth anniversary meeting and fair of the WNYASS.

Lucretia Mott, a leading Hicksite preacher and antislavery advocate, attended the 1848 Genesee Yearly Meeting and then traveled to Auburn to visit her sister, Martha Wright. The two were soon invited to a gathering at the home of Richard and Jane Hunt from which the call went out for a woman's rights convention to be held on 19 and 20 July at the Seneca Falls Wesleyan Chapel.[104] The call, published in the *North Star,* inspired at least five ultraist women from Rochester to make the fifty-mile trek east on only a few days' notice. Two of these, Amy Post and Catharine Fish Stebbins, participated in the debates

[102] *North Star,* 7 January 1848.

[103] GYMWF, June 1847 and June 1848, HRR. The minutes of 1848 indicate no serious disputes over the matters discussed. A different and more conflict-filled version of the same meeting appears in YMCF, *Proceedings of the Yearly Meeting of Congregational Friends, Held at Waterloo, N.Y., from the Fourth to the Sixth of the Sixth Month, Inclusive, with an Appendix, 1849* (Auburn, N.Y.: Oliphant's Press, 1849), pp. 5–6.

[104] On the Seneca Falls convention, see Miriam Gurko, *The Ladies of Seneca Falls: The Birth of the Woman's Rights Movement* (New York: Schocken, 1976). Judith Wellman has been extremely generous in sharing her research on Seneca Falls with me.

over the proposed Declaration of Sentiments and, with ninety-eight other women and men, signed the final document declaring that "woman is man's equal." Asserting that it was woman's "right and duty . . . to promote every righteous cause by every righteous means," they "regarded as self-evident falsehood" any "custom or authority adverse" to such claims, "whether modern or wearing the hoary sanction of antiquity." At the end of the two-day gathering, "there were still so many new points for discussion" that the participants appointed a committee to arrange a second meeting, a fortnight hence, in Rochester.[105]

The arrangements committee for the Rochester convention—Amy Post, Sarah Fish, Sarah C. Owen, Mary Hallowell, and Rhoda De-Garmo—met at Rochester's Protection Hall on the first of August to prepare an agenda and a slate of officers. Seeking the widest audience for their efforts, they appointed a committee to investigate the wrongs of the laboring classes "and to invite the oppressed portion of the community to attend the metings of the convention and take part in its deliberations."[106] While modeling the meeting itself on the Seneca Falls convention, the committee introduced two significant changes. First, the Seneca Falls convention had been called to discuss "the social, civil, and religious condition and rights of women"; the Rochester convention was to consider "the Rights of women, Politically, Socially, Religiously, and Industrially."[107] The greater emphasis on rights, and on economic rights in particular, showed the influence of women who were well practiced in public pursuits and productive labor. Second, a woman, Abigail Bush, was nominated to preside at the Rochester convention, for these female activists had come to believe that woman could only be redeemed from her "degraded position" by "the most strenuous and unremitting effort" to "claim an equal right to act."[108] Experienced in religious and reform meetings and emboldened by the experiences of Seneca Falls, the arrangements committee not only proposed Abigail Bush as president but also suggested four women to serve as vice-presidents and secretaries of the convention. At the opening session, Stanton and Mott proclaimed it "a most hazardous experiment to have a woman President and stoutly opposed it. . . . They were on the verge of leaving the Convention in disgust" when

[105] *Report*, p. 6; WRC, Minutes, 2 August 1848, PPWP.
[106] *Daily Advertiser*, 3 August 1848.
[107] *Report*, p. 3; WRC, Minutes, 2 August 1848, PPWP.
[108] WRC, Minutes, 2 August 1848, PPWP.

"Amy Post . . . assured them that by the same power by which they had resolved, declared, discussed, and debated, they could also preside at a public meeting. . . ."[109] The audience, filled with Amy Post's kin and coworkers, approved the proposed slate. Rather than being dependent on extralocal leaders, Rochester's ultraist women were here in advance of their more prominent organizers.

Seated at the front of the Unitarian Church, which housed the convention, the five women officers listened to the opening prayer by the Reverend Mr. Whicher of the Free Will Baptist Church.[110] The church was filled to overflowing, and when the woman began to read and speak, cries of "louder—louder" rang out, "nearly drown[ing]" the "low voices of the women." Yet they prevailed with the aid of Sarah Anthony Burtis, who quickly stepped forward. Her loud clear voice, trained in the travels of a Quaker ministry, proved a welcome addition to those with "trembling frames and faltering tongues" who "did not expect to be heard by all at first" but who "trusted in the sympathy of the audience and the omnipotency of Right."[111]

The presentation of the agenda revealed a startling, bold, and broad conception of woman's rights. The elective franchise, the ninth of eleven resolutions at Seneca Falls, topped the Rochester agenda. Yet political rights were only a small portion of the demands of the movement. The leaders of the convention urged "women no longer to promise obedience in the marriage covenant" and to allow "the strongest *will* or the superior intellect," whether man's or woman's, to "govern the household." They beseeched woman to claim equal authority not only within her own family but "on all subjects that interest the human family." One of those subjects, according to the convention's organizers should be women's work. The husband's "legal right to hire out his wife to service" and "collect her wages" was labeled "a hideous custom" that reduced woman "almost to the condition of a slave."[112]

Sarah C. Owen read an address concerning "woman's place and pay

[109] WRC, "Proceedings," in Mari Jo and Paul Buhle, eds., *The Concise History of Woman Suffrage* (Chicago: University of Illinois Press, 1978), p. 99.

[110] The Unitarian Church had gained a reputation for sympathy with the slave's cause and with antislavery women. The Free Will Baptists, an antislavery congregation, formally organized in Rochester in 1845. Unfortunately, no discussion of either the location of the meeting or the choice of ministers appears in documents relating to the convention. No records of the Free Will Baptist Church survive to indicate whether any woman's rights advocates were members of that congregation.

[111] WRC, Minutes, 2 August 1848, PPWP.

[112] Ibid.; The leaders specifically referred to this meeting as the "infancy . . . of the movement."

in the world of work," which was elaborated on by Mrs. Roberts in her report on "the average price of labor for sempstresses." Mrs. Galloy "corroborated the statement, having herself experienced some of the oppression of this portion of our citizens." The speakers claimed that many women were "ply[ing] the needle by day and by night, to procure even a scanty pittance for [their] dependent famil[ies]." Recognizing that most of the convention's participants were in more secure economic circumstances, the resolutions committee noted that "those who believe the laboring classes of women are oppressed" can aid their less fortunate sisters by doing "all in their power to raise their wages."[113]

Rochester's feminists predicated woman's political, familial, and economic rights on historical proofs of her capacity for equality. "From Semiramis to Victoria," declared one speaker, "we have found the Women of History equal to the emergency before them!"[114] Recognizing the failure of most women to match the achievements of such historical role models, ultraists reminded their audience that "only by faithful preserverance in the practical exercise of those talents, so long 'wrapped in a napkin and buried under the earth'" would woman "regain her long-lost equality with man." This mytho-historical perspective on woman's oppression and the possibility of its overthrow was combined with sensitivity to the powers of socialization. The conveners granted "that woman's intellect is feeble" but claimed it was so "because she has been so long crushed. . . . Let her arise and demand her rights and in a few years we shall see a different mental development." Here they compared women to the slaves of the South and saw women's rise foreshadowed in "the progress" made "within the past few years" by escaped slaves resettled in the free environs of the North.[115]

Ultraist woman's rights advocates harked back to the American Convention of Anti-Slavery women when they argued that woman had "too long rested satisfied in the circumscribed limits which corrupt customs and a perverted application of the Scriptures [had] marked out for her."[116] In 1837 such sentiments had supported perfectionist women's antislavery petition campaigns. In 1848 Amy Post and her coworkers demanded the same and added that "woman shall stand

[113] WRC, "Proceedings," p. 102.
[114] *Liberator*, 15 September 1848, reporting on speech by Rebecca Sanford at the WRC.
[115] WRC, Minutes, 2 August 1848, PPWP.
[116] *Report*, p. 5.

where God designed she should, on even platform with man himself";
but perfectionist women were not among their coadjutors.[117] The
Seneca Falls convention had drawn sharp criticism from Northern
editors, clerics, and politicians and led even Stanton to write, years
later, "If I had had the slightest premonition of all that was to follow
that convention, I fear I should not have had the courage to risk it, and
. . . it was with fear and trembling that I consented to attend another
. . . in Rochester."[118]

Rochesterians, however, even if unwilling to support ultraist demands, had apparently become more accustomed to hearing them than
the citizens of other Northern communities. Whereas editors in
Philadelphia, Albany, and elsewhere castigated woman's rights advocates for unwomanly behavior that threatened the natural order of
society, editors in Rochester responded with a mixture of humor,
curiosity, and support. The *Daily Democrat* of 3 August criticized the
convention participants for considering "some new, impractical, ab-
surd, and ridiculous proposition," but granted that they had introduced
one "practical good—the adoption of measures for the relief and
amelioration of the condition of indigent, industrious, laboring females." The editor claimed that the majority of those in attendance
were "drawn thither by motives of curiosity," yet concluded that the
"congregation of females . . . seem to be really in earnest in their aim at
revolution. . . . Verily, this is a progressive era!" The *Democrat*'s
major competitor, the *Daily Advertiser,* agreed that this was "an age of
'democratic progression,' of *equality* and *fraternization*—the age when
all colors and sexes, bond and free, black and white, male and female,
are, as they of right ought to be, tending downward and upward toward
the common level of equality." The editorial contained the standard
references to men and women exchanging their breeches and petticoats
and to ladies "scrambling for office." Nonetheless, the editor observed,
"the proceedings throughout were of a highly interesting character, and
the discussions of the convention evinced a talent for forensic efforts
seldom surpassed." In addition, local reform journals, like the *North
Star* and the *National Reformer,* covered the convention in detail and

[117] WRC, "Proceedings," p. 102.
[118] Elizabeth Cady Stanton, *Eighty Years and More, Reminiscences, 1815–1897* (1898;
reprint, New York: Schocken, 1971), p. 149. For critiques of the Seneca Falls convention
in the press, see Elizabeth Cady Stanton, Susan B. Anthony, and Matilda Joslyn Gage,
The History of Woman Suffrage, 4 vols. (New York: Fowler and Wells, 1881),
1: 802–808.

poured out encomiums to the "zeal, spirit, talent, and enthusiasm" of the meeting's leaders.[119]

Aware, however, that many of their neighbors retained serious reservations about their activities, ultraists sought to gain support and bolster their own commitment by seeking some higher authority to legitimate their demands for a re-formed world. Through the Yearly Meeting of Congregational Friends they attempted to define the character of that higher authority and to redefine humanity's relation to it. "War, Slavery, Sectarianism" in addition to the "unequal condition of Woman in society" were among the subjects discussed by the Congregational Friends. Yet no single subject was as important here as was attention to "the progressive principle in our nature" and a willingness to "live out the newly perceived truths that are ever dawning on the mind." No longer living in the closed environs of an agrarian Quaker community, ultraists now saw the need to spread the "fruits of the spirit" to "every member of the human family."[120]

The founding meeting of the Congregational Friends, attended by the Posts, Fishes, DeGarmos, Hallowells, and Burtises among others, was held in October 1848 at Waterloo, New York. The "Basis of Religious Association" adopted there noted that men and women "are made preeminently social beings" and that from "the exercise of the social principles of our nature, flow all the reciprocal benefits. . . ." To "attain these social [and] religious benefits in the highest degree, assemblies are needed," that is, "organization, or understood modes of action . . . not conflicting with man's prerogatives, nor God's." In the establishment of a new religious association, ultraists sought to institute "wise and right" relations among themselves and thereby provide a model for "freeing the entire human family from thraldom both physical and moral." That model included the autonomy of meetings, "perfect liberty of conscience," "equality in the human family, without limitation to sex, or complexion, or national peculiarities," and attention to the "Divine Light, in its present and progressive unfolding of truth and duty."[121]

---

[119] *National Reformer* (Rochester), 17 August 1848, in Susan B. Anthony, Scrapbook, vol. 2, Susan B. Anthony Papers, Library of Congress, Washington, D.C.

[120] YMCF, *Proceedings of the Yearly Meeting of Congregational Friends, Held at Waterloo, N.Y., from the Third to the Fifth of the Sixth Month, Inclusive, 1850* (Auburn, N.Y.: Henry Oliphant, 1850), pp. 7, 6.

[121] Ibid., pp. 44, 6, 44–48. Independent congregations were founded in Pennsylvania, Ohio, Michigan, and Indiana about the same time and many adopted Waterloo's "Basis of Religious Association."

Ultraists in pursuit of new bases of religious association were careful, however, to guard against spending their time "idly in discussing mystic theories, or observing lifeless forms, while so much is to be done. . . ."[122] Two weeks after the Rochester Woman's Rights Convention, Sarah C. Owen, Mrs. Roberts, Amy Post, and Mrs. Cavan, a tailor's wife, met at Protection Hall to form a Working Women's Protective Union. Declaring that "the laws of nature and of nature's God, entitle [women] equally with men to the products of their labor or its equivalent," the signers of the constitution agreed to "associate [them]selves together for the purpose of [their] individual and collective benefit and protection."[123] The Union met semimonthly, dues being five cents a year and one cent a meeting. Ultraist women also worked for the establishment of People's College in central New York and manual labor schools throughout the state. They aided Indians on the Cattaragus reservation and fugitive slaves fleeing to Canada, worked for dress and health reform, petitioned the state for women's property rights and against capital punishment, served as agents for reform journals, and sought to live out their social and political concerns in their daily lives.

At the same time, ultraist women extended their antislavery labors. Fourteen antislavery fairs were held and eleven stores for the sale of antislavery items were opened in western New York in the last half of 1848. Ultraists also opened an antislavery reading room in the center of Rochester "filled with some of the best Anti-Slavery, Temperance, Religious, Political and Literary papers in the country. An assortment of Anti-Slavery Books and Pamphlets" was offered for sale along with "a variety of rich, fancy and useful articles, made by the Ladies' Anti-Slavery Society." Each Thursday, the ladies' society met at the reading room "to sew, knit, read, and talk for the cause" and prepare items for sale.[124] Many of these items were prepared for the December antislavery bazaar, held on the twentieth and twenty-first despite "the exceedingly inclement state of the weather." While the crowd was apparently limited by the wintry storms that hit the city on opening day, the fair's managers were buoyed by the receipt of "a large and elegant assortment" of goods from the Misses Griffiths and other transatlantic friends of the cause. The total receipts of the fair

[122] YMCF, *Proceedings, 1849*, p. 10.
[123] *North Star*, 15 September 1848.
[124] Ibid., 1 September 1848.

amounted to $435, "a much smaller sum" than Amy Post and her coworkers "had reason to anticipate would result from [their] humble efforts the past year." Nevertheless, the fair's organizers reaffirmed their "confidence in the faithful and fearless proclamation of truth, as a means of reforming the world" and pledged themselves "to renewed efforts to hasten its spread over our slavery-cursed country."[125] The following week, they began preparations for fairs in nearby Henrietta and Williamson.

In the interim the fair organizers took part in the WNYASS annual meeting. Originally scheduled to begin on 22 December, the meeting adjourned until the following morning when "the operations of the Fair" would be concluded. Abigail Bush, Sarah C. Owen, and Amy Post served, respectively, on the committees of business, finance, and nominations. The executive committee reported that three antislavery lecturers had been supported for various periods, the circulation of the *North Star* had been extended, and an antislavery office and reading room had been opened. This latter was furnished by the women of the WNYASS, and Catharine Fish Stebbins had served as the office's first agent, followed by Sarah C. Owen. Both agents "made efforts to awaken interest, obtain funds, and keep the public aware" of the reading room's advantages. "The fact that it had been visited by but few, is a sad proof of the little desire for information on the part of the community." As in previous years, neither apathy nor opposition diminished ultraists' commitment to the cause nor led to a moderation of their views. Condemning "all ministers, laymen, legislators, or private citizens" who "stop their ears against the cries of the oppressed" as "traitors to the race of man," the convention advocated immediate emancipation, civil and political rights for blacks, and the complete integration of the two races in education, society, and "the intercourse of everyday life."[126]

The final resolution passed at the WNYASS meeting tendered thanks "to the untiring and devoted anti-slavery women . . . whose contributions of genius and industry" are "noble offerings upon freedom's altar."[127] During 1848 ultraist women's genius and industry reshaped the landscape of female activism in Rochester. Ultraists' demands at the Rochester Woman's Rights Convention, elaborated in

---

[125] Ibid., 12 January 1849.
[126] Ibid., 29 December 1848.
[127] Ibid.

the Working Woman's Protective Union, the Yearly Meeting of Congregational Friends, and the WNYASS annual meetings, provided a bold new measure of women's location in society. Though many continued to disagree with ultraists' vision of women's social roles, that vision redefined the terms by which the community and women themselves gauged woman's position and her progress.

This process of redefinition was particularly important for evangelical women. Having retreated from the moral crusades of the 1830s, many perfectionist leaders chafed at the narrow confines of benevolent activity. The collapse of perfectionist associations in the 1840s did not indicate members' lack of concern with slavery, intemperance, and vice, but rather their unwillingness to spearhead campaigns for eradication in the face of public censure. Now that a new circle of women activists, the ultraists, had emerged who were willing, indeed eager, to embrace the most extreme propositions of the day on any and every subject, it might be possible for perfectionists to rebuild their associations by presenting themselves as voices of moderation in the field of moral reformation.

[5]

Coalitions and Confrontations

Ultraists extended their militant and myriad labors after 1848 and seemed, briefly, to challenge benevolent ascendancy. The CS and OAA complained of a lack of community interest in the months following the Woman's Rights Convention and experienced a rapid turnover of officers and slight declines in membership. Yet the real threat to ultraist expansion and benevolent predominance in the 1850s came from the resurgence of perfectionist associations. Reclaiming the domains of moral reform, temperance, and abolition as their own, perfectionist leaders established in the 1850s more stable associations than those of the 1830s and appealed to women who desired a more expansive public role within the bounds of their own "proper" sphere. Moral reformers no longer sought out the perpetrators of vice but instead sheltered their potential victims. Abolitionists straddled the line between propriety and public action more tentatively. Nonetheless, by deferring to male kin and differentiating themselves from their ultraist counterparts, perfectionist antislavery women carved out forms of activism that they and a large proportion of the community deemed appropriate.

The hundreds of women who entered public paths on behalf of the poor, sick, orphaned, destitute, endangered, intemperate, and enslaved knew each other increasingly well, especially those few dozen who had led the various associations, institutions, and campaigns since the 1830s. As the fabric of local activism became more complex, however, the threads of three distinct networks could still be traced across it. At mid-century, that continued differentiation was a product of several factors, including the social and economic characteristics of the

139

women in the various clusters of organizations, the solidity of benevolent traditions, the refusal of benevolent or perfectionist women to accept woman's rights arguments, and ultraists' insistence on absolute racial as well as sexual equality.

Western New York ultraists were inspired to more radical endeavors by evidences of either public support or public censure. They were "cheered and gladdened by the progress already made,"[1] and, generally, they did not face the extreme ridicule, physical harassment, and mob violence that greeted and sometimes silenced woman's rights advocates and abolitionists in other Northern communities. At the same time, signs of "sectarian bigotry, anathema, and reproach" convinced ultraists that it was "necessary to strike deep at [the] root" of "social evils." "The more radical our exertions," claimed the Congregational Friends, "the more productive of the ends sought." While arguing for the ultimate triumph of "deep radical measures," however, ultraists attempted to divine "the most feasible method . . . of realizing [their] hopes."[2] Thus utopian goals were often pursued through mundane means.

The antislavery fair remained the primary means employed, and by mid-century ultraist women agonized less over the limited profits obtained and focused more on the erosion of prejudice effected. At Williamson Corners, Canandaigua, Lockport, and numerous towns in between, WNYASS fair organizers prided themselves on bringing "together persons who usually stand aloof from anti-slavery meetings," thereby helping to slay "the green-eyed monster—prejudice against color."[3] The success of these fairs depended particularly on the devoted labors of Amy Post and the experience of two British abolitionists, Julia and Eliza Griffiths. The Griffiths' move to Rochester in 1849 assured western New York ultraists of a continuous supply of elegant and exotic sale items and long lines of curious townspeople who wished to see what kind of British ladies would reside at the home of a black man. Not only did the Griffiths join Frederick Douglass's household, but Julia soon became his editorial assistant at the *North Star* and his most ardent advocate in the community.

The expansion of Douglass's editorial efforts and the entrance of

[1] *North Star* (Rochester), 9 November 1849.
[2] YMCF, *Proceedings of the Yearly Meeting of Congregational Friends, Held at Waterloo, N.Y., from the Fourth to the Sixth of the Sixth Month, Inclusive, with An Appendix, 1849* (Auburn, N.Y.: Oliphant's Press, 1849), pp. 6–7.
[3] *North Star*, 2 March 1849.

Julia Griffiths into WYNASS circles increased interest in the abolitionist cause by rejuvenating local efforts and attracting more national
figures to the city. Douglass presented his own Sunday evening lecture
series in the winters of 1849, 1850, and 1851, which brought relatively
large and respectful audiences into the new sixteen-hundred-seat Corinthian Hall. His efforts were complemented by those of Samuel J.
May, Giles B. Stebbins, Abby Kelley, Lucretia Mott, Sallie Holley,
Sojourner Truth, and other itinerant abolitionists. Local WNYASS
leaders met every other Tuesday evening at the antislavery reading
room to organize these affairs, plan strategies, and discuss national
events. The women's sewing circle gathered on alternate Wednesdays
to prepare items for fairs at which they also labored. In the spring,
ultraist women and men journeyed to New York City to attend the
American Anti-Slavery Society anniversary meetings, where a number
of the Rochester group were regularly elected to national offices.[4] In
the fall, planning began for the WNYASS annual meeting, culminating
in the December convocation of local ultraists, who shared their platform and their homes with prominent coworkers from Boston, New
York, and Philadelphia.

During the same period, ultraists continued their pursuit of "the
progressive unfoldings of Divine light."[5] Convinced that "*Church* is
Church wherever it be," ultraists "rejoiced in [their] freedom from
Sectarian Bondage."[6] "Thy sect," claimed Lucretia Mott, "is the righteous of the Earth," and ultraists agreed.[7] They believed that for "the
spread and carrying out" of "testimonies of truth," "associated action
increases efficiency, and the exchange of thoughts and feelings adds
strength to strength." Through the Yearly Meeting of Congregational
Friends, held each June at Waterloo, New York, and through more
frequent meetings in members' own towns and cities, ultraists sought
to unite, "all, of whatever name, or wherever scattered" who desired
the promotion of "truth, piety, righteousness, and peace in the earth."[8]

---

[4] Women were especially likely to attend the annual meetings in New York City because they could combine it with visiting family and because men often could not leave
their farms or shops for the regular May meetings.

[5] YMCF, *Proceedings, 1849,* p. 31.

[6] John Ketcham to Isaac and Amy Post, 11 March 1841; Amy Post to Isaac Post,
15 June 1855, IAPFP.

[7] Quoted in John Ketcham to Isaac and Amy Post, 11 March 1841, IAPFP.

[8] YMCF, *Proceedings of the Yearly Meeting of Congregational Friends, Held at
Waterloo, N.Y., from the Third to the Fifth of the Sixth Month, Inclusive, 1850* (Auburn,
N.Y.: Henry Oliphant, 1850), pp. 7, 48.

Congregational Friends charged that men and women had turned the "imperfect writings of men . . . into a great IDOL," "taking authority for truth, instead of truth for authority."[9] Ultraists thus refused to "set apart" any individuals as "ministers," asserting that between "the Infinite and all beings there exists an unbroken chain of communication." Without the interference of false prophets and profane authorities, "the Divine illimitable light" would reveal "a higher order" of society.[10] Many ultraists believed they were privy to such a revelation when news of mysterious spiritual rappings reached Rochester in the late spring of 1848. The two youngest daughters of the Hydesville, New York, Fox family heard strange noises that were interpreted as messages from the dead, sending fear throughout the local community. An older daughter, Mrs. Leah Fish, who resided in Rochester, decided to bring her infamous sisters to the supposedly more liberal environs of the city. There the rappings recommenced and Kate and Margretta Fox attracted a small following, including Isaac and Amy Post and George and Mary Willetts.

The cosmopolitan citizens of Rochester proved no less suspicious than their rural counterparts, however, and in November 1849 demanded a public demonstration and investigation. At the request of the spirits themselves, the Fox sisters' followers rented Corinthian Hall, and a committee of skeptics was appointed from among the four hundred spectators to ascertain the "true cause" of the rappings. Four committees and three demonstrations later, the city's investigative talents were exhausted and no fraud had been detected.[11] This finding aroused rather than calmed the audience, however. After the final demonstration, a " 'rowdy' element of the population, led by Josiah Bissell [Jr.], ex-alderman Seeley," and others "started to throw 'torpedoes'" at the stage, and in the resulting uproar the Fox sisters and their supporters fled to safety. Thereafter, several ultraists, including members of the Post, Hallowell, Willetts, Kedzie, and Burtis families, became more ardent champions of spiritualism, inspiring the ridicule of

[9] YMCF, *Proceedings of the Yearly Meeting of Congregational Friends, Held at Waterloo, N.Y., on the Sixth, Seventh, and Eighth of the Sixth Month, 1852* (Auburn, N.Y.: Henry Oliphant, 1852), p. 4.

[10] YMCF, *Proceedings, 1850*, pp. 47, 19, 5; *Proceedings, 1849*, p. 6.

[11] Blake McKelvey, *Rochester: The Water-Power City, 1812–1854* (Cambridge: Harvard University Press, 1945), pp. 288–290; Frank Wesley Clark, "The Origins of Spiritualism in America," (Master's thesis, University of Rochester, 1932), pp. 20–23.

the local press and causing evangelical and Unitarian ministers to denounce the rappings as the work of the devil.[12]

Ultraists antagonized their neighbors in a number of other ways
during this period. Just before the demonstration of their spiritualist
sympathies, the Posts exhibited their racial commitments by hosting
the wedding of ex-slave Benjamin Cleggett and free black Frances
Nell. This sanctioning of the social mingling of blacks and whites
"caused great dissatisfaction in the Rochester community."[13] Such activities also gained the disapproval of former Hicksite friends. Those
ultraists who had not yet been dismissed by the Genesee Yearly Meeting, including Sarah Fish, Sarah Hallowell, Sarah Burtis, and Rhoda
DeGarmo, were released in 1849, and soon thereafter the meetinghouse doors were closed "against anti-slavery and all other reformatory meetings."[14]

That winter the newly dismissed Hicksites joined Amy Post and
other ultraists in inviting "all classes and colours" to participate in their
seventh annual antislavery fair.[15] Blacks and whites responded, and
"one hundred people . . . sat down to one table" to share turkeys,
hams, chickens, salads, and other culinary delights. While the WNY-
ASS women were "grieved and mortified" that "the sum . . . left in
[their] hands" was "so small," they would not "despise even the sum of
one hundred dollars," for the "eating together of 'Colored with
White' " would "kill prejudice."[16] Thus Amy Post declared the event "a
glorious achievement." She was "soarly agrieved [*sic*]," however,
upon opening the *North Star* the next week to find Douglass's curt
dismissal of the affair. Noting that from "a financial point of view the
Fair must be considered a failure," he also asserted that "morally, it
has been far from successful." His only unguarded praise was bestowed upon a box of British goods "which formed the most saleable
part of the contributions."[17]

[12]Clark, "Origins," p. 26. See also, McKelvey, *Rochester,* pp. 347–348.
[13]Mary Robbins Post to Isaac and Amy Post, [1849], IAPFP.
[14]Rochester Monthly Meeting, Minutes, 27 July and 23 November, 1849, HRR; *North Star,* 31 August 1849.
[15]WNYASS, Anti-Slavery Fair Report, [1850]; Amy Post to Frederick Douglass, 2 February 1850, IAPFP.
[16]Ibid.; William C. Nell to Amy Post, 3 July 1850, IAPFP. The sum collected was $215 minus expenses.
[17]Amy Post to Frederick Douglass, 2 February 1850, IAPFP; *North Star,* 1 February 1850.

While anticipating the criticism of the regular press, WNYASS women were unprepared for condemnations from the very person who received the greatest share of their proceeds. Amy Post voiced the feelings of her coworkers in writing to Douglass, "I know this is a poor market but I know too that [it] is very bad polacy [*sic*] for a person to destroy the influance [*sic*] and character of his friends at home."[18] Ultraist women were simultaneously suffering the criticism of other male colleagues and the loss of female laborers. In 1849 the distaff members of the WNYASS complained to friends in Boston of "controversies with the 'Lords of Creation' . . . connected with the business operations of the WNYASS Executive Committee."[19] Some individual ultraist women also faced such controversies at home. Mary Fish Curtis, "an earnest worker for the equal political rights of woman," was married to newspaper editor Joseph Curtis, who "had little but ridicule for emancipation of women. . . ."[20] While Mary Curtis turned a deaf ear to her husband's objections, other female ultraists had little choice but to follow their spouse's dictates. Henry Bush, who fully supported his wife's public labors, nevertheless insisted on removing her from the site of her greatest triumphs. In 1850 he left Abigail, pregnant with their sixth child, and headed to California seeking gold and a new home. Though it took two years to resettle the entire family, Abigail finally boarded a ship west, lamenting those who were "leaving Home, its Comforts and Endearments" only to be "Doomed to Disappointment, Sorrow, & a Grave. . . ." For herself, she regretted leaving "Home's Loved Ones," never expecting to find others "to stand side by side with me, Heart to Heart, in our Labours of Love . . . to our Afflicted and Downtrodden Fellow Ones."[21]

Within the next two years, Catharine Fish Stebbins, Ann Braithewaite Clackner, and Sarah C. Owen also followed their families west, and those left behind found it increasingly difficult to recruit new workers.[22] Mary Springstead, a central New York Quaker, devoted herself to ultraist efforts after attending an antislavery meeting in the fall of 1850. Soon after, however, she wrote to Amy Post that the

[18] Amy Post to Frederick Douglass, 2 February 1850, IAPFP.

[19] William C. Nell to Amy Post, 11 August 1849, IAPFP. Nell is quoting from an earlier letter from Amy Post.

[20] Lucy N. Coleman, memorial tribute for Mary Fish Curtis, [1873], IAPFP.

[21] Abigail Bush to Amy Post, [185–], IAPFP.

[22] A few ultraist families moved to Michigan during this time, joining Quaker communities whose residents had been released from the Genesee Yearly Meeting in 1848 and had adopted the "Basis of Religious Association" of the YMCF of Waterloo.

"recent convention has caused great excitement" and "has been much misrepresented, and my friends and relatives in N York feel *dreadfully disgraced* in seeing my name associated with the business committee." She eventually chose ultraism over approbation, thanking God "for the strength to endure . . . reproach for the oppressed," but few others were willing or able to take on such burdens.[23]

Though attracting far more commendations than condemnations, benevolent leaders also found fewer women to bear their burdens at midcentury. Membership roles remained lengthy, but many declined to serve in CS or OAA offices. Both associations were concerned as well with diminishing donations, and the CS considered it "necessary" to bring "the claims of the Soc[iety] . . . before the public" in order to interest "strangers in its behalf" and swell "its list of members."[24] A year later the OAA sought "to secure a wider interest" in its efforts "among the Ladies of the City" by once again having "all the different Protestant churches fully represented on the Board."[25] The OAA also pressed the state legislators for funds, complaining of the uncertainty of local donations. Yet in 1849, when they finally obtained the requested monies, donations from local "Gentlemen" dropped to 5 percent of their previous level.[26]

Despite these complaints, benevolent associations remained active. The first six-hundred dollar appropriation from the state fund for orphan asylums was used for "an enlargement of the building . . . demanded by the yearly increasing number of children under the [OAA's] care."[27] Six new managers were added to the OAA board, and fundraising sermons were preached in a half-dozen or more churches annually. The CS soon adopted the same method, replacing an annual sermon in a single church with several sermons throughout the city. Under this plan, their receipts increased, as did the funds expended in the fifty districts that were now necessary to reach all corners of the city. Still, the CS was dependent primarily on volunteer labor, employing almost one hundred officers, managers, collectors, and visitors to distribute bedding, clothing, medical care, and less than five hun-

[23] Mary Springstead to Amy Post, 9 September 1850, IAPFP.
[24] CS, Minute Book, 3 October 1848, CSP.
[25] OAA, Minute Book, 9 October 1849, HCCP.
[26] OAA, Annual Report, 1847, 1848, and 1849, Scrapbook, HCCP. The drop in men's donations from about $950 to less than $100 was partly due to the increase in church donations, some of which certainly came from these gentlemen.
[27] Ibid., 1849, Scrapbook, HCCP.

dred dollars in cash.[28] In 1851 the CS and OAA were given a moral and financial boost by Jenny Lind. The "Swedish Nightingale" performed in the city in July and donated nine hundred dollars of the concert proceeds to the CS and five hundred dollars to the OAA, providing the societies with a "backwall of security" in coming years.[29]

Both the CS and OAA nonetheless had difficulty convincing women to serve as officers. The CS experienced its greatest problems in the summer, as affluent Rochesterians began escaping the heat, humidity, and illness of the city by taking up residence in the mountains or at the seashore. In addition, while the earliest CS leaders were an astonishingly healthy lot, by mid-century age began to take its toll on the benevolent pioneers; and the CS minutes became a record not only of charitable efforts but of deaths.[30] The OAA recorded far fewer deaths or retirements from service but still could not keep its offices filled. One of four directresses and three of nine managers elected in October 1849 had resigned by the following February. The same year almost the entire coterie of collectors, women who were to seek donations door to door, refused to serve. Collecting "money for the support of the Asylum by personal solicitation to the gentlemen of the City" had apparently "become very onerous."[31] The decision to apply to the state orphan fund and the Protestant clergy of the city eventually alleviated this problem, but women continued to decline serving as directresses or managers.

Despite the claims of the CS and OAA, most of the women who rejected benevolent, and particularly OAA, labors in 1849, 1850, and 1851 did not do so because they were uninterested in the cause or because the tasks were too burdensome. Rather, they sought to expand their labors into new areas. Mrs. Samuel D. Porter, Mrs. Selah Mathews, Mrs. Thomas Weddle, Miss Maria Porter, Mrs. David Scoville, Mrs. Ralph Lester, Mrs. Moses Matthews, and others left benevolent offices to return to the cause of moral reform, temperance, and antislavery. Female Finneyites and former perfectionist leaders shared their concerns with Unitarians, hovering between charitable

[28] CS, Minute Book, 1850–1860, summary of receipts and expenditures, CSP.

[29] Amy Hanmer-Croughton, "The Rochester Female Charitable Society," Rochester Historical Society, *Publications* 9 (1930), p. 73. See also, McKelvey, *Rochester,* p. 358; OAA, Minute Book, July 1851, HCCP.

[30] The CS Minute Book recorded deaths of trustees and some minor officers as well as major officers. The last were generally accompanied by a series of resolutions on the deceased woman's benevolent career.

[31] OAA, Minute Book, 30 October 1849, HCCP.

efforts they thought were too restricted and ultraist goals they thought too radical. Their first attempt to define a middle ground came in 1849 with the founding of the Home for Friendless and Virtuous Females, an institutional refuge for virtuous but vulnerable young women. Then, in 1851, several HF leaders helped establish the Rochester Ladies' Anti-Slavery Society, a single-sex association to aid free blacks and fund men's third-party political efforts. Neither of these societies attracted the hundreds of members claimed by their predecessors, the FASS and FMRS, but both remained active for many more years.

The home was "designed as a refuge for young females, destitute of home, friends, or employment, exposed to temptation and sin, and who might, if neglected, swell that already too numerous class sinking to ruin themselves, and drawing thousands of our youth into the vortex."[32] The plea for such an institution came from Mrs. Elizabeth Eaton, who had joined the American Female Guardian Society upon her removal to New York City and helped to found a Home for Friendless Women there.[33] The report of the New York society was read at the founding meeting of the HF, held in March 1849 at the third ward home of Mrs. Charles Church. Those in attendance immediately agreed to establish "a Retreat of like character" in western New York. At a second meeting, a fortnight later, a letter from Mrs. Eaton "was read containing many useful hints with regard to the formation of a Society." Mrs. Bissell and Mrs. Porter were appointed to draft a constitution, "which was hastily drawn up, presented," discussed and adopted the same afternoon. Less than three weeks later, on May Day 1849, the home was open "for the reception of that class of Individuals for whom it was designed."[34]

Like the OAA a dozen years earlier, the HF utilized the knowledge and resources of women long experienced in social activism to speed their translation of ideas into action. Also like the OAA, the HF combined the styles and programs of perfectionist and benevolent societies. HF meetings began with prayers and scriptural readings, and the society's primary concern was a direct extension of moral reform issues of an earlier era, while the structure of the association, the schedule of meetings, and the forms of assistance offered were heavily influenced by benevolent practices. The home's leadership reflected

[32] *Union and Advertiser* (Rochester), 9 November 1858.
[33] Blake McKelvey, comp., "Letters Postmarked Rochester," Rochester Historical Society, *Publications* 21 (1943), p. 103.
[34] HF, Minute Book, 11 March 1849, FHP.

the HF's complex origins. The association's first president, Mrs. Samuel Selden, was a charter member of the CS, an early officer of the OAA, and a devoted laborer for the FMRS. Mrs. Selah Mathews, the first directress, had served on the first board of managers of the OAA and later as directress of the CS, but she was most well known for her advocacy of Finneyite perfectionism and moral reform in the 1830s. The secretary, Mrs. Porter, was also strongly tied to early perfectionist campaigns. She entered local activism as an officer of the FASS and later devoted considerable energy to both the OAA and the FMRS. Of the eleven other officers elected in 1840, seven had previously served in the CS, OAA, or both while only one additional woman can be positively traced to earlier perfectionist labors and four may have served in such efforts.[35] The religious affiliation of the HF's first officers strengthens the connections between the perfectionist campaigns of the 1830s and 1850s. Two officers were members of First Presbyterian and one of St. Luke's Episcopal Church, but the majority were from the old Finneyite strongholds of Second and Third Presbyterian or the newer evangelical circles of First Congregational. In addition, the HF gained the support of two early perfectionists who had joined the antislavery Unitarian Society in 1842.[36] Finally, at least seven of the HF's leaders affixed their signatures to antislavery petitions a dozen years earlier. Thus, despite the suspension of FASS and FMRS activity for several years, perfectionists formed the core of HF leadership.

The day-to-day work of the home reflected the same complexities as its origins. The association continued to call for support from women of surrounding towns who had aided in FMRS work. They also maintained close ties with the Female Guardian Society of New York City and publicized their work through that society's journal, the *Advocate and Family Guardian*.[37] Yet the majority of HF women opposed a resolution to become an auxiliary of the New York society, seeking instead to integrate themselves more fully into the local benevolent network. The shift in focus from universal perfection to local ameliora-

[35] It is likely, given the numbers of experienced activists in Rochester, that members of a new organization would select experienced women to lead them.

[36] The Unitarian Society was established on a firm footing in the city in 1842 and attracted former Evangelicals, such as members of the Porter and Brown families, probably because of its antislavery pastors.

[37] The Female Guardian Society was an outgrowth of the Female Moral Reform Society in New York City and the *Advocate and Family Guardian* replaced the *Advocate of Moral Reform*.

tion was paralleled by the shift from the eradication of vice to its prevention, thus easing the work to be done and reassuring the community of the propriety of women's involvement. Home women sought to save deserving sisters from the "snares [of] the designing" by sheltering them in an all-female family, believing they would thus "prove a great blessing, both to humanity and the City." Although perfectionist women had begun this transition in the early 1840s, the FMRS along with the FASS were apparently too polluted by suggestions of impropriety and radicalism to be rescued. A temporary retreat, however, allowed for the resurgence of perfectionist concerns in more modest garb. HF leaders were sufficiently convincing of their purely charitable character that in 1851 these ex–moral reformers received several hundred dollars from Jenny Lind's contribution to "the recognized Benevolent Institutions" of the city.[38]

Providing services that complemented existing benevolent efforts was only one choice available to perfectionists at mid-century. The reemergence of evangelical women's antislavery work occurred in a significantly different context: the domination of a cause by ultraist women. Like evangelical women, ultraist women and men had initially isolated themselves from evangelical men's political abolitionism; but neither ultraist women nor men isolated themselves from the cause as a whole. Throughout the 1840s political abolitionists in western New York tried to assure their ultraist counterparts that they viewed a vote for the Liberty party as a moral as well as a political act; and antislavery agents, including those of the American Anti-Slavery Society, noted that relations between political and moral suasion abolitionists were relatively harmonious in the region. Samuel D. Porter was particularly vociferous in asserting that it was not electoral victory he sought with his "appeal to the Ballot Box" but the "*moral* effect of *numbers*."[39] Local Liberty party leaders' continued commitment to principled third-party politics in opposition to the more limited antislavery doctrines of the Free Soil party allowed them to coexist more peacefully with moral suasionists and may have encouraged their female kin to reenter the ranks of public antislavery activism at midcentury.[40]

---

[38] *Daily Democrat* (Rochester), 12 April 1851; 23 April 1853.

[39] Samuel D. Porter to Gerrit Smith, 14 March 1845, GSP.

[40] On differences between Liberty party and Free Soil party principles, see Eric Foner, *Free Soil, Free Labor, Free Men: The Ideology of the Republican Party before the Civil War* (New York: Oxford University Press, 1970).

The woman who led the resurgence of evangelical women's abolitionism was newcomer Julia Griffiths. By 1850 she wanted both to increase interest in the cause and to limit ultraists' influence. Griffiths had worked side by side with the ultraists in her first year in the city and helped to broaden the WNYASS's base by organizing sewing circles in surrounding towns. Griffiths was also a confidante of New York State Liberty party leader Gerrit Smith, however, and a friend of the Porters. In writing to Smith of her antislavery labors, she revealed differences with her ultraist coworkers. While noting her success in establishing "a large A.S. Sewing Society" among the ladies of Canandaigua, by talking herself "hoarse on *slavery*" in "a parlor," she assured Smith, "I am not 'woman's rights' or a public speaker."[41]

In 1851 Griffiths found her opportunity to bring new women into the cause whose views on woman's rights were closer to her own. The previous year, the passage of the Fugitive Slave Act had outraged abolitionists, and attempts by federal marshals and local police to force Northern blacks or escaped slaves into slavery kept the issue before the public. More immediately, the law-and-order editorials of the Rochester *Daily Advertiser* and the *American* and their outcries against the visit of British abolitionist George Thompson in January 1851 led local abolitionists to close ranks.[42] Bringing together the committed and the curious, Thompson attracted a massive audience to Corinthian Hall and was at once invited to speak there again in April at the end of his American tour. By organizing a fair to coincide with his return, ultraist women hoped to refill their coffers and broaden their popular appeal. They were thus pleased when Julia Griffiths, who was Thompson's countrywoman, convinced a wide spectrum of local women to share the management of this Grand Anti-Slavery Festival. The committee of ladies arranging the event included Griffiths and ten WNYASS women along with two former FASS members and eleven new recruits, several of whom were kinswomen of FASS founders. In addition, the committee included four members of the Union Anti-Slavery Sewing Society, a local association of black women who held fairs in support of the *North Star*.[43]

[41] Julia Griffiths to Gerrit Smith, 26 October [185–], GSP.

[42] *Liberator* (Boston), 4 April 1851, quotes several Rochester papers on Thompson's visit to the city.

[43] In 1842 perfectionist women had refused to join the WNYASS sewing circle because of black women's participation in it. See Sarah Anthony Burtis to Abby Kelley, 17 January 1843, AKFP. On the Ladies' Committee for the 1851 festival, see *North Star*, 24 April 1851. References to the Union Anti-Slavery Society fairs can be found in *North Star*, 21 July 1848 and 5 December 1850.

The collective efforts in behalf of the Thompson festival resulted in financial success, yet the affair was the culmination rather than the initiation of women's unity in the antislavery cause. In the months that followed, white female abolitionists broke into opposing camps. Their black coworkers, momentarily visible as their efforts converged with those of white women, once again faded from public record. In June 1851 Douglass helped to polarize local divisions when he announced his conversion to the Liberty party's brand of political abolitionism. By 1851 the Liberty party was all but defunct nationally. In Rochester, however, several of the most important leaders refused to accept the more limited antislavery stands of the Free Soil party and joined, instead, with the Gerrit Smith–led Liberty League. These Liberty Leaguers applauded Douglass's change of heart.

Applause did not always translate into subscriptions though, and, at least initially, the support of political abolitionists did not offset the loss of moral suasionists' contributions. Thus Julia Griffiths wrote to Gerrit Smith that Douglass's "change on the Constitution has thinned our Subscription list considerably. . . ." In response, Griffiths continued, she was "forming an Anti-Slavery sewing circle," which she trusted would be "influential, permanent, & efficient."[44] She and her followers repeated the almost mandatory wish for universal cooperation: "this association *did not deem it duty* to make an election between *old* and *new* organization, *'Liberty Party'* or *'Free Soil'*, but preferred to assume an independent position, with a view to cooperate with all whose love for the anti-slavery cause rises superior to their connection with any particular party or sect of abolitionists."[45] She complained, however, that "bigotry precluded many of the old friends from joining" the LASS.[46] Those old friends were her former ultraist allies who refused to accept self-imposed limits on their labors after a decade of struggling for equality.

Thus Rochester's white antislavery women replicated the 1840 division that first drove evangelical women out of public abolitionist efforts. WNYASS members continued to criticize churches' collaboration with slaveholders, advocated moral suasion, and insisted on equal roles within the abolitionist movement. The LASS, composed of former FASS members and newcomers of similar backgrounds and

---

[44] Julia Griffiths to Gerrit Smith, 26 August [1851], GSP.
[45] LASS, "Circular, the First Report of the Rochester Ladies' Anti-Slavery Sewing Society, 1852," SDPFP. See also Julia Griffiths to Amy Post, 16 October 1852, IAPFP.
[46] Julia Griffiths to Gerrit Smith, 26 August [1851], GSP.

presided over by Mrs. Samuel D. Porter, advocated continued faith in established churches and a morally self-conscious politics, the latter to be financed by the efforts of a separate and auxiliary women's association. Those women who had accepted Griffiths's invitation to the LASS were related to male political abolitionists, were evangelical or Orthodox Quaker FASS members or their kin, or were members of the First Congregational or First Unitarian churches.

Women of the Porter family met all three criteria. Samuel D. Porter was a Liberty party leader. His wife, Susan Farley Porter, was a FASS founder and first president of the new LASS, in which she was once again joined by sisters-in-law Maria, Almira, and Mary Jane Porter. While Samuel and Susan Porter now worshiped in the First Congregational Church, Maria, her father, and stepmother had joined the Unitarian Society. Among their coworshipers were LASS members Laura Farley, Mrs. James P. Fogg, and ex–Orthodox Quaker Mrs. Silas Cornell. The LASS gradually drew other early perfectionists back into the cause, including Mrs. Sarah Seward Gould, Mrs. Russell Green, Mrs. George Avery, Mrs. Ashbel Riley, Mrs. Abner Wakelee, Mrs. Lindley Murray Moore, Mrs. David Scoville, and Mrs. Elon Galusha, all of whom were wives of political abolitionist leaders.[47] In addition, the LASS attracted new recruits from Baptist and Methodist as well as Presbyterian and Unitarian congregations.

The LASS shared ties not only with its perfectionist predecessor, the FASS, but also with its perfectionist counterpart, the HF. In addition to Susan and Maria Porter, the LASS gained the support of HF founders Mrs. Weddle and Mrs. Squier. In more general terms, the HF and the LASS, like the FASS and FMRS, attracted women from the most dynamic economic sectors along with a significant number of single and widowed women bound to new wealth by ties of blood, residential proximity, and religious affiliation. Finally, both the HF and LASS pronouncements were richly bathed in religious rhetoric that matched the language of their perfectionist predecessors and male counterparts far more closely than that of their female competitors.[48] Thus, while the HF maintained connections with Rochester's other benevolent societies and the LASS emerged from a joint ultraist-perfectionist venture, the two societies formed a separate coterie within the activist

[47] It is possible that Mrs. Scoville and Mrs. Galusha were the second wives of Messrs. Scoville and Galusha. The others are definitely the same women who had joined the FASS in the 1830s.

[48] For a fuller discussion of differences in language, see Chapter 7.

community that drew as strongly on early perfectionist as on contemporary ultraist or benevolent models and concerns.

With the resurgence of perfectionism as a middle ground between benevolence and ultraism, contact and cross-fertilization among Rochester activists became more frequent and extensive. Yet none of the three groups—benevolent, perfectionist, or ultraist—were willing to sacrifice its own principles, goals, or tactics to combine efforts. In specific situations activists cooperated across associational lines, but such contacts were either brief or problematic. In part, perhaps the largest part, the continued distinctions among benevolent, perfectionist, and ultraist societies reflected the continued differences in the social and economic characteristics of their members. Bound to different communities of origin, residing in different neighborhoods and types of households, worshiping in different churches, marrying men of different occupational and social status, and having differential access to material resources and political power, women activists inhabited distinguishable if not entirely distinct worlds. They shared, with each other and with their nonactivist neighbors, exclusion from electoral politics and inclusion in a culturally defined female stereotype. Yet in their distance from the wielders of power and their deference to cultural norms, the three groups diverged; and in the 1850s as the 1830s these variations shaped significantly different responses to social change.

Benevolent women still represented the community elite; perfectionists, the most dynamic new urban sectors; and ultraists, the economically and socially marginal members of the new bourgeoisie. Since in absolute terms each group increased its wealth, power, and stability from first settlement to mid-century, relative differences among the groups remained the same.[49] For instance, ultraist men gradually began to enter the ranks of merchants, manufacturers, and professionals in the decade after the WNYASS's founding, with nearly one-quarter of them engaged in these pursuits. Yet by that time, 95 percent of benevolent women's husbands were merchants, manufac-

[49] Comparisons among activist groups at mid-century, including religious affiliation, occupation of husbands, residence, and household composition are based on data from a wide range of sources. Of particular importance for the last two topics was Seventh Federal Census, Manuscript Census for Monroe County, New York, 1850, and the "Genealogical Data for Monroe County and Adjacent Areas" compiled by Mary Moulthrop and housed at University of Rochester. For data on which comparisons are based, see Tables.

turers, bankers, or professionals, and they controlled the most lucrative sectors of those occupations.[50] Similarly, the husbands of
perfectionists gained firm control of third-party politics in the late
1840s and played increasingly prominent roles within the local Whig
party, but it was benevolent husbands who dominated the Whig party,
played significant roles in the Democratic party, and occupied the
largest portion of political offices.[51]

The CS, though fast approaching its thirtieth anniversary, was amaz-
ingly consistent in the type of leaders it recruited. Not only were they
the wives of affluent and politically powerful men, but nearly one half
were still New England–born at mid-century and nearly 60 percent
were First Presbyterian or St. Luke's communicants. In part, the extension of early patterns was due to the lengthy careers of CS founders,
many of whom were reaching their thirtieth anniversary in benevolent
office along with the CS itself. The HF also attracted many Yankee-
born leaders in its early years, but among perfectionists as a whole the
largest number came from eastern or central New York. In addition,
the LASS attracted several women who gained their abolitionist experiences in Great Britain. As the perfectionists of the 1850s were more
geographically diverse than their 1830s predecessors, so too were they
more religiously diverse. One quarter did attend one of the major
evangelical churches, but an equal number changed church affiliations
so often in this period that they could not be definitely traced to any
congregation. A significant number of LASS women, on the other
hand, worshiped at the First Unitarian Society whatever their formal
religious affiliation. Ultraist leaders, though the last to arrive in
Rochester, were most likely to be native-born central or western New
Yorkers. Smaller but still significant numbers arrived from New England, eastern New York, or Long Island; but whatever the region
from which they emerged, the vast majority had lived in Hicksite
Quaker communities. In the late 1840s many Hicksites became, in
addition to or as a substitute for Quakerism, Congregational Friends,
Unitarians, spiritualists, or all three.[52] Thus, while each group

---

[50] In the category of professionals, for example, benevolent husbands were doctors and
lawyers, while ultraist husbands were itinerant lecturers.

[51] There was some shift of elites out of politics as it became more partisan, especially
among the Rochester clan. Many fewer Democrats had activist wives than did Whigs or
third-party leaders, unless large numbers of Democrats' wives are among the large
numbers of unrecorded perfectionist workers.

[52] A few ex-Evangelicals and some Orthodox Quakers also joined the Unitarian Society. Generally, only the ultraists maintained multiple religious affiliations.

diversified by mid-century, the differences were still greater among the three groups than within any single group.

Ultraists' roots in the Quaker communities of New York and New England went deep into the soil: more than a third of ultraist families continued to subsist on products and profits from farming. Younger ultraists were more likely to depend on incomes from shopkeeping or artisan husbands, and single and widowed women often contributed to household incomes. It was the rare commercial farmer or clerk who linked ultraist families to the more dynamic economic sectors of the urban economy. LASS husbands occupied the lower rungs of the commercial economy as shopkeepers, business agents, commercial farmers, and clerks, while the HF was comprised by their richer relatives—merchants, manufacturers, lawyers, and judges. Thus HF women came closest to achieving benevolent women's economic status. Benevolent women's control of the city's wealth was, however, never actually challenged by any other group of activist women. Not a single shopkeeper, clerk, or farmer's wife graced the roster of the CS or OAA board members, though lawyers, physicians, bankers, textile and tool manufacturers, and the town's largest merchants were well represented. And, as commercial ventures became more established and profitable, benevolent women's husbands began to appear among the city's leading forwarding and commission merchants, warehouse owners, and railroad and shipping agents. Because of their husbands' financial successes, not a single benevolent woman worked for wages. Among perfectionists, several women worked in "genteel" occupations, as teachers, seminary school directors, or boardinghouse keepers, often in addition to directing home or antislavery affairs. Ultraist women engaged in paid labor most often and in less remunerative employments—nursing, needlework, and lecturing.[53]

The primary reason that benevolent women were able to escape wage labor was that their families were affluent. In addition, virtually all benevolent women were married, and those who were widowed were left with healthy estates. Only one or two single women ever appeared on the annual lists of OAA or CS officers, while the LASS and WNYASS were likely to have six or seven such women among

---

[53] In this period, nursing was neither considered a profession nor did it pay well. It was sometimes viewed with as much suspicion as lecturing was in terms of its respectability for women.

their leading circle at any one time.[54] It was primarily these single and widowed abolitionists who formed the ranks of activism's waged women. Labor within the household probably varied as much among activist women as labor beyond the household, since there was significant variation in the size of families, number of servants, access to manufactured goods, and other attributes of domestic life. Among female activists, benevolent women were most likely to invite parents, sisters, or other relatives into their households, to have children, and to have large numbers of children living at home. Nearly 40 percent of benevolent households also contained servants, laborers, or boarders. Over half contained 6 or more members at mid-century, clearly exceeding the national average of 5.6. And several benevolent officers supervised households of 9 or more members.

Perfectionist and ultraist households were smaller and children were fewer. Only 85 percent of perfectionist leaders were married in 1850, compared with over 90 percent of benevolent officers, though in both groups over 90 percent of married women bore children. Perfectionist women, however, rarely had more than three children, or at least rarely more than three living at home, while benevolent women had four or five. Several perfectionist women—single, widowed, or married—boarded with other families; only a quarter lived in nuclear families. Those who managed their own households were much more likely to shelter servants, laborers, or boarders than relatives, creating households that matched the national average in size. Ultraists, though the most agrarian and therefore apparently the most likely to house large extended families, were in fact the most modern in their household structures, being most likely to live in nuclear families and averaging only four persons per household.[55] While the largest number of ultraist women lived in households of five or six people, the average was lowered by the number of young married couples living alone or with only one other household member. Ultraist circles contained the lowest proportion of married women. Just under 75 percent were married as of 1850, and just over 80 percent ever married. Moreover, a smaller number of these women bore children, and those who did had fewer children living at home. In this last case at least, ultraists seemed

[54] The HF had more single and widowed leaders than the CS or OAA and fewer than the LASS or WNYASS.
[55] The smaller family size of ultraists is partly due to their younger average age, but even when age is held constant there is a significant difference between ultraists and other groups.

to draw more heavily on eighteenth-century agrarian traditions than on modern family precepts, sending their young children to friends or relatives to gain education and discipline that overfond parents might find hard to impose.[56]

The translation of these structural features into daily experience was affected by several factors that, while less concrete, were equally important. For example, the smaller families of the ultraists did not necessarily reflect different or more modern attitudes about the family, nor did they necessarily diminish the burden of domestic labor. Impressionistic evidence from private letters and church records, particularly mothers' own expressions of grief over the loss of children, suggests that ultraist women suffered more infant deaths than other activist women. In addition, ultraist families moved more frequently than other activists, and older children either remained behind or younger children returned to former homes for extensive visits. Thus ultraist women may have desired larger families and endured equivalent periods of pregnancy but, because of greater geographic mobility, more limited resources, or higher infant mortality, ended up with smaller families. Moreover, since ultraist women were younger on the average than their benevolent and perfectionist counterparts, they often cared for infants or young children in conjunction with public labors and did so without the degree of extra household help employed by other activist women. Over 80 percent of benevolent women had at least one other adult female living in their household in 1850, and these women, whether children, servants, or other relatives, provided additional domestic labor.[57] Sixty-five percent of perfectionist households contained such extra helpers, and a larger number of perfectionist leaders hired women specifically as servants rather than relying on the more ambiguous domestic roles played by female kin. Less than half of ultraist households contained an adult female other than the ultraist leader herself, so that virtually all domestic burdens fell on her shoulders.

The extent of domestic burdens in this period was shaped by a husband's place of business as well as by his occupation and income. In

[56] On seventeenth- and eighteenth-century practices of sending out children, see Alan MacFarlane, ed., *The Diary of Ralph Josselin, 1616–1683* (London: Oxford University Press, 1976), intro.

[57] The category of adult women includes any female sixteen years or older. In the 1820s and 1830s, as benevolent women entered activist ranks, they had fewer adult children but apparently more sisters and sisters-in-law living in the household. For a general view of domestic help in this period, see Faye Dudden, *Serving Women: Household Service in Nineteenth-Century America* (Middletown, Conn.: Wesleyan University Press, 1983).

Rochester the shift in the household as being an arena of production to an arena of consumption was gradual and not yet complete at mid-century. Even in affluent families, husbands had not entirely separated their business from their wives' domestic affairs. At least a third of benevolent leaders had husbands who used their home address as a business address, including several lawyers and physicians as well as the owners of a cotton mill, a construction company, and a wool dealership. Moreover, many professional men had offices near their residences, so that even separate addresses did not always indicate a neat division between public and private domains. Yet legal, medical, and financial counseling could be confined within the household to discrete spaces, and it is unlikely that wives would have been requested to assist in such endeavors. Half or more of perfectionist women had husbands working out of the household, including lawyers, land agents, grocers, a newspaper publisher, and a carriagemaker. Both the greater proportion of husbands in the home and the greater likelihood of shopkeepers and artisans calling on wives for assistance would have increased the workload of perfectionist leaders and may account for the larger numbers of servants they hired. Over 60 percent of ultraist men worked within their households, and the farmers among these would certainly have called on family members to aid in harvest and planting seasons. Ultraist jewelers, tailors, nurserymen, and shopkeepers were also likely to seek help from family members, and the relative absence of adolescent or adult children, other relatives, servants, or laborers would have increased wifely burdens.

Finally, benevolent women lived closest to city shops and services and to each other, whereas ultraist coworkers were more scattered throughout the city and, indeed, throughout western New York. By the 1850s many household items could be purchased rather than produced, and benevolent women had the greatest access to both money and marketplaces. Such access did not mean idleness, however. The eight-room, double-story homes that were popular with Rochester's elite in the 1830s and the Greek Revival mansions built in the following decade required more furniture, candles, curtains, chamberpots, utensils, and supervision than the smaller abodes of ultraists. It did mean a greater emphasis on consumer and supervisory than productive activities, especially since benevolent women could easily survey the domestic order maintained by their sister activists. Over two thirds of the thirty-six women serving in CS and OAA offices at mid-century were third ward neighbors. Seven lived between number 59 and number 91 South Fitzhugh Street, and ten others lived one street over, between 44 and 97 South Sophia. A twenty-block area in this Ruffled Shirt ward contained the homes of at least twenty-eight benevolent officers. Both the concentration of these officers' residences and their elegance lent an aura of prestige and propriety to benevolent leadership that was transferred from domestic to public domains.

Perfectionist women also clustered in city neighborhoods but never as densely nor as often in opulent surroundings. Eight of the HF's first fourteen officers did live in the third ward, four amid their benevolent counterparts. Others lived on the fringes of the district, in pleasant and established neighborhoods in bordering areas, or in the more remote sixth ward, which was fast becoming a rival social center to the old Ruffled Shirt ward. LASS members were more widely scattered. Society president Mrs. Samuel D. Porter resided in the third ward along with her sister, Mrs. John Wilder, and Mrs. Weddle, Mrs. Gould, and Mrs. Fogg. The rest of the Porter women lived in the first ward with four other antislavery leaders, and a dozen coworkers were dispersed in four other wards and five bordering towns. Nevertheless, even these women had greater access to urban resources and to each other than did ultraists. Only in the first ward did a few ultraist families—the Posts, Willetts, Halsteads, and Curtises—live in close proximity to each other and to other activists. Some of the extended families who shared reform work and residences in 1842 had broken into smaller units by 1850; in the town of Gates several families lived as neighbors, but the size of their farms impeded their interactions far more than the smaller yards of urban enclaves. By mid-century, ultraists could be found in every city ward but the third; in surrounding towns such as Gates, Chili, Henrietta, and Perinton, and in agricultural outposts such as Darien, Bath, Farmington, Port Byron, and Waterloo. Altogether, the women who shared ultraist labors covered nearly one hundred miles of upstate New York territory.

Despite the religious, economic, domestic, and residential diversity of the three groups, those activist women who resided in the city proper attempted to work together on a few occasions. As early as the 1830s perfectionists had gained some benevolent and ultraist signatures on antislavery petitions. In the same decade, collectors for the orphan asylum were given donations by at least two future woman's rights advocates. The HF modeled certain of its features on benevolent enterprises and worked closely with the OAA in placing adolescent girls or caring for the children of friendless young widows. In 1851 ultraist and perfectionist abolitionists had merged their efforts successfully if briefly at the Thompson antislavery festival. Yet the only social problem that garnered significant attention over a long period of time in all three activist networks was intemperance.[58] Benevolent women aided its victims, perfectionists first sought its eradication and later the salvation of its potential prey, and ultraists urged that it be accepted as grounds for divorce. Within their individual households and religious meetings, female activists of each group urged teetotal practices and expected them of male kin and coworshipers. In 1852 a wide spectrum of activist women finally attempted to forge an association to fight the evil. Though called the New York State Women's Temperance Society, the organization was based in Rochester and was led by Rochesterians. Its history reveals the potential for alliances among activist women in the final decade of the antebellum era.

In the winter of 1851 a small group of ultraists, including the Anthonys and the Burtises, joined with some relatively new entrants to local activist circles, such as Mrs. H. Atillia Albro, to organize a Daughters of Temperance festival at Rochester's Minerva Hall. Attended by local political officials and receiving favorable coverage in the press, the festival suggested that ultraists' advocacy of temperance could moderate community criticism of their activities. Many local women applied their talents and influence to the temperance cause throughout the late 1840s and early 1850s. When Amelia Bloomer began publishing her temperance journal, *The Lily,* in Seneca Falls in 1849, she received support and subscriptions from numerous Rochester sympathizers. Letters to the editor revealed that a temperance " 'Union' " had been organized among local ladies and that "pieces from the Lily" were read at the meeting. These women were convinced of the importance of their continued labors when alleged chicanery among some common council men assured that Rochester would "be cursed with licensed grog shops."[59] Women were encouraged to ostracize male drinkers, attend temperance gatherings, distribute literature, and petition state legislators. It was Samuel Chipman, evangelical

[58] Few records on specific temperance organizations and events exist for Rochester despite evidence that the cause had the widest appeal among all groups of women activists.
[59] *The Lily* (Seneca Falls), 1 May and 1 July 1849.

editor of the Rochester *Temperance Journal,* who urged local ladies to lay siege to the hundreds of taverns that "pour poison into the city," and thereby fostered the formation of the Anthony-led Daughters of Temperance to rally support for a state prohibition law.[60]

As temperance men turned increasingly to political action in the late 1840s, temperance women lamented their lack of political influence. Susan B. Anthony hoped that the Sons of Temperance would support their female counterparts on this issue, and in January 1852, attending the state Sons' meeting as the delegate of the Rochester Daughters, she decided to speak directly to her male allies about women's exclusion from the electoral process. The Sons of Temperance viewed the Daughters more as subordinates than sisters, however, and informed Anthony "that the ladies had been invited to listen and not to take part in the proceedings." Those women "who were not satisfied with such a position withdrew, announcing that they would hold a meeting . . . in which men and women would stand on equal ground." Mary C. Vaughan presided at the evening convocation, and several speakers called for a new women's society that would not be subordinate to any male society. Thereupon the participants elected a three-member executive committee, which included Anthony and Albro, to organize a women's state temperance society.[61] The committee drafted an agenda and called for an April meeting in Rochester.

As temperance women demanded political rights for themselves, they lost the support of many male colleagues. Even Samuel Chipman criticized women's direct entrance into political battles. He did agree to publish the proceedings of the January 1852 meeting in his *Journal* but apologized to his readers as he deemed it more of a woman's rights than a temperance gathering.[62] Nevertheless, Chipman and such other male temperance advocates as George Avery, Samuel Richardson, and James Fogg were sufficiently confident of limiting women to useful but restricted roles that they endorsed the call for the women's April meeting. With encouragement from the Daughters of Temperance, the *Temperance Journal,* and male leaders, hundreds of women gathered at Corinthian Hall, including a large contingent of local perfectionists and ultraists and a sprinkling of benevolent leaders.

The meeting was led by Anthony and Albro, who, though more

[60] *Temperance Journal,* 28 November 1851, quoted in McKelvey, *Rochester,* p. 348.
[61] Elizabeth Cady Stanton, Susan B. Anthony, and Matilda Joslyn Gage, *The History of Woman Suffrage,* 4 vols. (New York: Fowler and Wells, 1881), 1: 476.
[62] *Temperance Journal,* 30 January 1852.

radical than their evangelical peers, were less doctrinaire on the subject of woman's rights than the leading ultraists.[63] At the initial session, restricted to women only, the election of convention officers revealed that ultraists were well-organized and were attending in full strength. Though they were the smallest of the city's three activist circles, the ultraists elected four of their own—Rhoda DeGarmo, Sarah Fish, Amy Post, and Mary Hallowell—to NYSWTS offices. There they joined Anthony and Albro, six women from other parts of the state, and only two local perfectionists—Mrs. Avery and Mrs. D. C. Alling.[64] In addition, Elizabeth Cady Stanton, western New York's most infamous feminist, was elected to preside.

Stanton attempted to alleviate the fears of the convention's more moderate participants by "immediately proceed[ing] to explain her position" on the relation between drunkenness and divorce, disclaiming any proposal that viewed "divorce as a *remedy* for the evil" and arguing only that it was "a moral duty on the part of the wife" to leave an intemperate husband. Several women quickly expressed "their concurrence in the views of Mrs. Stanton."[65] Yet debates on issues of membership and organization revealed basic disagreements over the character of the new association. Some women, joined in the afternoon discussions by temperance men, wished simply to become members of the existing New York State Temperance Society rather than form an independent association. The ultraist organizers were accused of being "unjust towards temperance men of the Empire State," who they claimed would never acknowledge women's right "as equals to speak and vote."[66] Despite objections, the ultraists prevailed, and an independent women's society was formed that then selected delegates to attend the state meetings. Advocates of opposing positions agreed to serve together in the society's offices the first year, and the three-member executive committee, composed entirely of Rochesterians, cut across all groups of local activists. Sarah Gould represented the CS and the HF as well as First Presbyterian Church and the old wealth of the third ward, though her roots were in Finneyite perfectionism. Mrs. Samuel Richardson represented the evangelical tenets of Methodism yet had been a CS member since the early 1840s. She married into new

[63] In this period, Susan B. Anthony was not widely known as an ultraist; her primary concern until the early 1850s was temperance.

[64] *The Lily,* 1 May 1852.

[65] Ibid.

[66] Ibid., 1 June 1853. This issue contains a review of the 1852 proceedings.

wealth, becoming Samuel Richardson's wife after his rise from artisan to merchant and at the beginning of his ascent from alderman to mayor, a position he achieved in 1850. The third committee member was Mary Hallowell, who represented the ultraist network though the successful manufacturing ventures of her husband and her affiliation with the Unitarians may have made her a less threatening coworker than her mother Amy Post or other more outspoken ultraists.

It was Stanton as president who articulated the initial program of the NYSWTS. She attempted to appeal to every woman, claiming that "every relation which binds her to the race" also binds her to the temperance cause. She focused first on family relations, desiring that "no woman" would "form an alliance with any man who has been suspected even of the vice of intemperance." She extended this plea to all social circles: "Let us touch not, taste not, handle not, the unclean thing in any combination . . . refuse it in all its most tempting and refined forms." She urged women to foment a "moral revolution" through "lectures, tracts, newspapers, and discussion," suggesting that they temporarily withdraw support from "all associations for sending the Gospel to the heathen across the ocean" and instead devote all their resources to "the poor and suffering among us." As long as they were directed toward home missions, Stanton approved of those strategies already tested by benevolent and perfectionist societies: "Let us," she stated, "feed and clothe the hungry and naked, gather children into schools, and provide reading rooms and decent homes for young men and women thrown alone upon the world." Finally, Stanton downplayed the most volatile issue of the woman's rights program—the vote. She did suggest that women "petition . . . State governments so to modify the laws affecting marriage and the custody of children, that the drunkard shall have no claims on either wife or child," but she added that she "would give more for the agitation of any question on sound principles, thus enlightening and convincing the public mind, than for all the laws that could be written or passed in a century."[67]

Initially, the implementation of Stanton's program suggested that ultraist leadership might be the stepping stone to success. Susan B. Anthony and Emily Clark, of nearby LeRoy, were hired as agents of the NYSWTS and visited nearly every county, enrolling two thousand new members and collecting twenty-eight thousand signatures on a

[67] Stanton, Anthony, and Gage, *History,* 1: 481.

women's petition favoring statewide prohibition. Anthony and Clark, however, frequently found themselves defending or attempting to moderate positions expressed by Stanton as her true political colors were unveiled. Within months of assuming the society's presidency, Stanton was proclaiming that "woman's rights predominated over temperance" and "uniformly pressed" the divorce issue as central to the cause. In June 1852 she sent an epistle to the New York State Temperance convention that was "so radical that the friends [of the NYSWTS] feared to read it."[68] At the same time that Anthony attempted to offset Stanton's radical pronouncements by describing women's temperance work as "a missionary effort," male temperance advocates confirmed ultraists' suspicions of the state society's male leadership by denying women the right to speak or vote at the state convention.[69]

Throughout the next year temperance and woman's rights advocates crisscrossed New York State. The appearance of a handful of female temperance advocates at a woman's rights convention in Syracuse that fall reinforced the fears of more conservative NYSWTS workers. Moreover, by this time, not only Amelia Bloomer and Stanton but also Susan B. Anthony, Sarah Fish, and other ultraist temperance advocates had donned the new bloomer costume and argued vociferously for its acceptance as both a symbol of woman's freedom and a practical addition to her wardrobe. Rochesterians had a chance to observe the bloomer wearers in March 1853 at a women's temperance convention in Rochester where the issues of women's dress and woman's rights seemingly dominated the proceedings. Thus when the NYSWTS reconvened on June 1, 1853, tension was running high.

Four hundred women and men attended the first day's meeting to hear speeches by such "distinguished ladies" as Lucy Stone, Amelia Bloomer, Antoinette Brown, and others. While these spokeswomen had feminist sympathies, it was not until Stanton rose to speak that woman's rights became the focus of the convention's proceedings. Stanton noted that owing to the "radical and liberal" character of the society's leaders, all persons were welcome to join in the association's activities "without regard to sect, sex, color, or caste." It was thought necessary in the first year, however, to exclude men from office holding in the NYSWTS in order that women might learn "how to stand and

---

[68] Ibid., p. 485.
[69] *The Lily,* 1 July 1852. Several men argued for women's equal participation but were defeated by the more conservative male delegates.

walk alone." Now having demonstrated their "self-reliance, dignity, and force," it was time for women to open the society's offices to all persons. Arguing that there was a "growing recognition of woman's power and her right to act," Stanton and her supporters wished to use the current women's society as the basis for a new "People's New York State Temperance League."[70]

A heated debate ensued, joined by men and women, in which all sides of the question were argued. A few men, including Frederick Douglass, favored the change on the principle of absolute equality, but others wished to maintain sex-segregated societies, in part to keep woman's rights issues out of male temperance gatherings.[71] Several women also eloquently sustained the resolution for an all-female society. Emily Clark stated that "her experience of one year as an agent had taught her that the power of the Society lay in the fact of its being a Woman's Society." Amelia Bloomer claimed, "It is because we are an advocate of *woman's* rights that we object to yielding up the rights we have gained to men." Pointing to "the conduct of the men in this Convention," who occupied the floor at length without letting women voice their own preferences, she concluded, "The time has not come when *men* are prepared to come on a platform with us and acknowledge our equality."[72] The perfectionists and the ultraists had virtually changed positions from the previous year, the latter gaining faith in men's willingness to accept them as coworkers and the former losing such faith. Thus by 1853 ultraists, whose own activist skills were developed in such joint-sex organizations as the WNYASS, argued that equality of opportunity for officeholding was more important than whatever advantages accrued from sex segregation.

The arguments of Amy Post, Mary Hallowell, and Susan B. Anthony could not convince the members to accept Stanton's resolution, but they were forceful enough to forestall its defeat, postponing a decision to the following year. Yet just as the issue seemed to be laid to rest, the election of officers refueled the dissent. Mrs. Mary C. Vaughan, an advocate of separate societies, was easily chosen over Stanton as the next NYSWTS president. Anthony, however, won the position of secretary with equal ease but declined to serve because "the Society had

[70] *The Lily*, 15 June 1853.

[71] Ibid. Amelia Bloomer points out in this issue that Douglass supported the exclusion of whites from black antislavery and Negro convention organizations to allow blacks to gain leadership skills and experience denied them in racially mixed associations.

[72] Ibid., 1 June 1853.

taken a position in opposition to Woman's Rights."[73] Amy Post also refused to serve in the society, and her position was then filled by Maria G. Porter. As other ultraists withdrew, they were similarly replaced by local perfectionist leaders, while only the more moderate founding members—Atillia Albro, Mrs. Alling, Mrs. Gould, and Mrs. Richardson—accepted offices for the following year. These women kept the NYSWTS functioning for two more seasons on a limited basis but then turned their full attention back to local labors. They were encouraged in this transition by city editors who ridiculed both the "strong-minded and able-bodied women" who had first offered men offices in the NYSWTS and "the 'men' who are hankering for these offices." The latter, the *Daily Union* argued, "have not enough masculinity to hurt themselves nor anybody else."[74] Conservative women of Rochester agreed, expressing their disapproval of the "Female Garrisons" who tainted women's joint temperance venture and then abandoned it for woman's rights.[75]

By fall 1853 Rochester women activists had once again divided. This time the faultline lay between affluent activists, both perfectionist and benevolent who argued for women's influence through ameliorative and auxiliary efforts and ultraists who advocated woman's right to wield equal power with men. Ultraists' rejection within the NYSWTS of any position less than full equality was consistent with other actions taken by them in this period. Though immediately after the founding of the NYSWTS ultraists seemed willing to ally themselves with perfectionists in the temperance cause, they were simultaneously rejecting a similar alliance in the antislavery movement. As Frederick Douglass applied himself more fully to political abolitionism and Julia Griffiths forged an evangelically based ladies' society to aid his efforts, ultraist women increased their activities on behalf of moral suasion and the Garrison-led American Anti-Slavery Society.

In 1850, when WNYASS women had first met Douglass's criticism of their efforts, they responded with anger but also with uncertainty and with reassurances of the moral intent of their enterprise. In 1852, however, when Douglass applauded the LASS for its "self-denying labors" and assured them that "at present you have the field to your-

[73] Ibid.
[74] *Daily Union* (Rochester), 2 June 1853.
[75] Quoted in McKelvey, *Rochester*, p. 349.

selves," ultraists responded swiftly and without apology.[76] In a letter to *Frederick Douglass' Paper,* Sarah Hallowell chided Douglass for his feigned ignorance of WNYASS efforts. "For years," she wrote, "(as we need not remind you,) we have labored earnestly and trustingly to get up Annual Fairs as a means of aiding our great cause." The small number of workers, competition from church and charitable societies, and divisions within the antislavery movement caused WNYASS to "change [its] modus operandi," Hallowell admitted, but the society had never considered this "a final cessation of [its] associated efforts for the *slave.*" Noting that by Douglass's comments on the LASS "it might be supposed *we* [WYNASS] had no existence, were dead, disheartened, disbanded," Hallowell concluded, "Justice to our friends, and a due self-respect, alike prompt us to make our existence known."[77]

Julia Griffiths continued to solicit ultraists' aid for a brief period after this exchange. When Amy Post visited relatives on Long Island in fall 1852, Griffiths wrote, "I miss you very much, I assure you—for although we differ on 'the Constitution', we agree to differ & that's a good thing!" Reminding Amy of her long friendship with Douglass, Griffiths begged her to "re-read our *Rochester Society Constitution*— consider the strictly *independent ground we have taken,* and *reject it if you can.*" She noted that Mrs. Weddle, who had been drawn to ultraist efforts at one time, "was with us," and that LASS members "would *all* like to have Mrs. Post with them. Can you say no?"[78] Mrs. Post could, and did. For her, the LASS's claim that "the National Constitution" was the means by which abolitionists "could secure the blessing of Liberty"[79] for the enslaved indicated support of a government that oppressed not only blacks but Indians, workers, and women as well. Nor did LASS women intend to confront directly governmental authority—they would rely instead on male spokespersons. Certain that public opinion rather than politicians was the key to social change, including the abolition of slavery, ultraists initially considered the LASS well intentioned but misguided. As competition between the two groups increased, Amy Post and her coworkers were less convinced of

[76] Frederick Douglass to Mrs. Samuel D. Porter, president, LASS, 27 March 1842, printed in LASS, "Circular," SDPFP.

[77] Sarah Hallowell Willis to Frederick Douglass, 19 April 1852, printed in *Frederick Douglass' Paper,* 22 April 1852.

[78] Julia Griffiths to Amy Post, 16 October 1852, IAPFP. Griffiths refers first to the national Constitution and then to the LASS constitution.

[79] LASS, "Circular," SDPFP.

the LASS's intentions but more convinced that moral suasion tactics with the full and equal participation of women and blacks was the only antidote to oppressive institutions.

Throughout 1852 and 1853, WNYASS women made abundantly clear their commitment to the American Anti-Slavery Society and its support of moral suasion and female equality. Lecture tours by Abby Kelley (now Abby Kelley Foster) and Sallie Holley, the former appearing with "the Boston Liberator in one hand and Uncle Tom's Cabin in the other," aroused ultraist women to renewed efforts and local editors to renewed attacks.[80] The editor of the *Democrat*, for instance, found it difficult to believe "that one [Sallie Holley] so eminently fitted for the acknowledged sphere of woman . . . should be withdrawn from it to enter an arena full of incongenialities." Holley responded in the style of any good ultraist, "Everyday I feel more and more how great the work is," and announced plans to join Kelley Foster on a lecture tour of Massachusetts.[81] The WNYASS women funded tours of Kelley Foster and Holley through western New York and sent items to the Boston fair, the proceeds of which supported the American Society and the *Liberator*.

In spring 1852 the decade-long commitment of the Rochester ultraists was rewarded when the American Society decided to hold its annual meeting in the city. Rochester ultraists had often traveled to New York City to attend such meetings, but now they could gather with the nation's most famous abolitionists in their own Corinthian Hall. Amy Post, Mary Hallowell, and Abigail Bush served alongside Wendell Phillips, Parker Pillsbury, and Henry Wright on the business committee, while the citizens at large heard Garrison, Kelley Foster, Douglass, and others debate the great issues of the day. In the concluding session of the three-day meeting, the society both demanded the recommitment of individuals to an unpopular cause and applauded Rochesterians as a whole "for their courteous and candid hearing of the views which had been expressed." The meeting did not transform Rochester into a haven for abolitionists nor heal divisions within local ranks. For ultraist women, however, it did "strengthen them all for a

[80] Laura Wilcox Ramsdell to Susan B. Anthony, 20 December 1896, Unitarian Society of Rochester Records, University of Rochester. Ramsdell is recounting her conversion to abolitionism.

[81] Sallie Holley to Abby Kelley Foster, 17 February 1852, AKFP. Holley encloses the clipping from the *Daily Democrat*, n.d. Holley was active in Rochester in 1852 and 1853 primarily.

faithful and life-long warfare upon the accursed system of slavery in our land."[82]

During the early 1850s ultraists avidly pursued spiritualism and woman's rights as well as abolition. A circle of believers and mediums met regularly, led by Isaac Post, George Willetts, Sarah Burtis, and the Kedzies. Isaac Post developed an alphabetical code by which the rappings of spirits could be translated into words. Employing this method, he produced *Voices of the Spirit World*, a compendium of communications from Quaker luminaries Elias Hicks and George Fox as well as Benjamin Franklin, John C. Calhoun, Margaret Fuller, Martha Washington, and other spirits. Some spirits retracted ideas proclaimed during their earthly sojourn, while others elaborated on them: all agreed that if they had their lives to live over, they would follow the ultraist path.[83] In Rochester, no ultraist women gained the public visibility of male mediums, but they nevertheless gained a private sustenance from spirit communications that had direct feminist implications. As spiritualist Sarah Thayer wrote Amy Post, a mother "ought to be better qualified to direct the spiritual life of her own sex than any belov'd disciple or even Jesus himself as a man or a brother."[84]

In general, female ultraists were more interested in talking to each other than to spirits when it came to the subject of woman's rights. Rochester ultraists hosted a county woman's rights convention in January 1853 and a statewide meeting the following November. Here Amy Post, Mary Hallowell, Rhoda DeGarmo, Lemira Kedzie, Sarah Burtis, and "others who have been prominently identified" with the cause in Rochester shared the stage with nationally known feminists Ernestine Rose, Antoinette Brown, Elizabeth Cady Stanton, and Susan B. Anthony.[85] Yet with the exception of Rose, the national figures had gained their first woman's rights experience in western New York and had often been led by as much as they had led their grassroots supporters. At the January meeting, representatives from more than a dozen towns as well as from Rochester itself discussed "the disabilities which the customs and laws impose on the industrial rights and powers of Woman" and listened to Rose address the "Legal Wrongs of Women."

[82] *Liberator*, 21 May 1852. The convention drew some political abolitionists, including Douglass and Porter, but ultraists dominated the proceedings.

[83] Isaac Post, *Voices of the Spirit World, Being the Communications from Many Spirits, by the Hand of Isaac Post, Medium* (Rochester: Charles H. McDonnell, 1852).

[84] Sarah [E. Thayer] to Amy Post, 9 March 1853, IAPFP.

[85] *Daily Democrat*, 15 June 1853.

Corinthian Hall was "nearly filled" as Rose extolled the virtues of the "woman's rights movement, which claims equality for all the sons and daughters of man" and proclaimed it "one link in the chain of progressive reform." She then claimed for women not only the right to vote but also "the privilege of being voted for."[86]

On November 30 and December 1, woman's rights advocates again met in Rochester, devoting their attention to "Woman's legal and civil disabilities." This time they adopted a plan for a massive petition campaign to extend the reforms already made in the "barbarous usages of Common Law . . . until every vestige of *partiality* be removed" from New York State law.[87] For the remainder of the decade, woman's rights activities centered around the universal improvement of women's political and property rights through legislation and on individual women's achievements in new fields of endeavor. Thus local feminists, who had applauded Elizabeth Blackwell's graduation from medical school at their 1848 convention, were pleased to note in 1851 that the nation's second woman medical school graduate was Rochesterian Sarah R. Adamson. In September 1853 Antoinette Brown became one of the first ordained women pastors in the country, occupying a pulpit in South Butler near Rochester. Her ultraist neighbors invited her to address their convention in November, the same month that she presided at the marriage of Rhoda DeGarmo's daughter.[88] While receiving less widespread attention, Sarah Anthony Burtis's pioneering efforts affected the lives of greater numbers of women: she broke the male-dominated ranks of store clerks and thereby opened a whole new field of employment to local women.[89]

As ultraist women became more outspoken on their own behalf, they lost some of their early coworkers. This time the women who retreated from ultraist circles did not also retreat from the antislavery cause, but they refused to combine abolitionism with feminism. One such woman was Phoebia Pickard, whose husband, Daniel, had been a vocal critic of woman's equality within the family at the Rochester Woman's Rights Convention of 1848. The husbands of other ultraists-turned-LASS-members were also critics of woman's rights and supporters of

[86] Ibid., 17 January 1853.
[87] *Frederick Douglass' Paper*, 23 December 1853. Despite divisions between Douglass and the ultraists over abolitionist tactics, he continued to publicize woman's rights events in his paper.
[88] Stanton, Anthony, and Gage, *History*, 1: 473.
[89] McKelvey, *Rochester*, p. 349.

political abolitionists. The women themselves were generally younger than their more militant counterparts who remained in the WNYASS. They were more likely to have been raised outside agrarian Quaker communities, to reside outside farm families, and to attend the Unitarian Church rather than the Congregational Friends meeting.[90] In the decade before the Civil War both the LASS and the HF gained the support of those Quakers and Unitarians who rejected the woman's rights arguments of ultraists.

No longer seeking recruits only from evangelical churches and less immediately concerned with the perfectability of the world, the leaders of the LASS and the HF sought to define a specific role for themselves within local activism. Both societies castigated leisured women who failed to obey godly admonitions to useful labor just as vehemently as they denied ultraist women's claims to equality. They condemned "extravagance" and "ostentatious display" among women "addicted to society." Women, they declared, must play "a dignified part" in "the world's affairs." The "moral sentiment of the people must be purified," and this was woman's "true mission." Once accomplished, women would claim nought for themselves but "leave with the Eternal Father the honor and glory of all our endeavors."[91] While thus distinguishing themselves from ultraists, HF and LASS leaders distanced themselves from benevolent efforts. Whereas mid-century perfectionists still envisioned women's mission as a finite one, benevolent leaders of the same period concluded that "the poor ye have always with you."[92] By the mid-1850s, however, this latter disparity paled in comparison with perfectionists' disdain for woman's rights. After the failure of ultraist-perfectionist alliances in the temperance and antislavery movements, LASS leaders sought closer ties with their benevolent sisters and adopted, where possible, the forms of organization and the language of benevolent enterprises.

The OAA had made a successful transition from a joint perfectionist-benevolent venture to an almost purely benevolent enterprise, and the HF initially hoped to follow its path. They replicated many of the

---

[90] Several persons maintained affiliations with the YMCF and the Unitarians, and all of them were ultraists.

[91] *Journal of the Home* (Rochester), 1 September 1860; LASS, "Circular," SDPFP.

[92] CS, *Charter, Constitution, By-Laws, and Officers of the Rochester Female Charitable Society (for the Relief of Sick Poor), Together with Its History and Annual Reports for the Year 1860* (Rochester: C. D. Tracy, 1860), p. 15. This was one of the CS's most frequently employed biblical quotations.

OAA's features—its early recruitment of both benevolent and perfectionist officers, its institutional structure, and its solicitation of funds from philanthropic gentlemen and state legislators. With its focus on slavery, the LASS was a less likely candidate for benevolent support, yet the association tried to mitigate its more radical side by emphasizing its ameliorative and auxiliary character. Far more self-consciously—and successfully—than the WYNASS, the LASS imitated church and charitable society models in its annual fairs. It also relied on male, and especially ministerial, spokespersons, asserted its members' subordination before God and man, and described slaves as proper objects of Northern charity rather than in ultraist terms, as brutalized victims of Northern indifference and Southern tyranny.[93]

The HF was the most successful in its pursuit of benevolent credentials. As early as 1850, home leaders clarified their connection to, or rather distance from, earlier moral reform labors. When the city's Poor Master applied to the home for a room for a young unwed mother to save her from the gloomier prospect of public support at the alms house, "it was deemed inexpedient to receive her . . . as it would be in violation of the Constitution," which expressly stated "that 'virtuous females' alone" were to be aided.[94] In its early annual reports, the HF assured the public that the few unworthy individuals admitted to the home were quickly discharged and were "more than counterbalanced by the numbers in which deserving poverty has been saved from humiliating dependence on public charity. . . ." Appealing to public civic pride as well as public economy, HF leaders noted that "many a virtuous and indigent female will have cause to bless the day when the benevolent of the city and surrounding country laid the foundation for a 'Home.'" By 1853 home leaders pronounced their institution "a *'fixed fact,'* and one of those means of public usefulness, which it will be alike the duty and the pleasure of the community to sustain and to consider as one of the recognized Benevolent Institutions of our city."[95]

In the same year the LASS, only in its second year of activity, was gaining far wider acceptance than its ultraist competitor. The December 1853 LASS festival "passed off pleasantly and to the entire satisfaction" of the society's members, making "a very favorable impression,"

[93] For further comparisons of the LASS and WNYASS on racial attitudes, see Chapter 7.
[94] HF, Minute Book, 18 June 1850, FHP.
[95] *Daily Democrat,* 12 June 1851, 28 April 1852, and 23 April 1853.

they thought, on the community. According to *Frederick Douglass' Paper,* "there was a quiet earnestness observable in the faces and movements of the officers and members of the Society, which impressed spectators with a sense of the dignity of the disinterested work to which they were devoting their time, their talents and position." Reporting on the WNYASS fair of 1850, Douglass had dwelt on the financial and moral failures of the occasion. Now he praised both "the dissemination of light and knowledge" afforded by the LASS festival and the sale items, which "exceeded in beauty, richness and abundance those exhibited on any previous occasion."[96] Whereas the 1850 fair had aroused public indignation by the social mingling of blacks and whites, the "interest of [this] occasion was much enhanced" by the "eloquent and energetic" addresses of William J. Watkins, Esq., and the Honorable William C. Bloss and by "the brilliant performances of Prof. Gustave de Speiss on the Piano Forte." Moreover, the festival garnered five hundred dollars for the cause, surpassing the previous year's "highly encouraging" proceeds by a hundred dollars.[97]

One year later the LASS reported annual receipts of more than $1,200, clearly making it competitive with the benevolent associations of the city for the community's charitable contributions. The LASS's choice of tactics certainly aided in that competition. In addition to the annual festival, the society sponsored lectures by "some of the most gifted, fearless, earnest, thorough, and indomitable men in the anti-slavery ranks." The winter series for 1855 included speeches by the Reverends John Pierpont, Thomas W. Higginson, and Theodore Parker, and by Ralph Waldo Emerson and the Honorable Salmon P. Chase. The proceeds of Rev. Henry Ward Beecher's lecture "Patriotism" amounted to $195, of which "the distinguished Lecturer and Philanthropist refused to touch a single cent." Without one agent of the American Anti-Slavery Society or one woman on its roster of speakers, the LASS avoided the public criticism that so often met WNYASS efforts and was thereby assured greater financial success. Douglass soon predicted that "the usefulness of this young Association . . . is about to be greatly increased, and the sphere of its operation widely extended."[98]

Douglass's prediction failed to materialize, however. Though the

[96]*Frederick Douglass' Paper,* 30 December 1853.
[97]LASS, "Circular," SDPFP.
[98]*Frederick Douglass' Paper,* 12 January, 16 March, and 12 January 1855.

LASS continued to report healthy profits from its festivals and large audiences at its lectures, the association never numbered more than a couple of dozen active members. Susan and Maria Porter, Mrs. James P. Fogg, Sarah Seward Gould, and Mrs. Russell Green supplied the only active links between perfectionist abolitionists and the CS or OAA.[99] Bonds between antislavery women and the HF were more extensive, yet only the Porters managed to remain equally active in both associations. At the same time, the most active HF women evinced almost no interest in LASS labors. Mrs. Selah Mathews, Rochester's leading perfectionist of the 1830s and president of the HF from 1851 to 1871, never appeared in LASS reports or donation lists, nor did her most active coworkers, such as Mrs. James K. Livingston, Mrs. Moses Matthews, Mrs. Edwin Scrantom, Mrs. James Gregory, or Mrs. Samuel Selden.

HF leaders' general neglect of the antislavery cause, despite their religious, economic, and residential ties to the LASS, may have resulted from their desire to integrate themselves more fully into the local benevolent order. In the 1850s they sought to *"put away [the] evil thoughts"* of which they had been accused a decade earlier.[100] They were somewhat successful, achieving far greater support, at least in the number of members they recruited, than the LASS. Yet the home still did not attain the acceptance accorded its sister institution, the orphan asylum. Whereas the OAA obtained some $3,800 in its first two years of operation, the HF collected but $700 in the same period. Given this knowledge of their own marginality to the benevolent network, HF leaders may not have been eager to risk tainting their reputation further by mixing in antislavery politics. At the same time, the CS and OAA gained little from accepting the HF as a full-fledged benevolent partner. In 1855 the CS first reached the $1,000 mark in private donations for a single year. The same year, it received the promise of a $5,000 matching grant from the common council to erect a hospital, obtained a charter of incorporation and selected its first male board of trustees, and acquired a $2,500 donation from Phineas T. Barnum's "Moral Lectures" by the arrangement of a number of "prominent citizens of

[99] Mrs. Green, assuming that she is the first wife of Russell Green, was a charter member of the CS and the only connection between the LASS and the CS. Despite the thirty years between the foundings of the CS and the LASS, the evidence that this is the same Mrs. Green is strengthened by the fact that the woman has the same first name, religious affiliation, and residence.

[100] *Daily Sun* (Rochester), 27 June 1839.

Rochester."[101] The CS retained some one hundred thirty officers, collectors, and visitors to oversee sixty-one districts and sixteen church collections on behalf of its nearly five hundred members. Its visitors, moreover, included some of the leading lights of the OAA, HF, and LASS. Clearly, the CS had successfully passed through the crisis period of the early 1850s. While it was eager to send young women among the "sick poor" for care at the HF, the CS now saw little reason to forge more intimate ties to the new association.

THE OAA worked more closely with the HF, especially in the placement and care of young mothers with children, but it, too, favored relying on its own, relatively abundant, resources over merger with the HF. In the annual report presented in October 1854, the OAA managers noted that at "no period since the commencement of this labor of love for 'orphan and destitute children' has the Institution presented a more prosperous and happy aspect."[102] Membership dues accounted for over one quarter of the institution's $3,000 receipts that year, with church collections providing an equal portion. Bequests from early supporters increased during the 1850s, while "Orphan's Concerts" raised over $300 annually. In the battle for financial stability, the OAA was successful on its own terms. There was one battle, however, in which it did seek the HF's support, the fight to deny Catholics admission to the city's foremost benevolent institutions. The HF obliged, and both societies passed resolutions at the height of the nationwide nativist panic to deny Roman Catholics entrance to or influence in their institutions. The OAA went so far as to change its name formally to the Rochester Protestant Orphan Asylum.[103] It was only on this ground of shared religious intolerance that the HF and OAA met as equals.

Thus by 1855 the HF and LASS were well-established activist associations that were integrated into neither existing benevolent nor existing ultraist networks. At the same time, the HF and LASS provided more acceptable public roles for women, according to prevailing community standards, than their predecessors, the FMRS and FASS. In the 1850s perfectionists were willing to accept their own subordination, to attend to primarily local concerns, and to ally with the most

[101] Hanmer-Croughton, "Rochester Female Charitable Society," p. 73.

[102] OAA, Annual Report, 1854, Scrapbook, HCCP.

[103] On anti-Catholic stands of OAA and HF, see *Daily Union,* 7 November 1854; HF, Minute Book, 29 March 1854, FHP; OAA, Minute Book, 26 July, 29 November, - 27 December 1853 and 28 February 1855, HCCP.

respectable circles of Rochester society. Members of the HF, drawing on the more stable, married, and affluent segments of early perfectionist ranks, made their primary alliances with the CS and OAA whenever possible and gained respectability through the institutionalization of the still virtuous. Members of the LASS, on the other hand, rejected institutionalization and a larger share of respectability to pursue the antislavery cause, but they presented themselves as disinterested and self-denying laborers, removed from the taint of partisan politics, racial mixing, and woman's rights. Both groups rejected ultraist demands for racial and sexual equality at the same time that they were rejected as equal partners by their benevolent peers. Thus, more by default than design, the LASS and the HF preserved the perfectionist network in the early 1850s. The return of Finney to Rochester in 1855 and the outbreak of war five years later promised an influx of women into public labors, presenting perfectionists with a chance to recruit new members and female activists in general with the opportunity to realign old networks.

[6]

Union or Liberty

Many years had passed since the Burned-over District was first swept by the fires of revivalism and more than a dozen since the last great outburst of religious enthusiasm in Rochester. The most intense spiritual outpourings in the city had been directed by Charles Grandison Finney and in the autumn of 1855 he was called back once again "to labor for souls." First and Third Presbyterian churches, led by stalwart Calvinists, refused to aid the Evangelist's efforts, but the other Presbyterian churches along with the Congregationalists, Baptists, and Methodists "took hold of the work and entered into it with spirit and success."[1] Finney himself "preached in several of the churches twice or three times every day and Sunday for about eight months" and held prayer meetings each morning "at 10 o'clock A.M., averaging from 800 to 1000" participants. One of Finney's staunchest opponents, First Church pastor J. H. McIlvaine, recalled some thirty-five years later that "the whole population of Rochester rocked, as if the city had been shaken by an earthquake."[2]

As did Finney's earlier revivals, this one commenced "among the higher classes of society." Lawyers, judges, and merchants were particularly affected, as were students at the newly established University of Rochester. By the end of the winter, however, "all classes of persons, from the highest to the lowest . . . were visited by the power of the revival. . . ." Women were often visited first by Mrs. Charles

[1]Charles Grandison Finney, *The Memoirs of Rev. Charles G. Finney, Written by Himself* (New York: F. H. Revell, [1876]), p. 435.

[2]J. H. McIlvaine to Mr. H. Pomeroy Brewster, 30 September 1891, in H. Pomeroy Brewster, "The Magic of a Voice, the Rochester Revivals of Charles G. Finney," Rochester Historical Society, *Publications* 4 (1925), p. 284.

Finney, who labored "as usual, with great zeal and success."[3] This Mrs. Finney was the Evangelist's second wife and well acquainted with Rochester, having lived there as Mrs. William Atkinson from 1821 to 1848. The wife and then widow of miller William Atkinson, she had been a CS charter member, a seminary principle, and an Episcopalian who learned to love Finney's views of sanctification years before the man himself. In 1837 she was president of the CS, a founding member of the OAA, and an antislavery petitioner, and five years later she joined the evangelical First Congregational Church. As the Evangelist's wife, Elizabeth Atkinson Finney "perfected a style of ministry that both allowed her an independent arena for her talents and permitted her to work in tandem with her husband until he became dependent on her as a primer for his own revivals."[4] She was particularly important in directing female prayer meetings from which she recruited spiritual sisters for door-to-door and, in 1856, store-to-store canvassing for converts. Surrounded in Rochester by former neighbors and coworkers, Mrs. Finney was especially successful. "Many of the ladies . . . exerted their utmost influence to bring all classes to meeting and to Christ," visiting "stores and places of business" as well as private homes.[5]

By such means female perfectionists helped themselves as well as Mrs. Finney. The HF board observed that the home had "gained rapidly on the estimation of the Community," and the LASS noted that its January 1856 festival "was crowned with abundant success."[6] Even the OAA, though predominantly a benevolent institution by this time, benefited from its perfectionist roots. In October 1856 the board reported that "the past year has been especially crowned with His goodness," the institution being granted all necessary supplies "and means also . . . for moral and mental training" of its peculiarly healthy inhabitants.[7] The HF always invoked the "Providence of God" and "the Lord's favor" as explanations for success, but these blessings were more closely tied to evangelical religion in 1856 than at any time since the society's founding. At the 1856 annual meeting, evangelical

---

[3] Finney, *Memoirs*, pp. 437, 438.
[4] Leonard I. Sweet, *The Minister's Wife: Her Role in Nineteenth-Century American Evangelicalism* (Philadelphia: Temple University Press, 1983), p. 192.
[5] Finney, *Memoirs*, p. 438.
[6] HF, Annals of the Home, 1849–1858, FHP: *Frederick Douglass' Paper* (Rochester), 1 February 1856.
[7] OAA, Annual Report, 1856, Scrapbook, HCCP.

churches were especially well represented by the officers, while those representatives of First and Third Presbyterian were Finney converts of an earlier era, such as Mrs. Selah Mathews, Mrs. Jacob Gould, and Mrs. John Bush. For the first time not only were the society's reports printed in the daily papers and the *Genesee Evangelist,* but "six hundred copies" were also to be published "in pamphlet form" for distribution throughout the city.[8] In the following year, "253 patrons" were admitted to the home, a school was opened for the youngest residents, and a lengthy donations list provided "testimony to the goodness of God."[9]

The LASS also hoped for more bountiful returns on its labor. Members initially feared that the "extended revival" might preclude "many, who are usually quite interested in our success" from exhibiting "that liberality" at the LASS festival "which has hitherto characterized them." Yet once it was clear that the festival had succeeded, even Frederick Douglass abandoned his skepticism of revivals, convinced that "many friends of the slave" would "rise up in the wake of President Finney's preaching." The result, he hoped would be that the "friends of emancipation will not hereafter be confined to the sewing circle of a few devoted Anti-Slavery Ladies. . . ." Several new women did take up the slave's cause, and by the fall, sixty-eight fugitives had been aided in their flight to Canada, several hundred dollars had been donated to *Frederick Douglass' Paper,* and sufficient goods had been solicited, mostly "fine foreign items," to stock an antislavery sale at Samuel Hamilton's store.[10]

Female Finneyites also extended their labors by forming a new association, the Industrial School of Rochester. The IS offered a combination of religious and vocational training to boys and girls from needy families. The society was formed at the city's newest evangelical home, Plymouth Congregational Church. OAA and HF members, who constantly confronted the difficulties of placing orphans and friendless women in jobs, had noted the need for such a school for years. Mrs. Ebenezer Griffin's visit to an "industrial home" in Brooklyn, New York, in fall 1856 gave the final impetus to local efforts. An informal meeting of "interested ladies" was held at the home of Plymouth

[8] HF, Minute Book, 2 April 1856, FHP.
[9] *Daily Union* (Rochester), 12 April 1857.
[10] *Frederick Douglass' Paper,* 14 and 28 March, 4 April, and 21 November 1856, and 19 June 1857. For an example of Douglass's earlier skepticism regarding revivals, see *North Star* (Rochester), 3 March 1848.

Church founder Mrs. Henry A. Brewster. The IS association was then formally organized on 17 December, and the school began operations the following spring.[11] The IS was led by Mrs. D. C. Alling, who had ended her labors in the NYSWTS a year earlier. Several of her coworkers in the IS also served the temperance cause, and all had experience in the CS, OAA, HF, or all three. All devoted Evangelicals, the new society's directors were nonetheless a heterogeneous group, including two Episcopalians who had converted in the Finney revivals of 1830–1831, several Plymouth Church members, and a number of Methodists. These women collected funds, provided school supplies, assisted in teaching and sewing classes, visited children in their homes, made and repaired their school clothes, and offered each child one substantial meal per day. Since they did not provide a full-time residence for their charitable charges, IS women were able to aid a large number of disadvantaged youths, including some 264 girls and an equal number of boys the first year.

Credit for the advances made by the HF, LASS, OAA, and IS in the aftermath of Finney's final Rochester revival could not, however, be laid solely at the Lord's feet. In 1855 and 1856 Rochester was in the midst of boom times, and so the city's female-led welfare institutions were assured of adequate funding and women were encouraged to extend their labors into new domains. Antislavery perfectionists were among the beneficiaries of community prosperity, but their success was due as well to national events that thrust their male allies into the political spotlight. In the mid-1850s the Republican party emerged as the most viable national body to advocate antislavery positions. Long "in favor of Constitutional Liberty," the men of the Porter, Cornell, Galusha, and Fogg families finally abandoned Liberty party principles to join the Republican bandwagon and seek electoral victories.[12] The Republicans, like the Free Soilers before them, opposed the extension of slavery into the territories but accepted its continued existence in the South. When local Liberty party leaders accepted this platform, they received the support of leading editors and politicians in Rochester. Republican Samuel G. Andrews, whose stand on slavery was far less radical than that of Liberty party men, ran virtually unopposed for

[11] William Farley Peck, *A Semi-Centennial History of Rochester with Illustrations and Biographical Sketches of Its Prominent Men and Pioneers* (Syracuse: D. Mason, 1884), p. 422.

[12] LASS, "Circular, The First Report of the Rochester Ladies' Anti-Slavery Sewing Society, 1852," SDPFP.

mayor in 1856, receiving the endorsement of political abolitionists, former Whigs, and local Democrats.[13] That spring, Andrews chaired a meeting of local politicians that attracted an audience of six hundred by denouncing proslavery Congressman Preston Brooks's attack on abolitionist Senator Charles Sumner. Summer performances of *Uncle Tom's Cabin* received an enthusiastic reception from reviewers and audiences alike, the male portion of which guaranteed the Republicans a five-thousand-vote margin in the fall presidential sweepstakes. A city hall protest meeting, occasioned by the Supreme Court's 1857 Dred Scott decision, brought together early Whig leader Thomas Kempshall, Democratic Judge John Chumasero, and Liberty party leaders Samuel D. Porter and William C. Bloss.

Several months later, members of the LASS pointed to the Court's decision and to "the danger that [seems] to threaten the small amount of liberty" free blacks "have hitherto enjoyed" as "the most urgent reasons for unwearied effort." Specifically, they sought customers for their annual antislavery bazaar.[14] Yet the receipts on that occasion did not bear out the expectations raised by recent events. National affairs once again shaped local responses, but this time in ways less providential to the antislavery cause. By spring 1857 "business of all kinds" was "unusually dull" in Rochester as elsewhere, and "merchants of small capital doing a credit business" were "falling in every direction. . . ."[15] Simultaneously, conflicts in the Kansas territory, which resulted in bloodshed by both antislavery and proslavery forces, slowed the turn to abolitionism by local politicians and exacerbated differences in antislavery ranks.[16] The same year, the American Anti-Slavery Society held a major convention in Rochester, boosting ultraist zeal as Julia Griffiths's return to England diminished perfectionist prospects.

While many of the LASS's difficulties stemmed from the antislavery issue, the recession of 1857 affected fund-raising efforts of this as well as other associations. The HF and IS attempted to stave off a contraction of efforts by fortifying their support. The IS incorporated in the spring of 1857, appointing a male board of directors that included the

---

[13] Adelaide Elizabeth Dorn, "A History of the Antislavery Movement in Rochester and Vicinity" (thesis, University of Buffalo, 1932), pp. 87–91. See also *Frederick Douglass' Paper,* 11 July 1856.

[14] *Frederick Douglass' Paper,* 24 April and 11 September 1857.

[15] Henry Morse to Aaron Erickson, 18 May 1857, in Blake McKelvey, comp., "Letters Postmarked Rochester," Rochester Historical Society, *Publications* 21 (1943), p. 98.

[16] Dorn, "History," p. 93.

leading philanthropists of the city. The HF, less willing to depend on gentlemanly assistance, turned to women of nearby towns for help. The question of "Publishing a Journal" had been "often laid on the Table" at HF meetings in the past, "the demand" being "mainly felt in the country." In July 1857, however, the HF board suddenly decided that "the great Interest expressed in such a work by the Ladies living in the adjoining Towns & their offers of tangible aid" seem "to call for some effort on our part."[17] In the first issue of the *Journal of the Home,* published in October 1857, the editor assured the HF board that many would receive the paper who "only lacked information and direction to spring into active charity." While admitting the "wide spread distress" of the previous year, the *JHF* claimed that these were "retributive judgments," making clear the responsibilities of those "in high places." The "wickedness" of some in these ranks "brings ruin upon thousands of the lowly who have not shared [the] guilt," and thereby necessitates the intervention of others in that class to save the poor who are unjustly victimized.[18]

The revivals and the recession of the late 1850s alternately rejuvenated and restricted perfectionist labors. Benevolent and ultraist ranks, on the other hand, were not significantly expanded by the revivals, while they were somewhat contracted by the recession. Economic retrenchment was the only factor that periodically impeded the extension of female benevolence. While financial reverses did not undercut the moral support of such endeavors, they did temporarily limit these endeavors' material base. After a decade of negotiation the CS obtained a site for the erection of a city hospital, a pledge of seven thousand dollars from the common council, and papers of incorporation to legalize the society's control over hospital functions. Yet the final land grant was made just as the recession hit. In stark contrast to the speed with which the asylum, home, and industrial school were put into operation, the hospital project, which required significant technical and financial support from male professionals and politicians, was long delayed. Similarly, the OAA, which had collected nearly six thousand dollars in the revival years, experienced a temporary circumscription of its work in 1857 and 1858. Its annual income dropped to below five thousand dollars and the number of children aided annually fell below one hundred.

[17] HF, Minute Book, 21 July 1857, FHP.
[18] *JHF* 1 October 1857 and 1 January 1858.

The late 1850s were years of retrenchment rather than retreat for the CS and the OAA. Both associations introduced programs and precedents in these years that would, with the return of prosperity, lead to further expansion. The OAA, for instance, convinced the state legislature to maintain relatively high levels of funding during the recession, establishing a strong base upon which to build in 1859 and 1860. In addition, in the midst of the recession the local Knights Templar lodge came to the rescue of the asylum. On New Year's Day 1858, a group of Templars "visited the Asylum, leaving a substantial proof of their interest in the Orphan." Even after the return of prosperity, 1 January remained a donation day for the OAA.[19] That same winter, the "need of some place where vicious girls could be reclaimed and kept from harming others" became unavoidably apparent; and the OAA, CS, HF, and IS petitioned "the Legislature of the State of New York for an appropriation for a Reformatory School for Juvenile Females."[20] As happened with the city hospital, several years passed before politicians responded to women's pleas, but the first step had been taken.

Unlike the Panic of 1837, that of 1857 claimed few benevolent supporters; it simply moderated their philanthropy for a season. The husbands of CS and OAA leaders were more financially secure than ever on the eve of the recession, and, if they could wait out the hard times, the demise of smaller competitors promised to improve their economic status. Their political power had also been expanded as local leaders moved into county, state, and even national positions. Thus as benevolent societies' need for institutional charters, legislative approval, and public funds increased, so did their access to county and state offices. From the early 1850s through the Civil War, a sprinkling of benevolent leaders resided in Albany as well as in Washington, D.C., and continued their appeals on behalf of Rochester's needy from those arenas of power.

Ultraists suffered more serious setbacks in these years and in response intensified their efforts. Anticipating a new wave of revivalism, ultraists of the early 1850s sought only to weather the evangelical storm. They knew that for a season local energies would be absorbed by revival enthusiasms, but they assured themselves that it was better

[19] OAA, Annual Report, 1858, Scrapbook, HCCP.
[20] Peck, *Semi-Centennial History*, p. 423; OAA, Minute Book, 23 February 1858, HCCP. An increase in female delinquency and prostitution may have been feared because of the deepening recession.

to heed the "still small voice" within their own circle than to go "thrashing about" in the protracted meetings induced by evangelical preachers.[21] At the same time, Rochester's religious radicals tried to broaden their appeal before Finney's fires swept the city. The Yearly Meeting of Congregational Friends, believing that their name conveyed "a sectarian [i.e., Quaker] feeling . . . to the public generally," adopted the *"Friends of Human Progress"* as their new appellation.[22] Not counting on titles alone to attract interest, they maintained a full schedule of lectures, meetings, conventions, and speaking tours. In these endeavors, they gained the aid of at least one Yankee Evangelical, Lucy Coleman.

Lucy Coleman embraced spiritualism, abolitionism, and feminism in rapid succession in the early 1850s and never retreated despite fervent appeals from Evangelicals in the revival years. It was in her company that Amy Post attended a Western Anti-Slavery Society meeting and a Cincinnati woman's rights convention in 1853, surveyed fugitive slave communities in Canada, and led a Friends of Human Progress gathering.[23] These experiences encouraged Amy Post to forward tactical suggestions to Abby Kelley Foster for her 1857 Midwest antislavery tour.[24] At the same time, Amy's sister, Sarah Hallowell, accompanied Sallie Holley on a lecture tour of western New York. Within Rochester, meetings led by abolitionists Lucretia Mott and Wendell Phillips and spiritualists John M. Spears and Andrew Jackson Davis kept ultraist fires burning despite the general shift away from moral suasion in the wake of Republican electoral victories. Within the political domain, Rochester remained the center of ultraist-led petition campaigns for woman's rights, and national feminist journals such as the *Una* and the *Woman's Advocate* requested periodic reports from Amy Post.[25]

Nevertheless, in 1856 and 1857 the rising star of political abolitionism, the recession, continuing disagreements with the LASS, and increasing internal dissension jeopardized ultraist antislavery and woman's rights labors. Amy Post complained to itinerant lecturer

[21] Nathaniel Rundall to Amy Post, 26 January 1852, IAPFP.
[22] YMCF, *Proceedings of the Annual Meeting of Friends of Human Progress, Held at Waterloo, N.Y., on the Fourth, Fifth, and Sixth of the Sixth Month, 1854* (Oswego, N.Y.: Pryne and Stickney, 1854), p. 3.
[23] Lucy N. Coleman, *Reminiscences* (Buffalo: H. L. Green, 1891), pp. 3, 20–41.
[24] Abby Kelley Foster to Amy Post, 12 September 1857, IAPFP.
[25] S. C. and D. R. Hewitt to Amy Post, 27 February 1855 (on Amy Post as an agent of *Una*) and A. E. W. Dowell (editor, *Woman's Advocate*) to Amy Post, 2 January 1855, IAPFP.

J. Elizabeth Jones in the winter of 1856 that ultraist lectures had not been well attended while revival meetings and political rallies were attracting massive audiences. Jones commiserated but noted that it was "the general complaint everywhere."[26] The Posts were soon faced with more immediate problems when the death of a Long Island friend left the unsuspecting Isaac saddled with a six-thousand-dollar mortgage debt. Soon after, the Post & Willis pharmacy declared bankruptcy, and the Posts temporarily retreated to farming and a smaller home.[27] For the first time in years, neither Isaac nor Amy attended the American Anti-Slavery Society annual meeting in New York City, though they continued to host its agents who sojourned in Rochester. It was a year and a half before the "privations" consequent upon "heavy losses" began to lift and the Posts had an "improved prospect of a calm and quiet old age."[28]

At the same time that the collapse of the Posts' finances restricted the family's ultraist activities, the LASS announced reorganization and again sought Amy Post's and other ultraists' entrance into perfectionist antislavery circles. Julia Wilbur, a LASS worker since the early 1850s and a boarder in Mary Hallowell's household, was the primary recruiting agent. While ultraists thought of admitting her to the "confidence of [their] circle," they were warned by Boston friends that "the position she occupies of close fellowship with your enemies materially unfits her" for such inclusion. At the same time there was considerable suspicion over just how different the reorganized LASS would be. "The fact that the new organized Women's Anti-Slavery Society . . . secured Rev. George B. Cheever to lecture for them induces" the belief, wrote William C. Nell, "that some one among them wears Julia Griffiths [*sic*] mantle."[29] That fall, Griffiths briefly returned to Rochester, thus convincing the LASS's detractors that the new organization was no different from the old.[30]

While once more rejecting perfectionist alliances, female ultraists were experiencing dissension in their own ranks. As Lucy Coleman toured the Midwest, she longed for Amy Post's companionship—"You like to travel," she wrote, "and the scenery is so strange, I wish you could see it." But she charged others among the circle, specifically the

[26] J. Elizabeth Jones to Amy Post, 4 February 1856, IAPFP.
[27] William Titus to Isaac Post, 28 February 1856, IAPFP.
[28] Sarah E. Thayer to Amy Post, 23 December 1857, IAPFP.
[29] William C. Nell to Amy Post, 12 April 1856 and 23 August 1857, IAPFP.
[30] Sarah Hallowell Willis to Amy Post, 7 October 1857, IAPFP.

Burtises, with "nonsense," berating them for wanting *"to practice 'free love' "* and for placing *"responsibility"* for their actions *"on the Spirits of Heaven, or Hell."*[31] Susan B. Anthony, also on a lecture tour, was satisfied with her own efforts and voiced no complaints about her Rochester supporters, simply informing them of upcoming arrangements and seeking their attendance at her meetings.[32] Yet Anthony's frequently curt orders and her relatively late conversion to the woman's rights cause led more than one local activist to claim that they did "not like S B Anthony at all" and were not about to install her as chief organizer.[33]

Moreover, as human and financial resources dwindled and divisions intensified, ultraists were faced with a proliferation of social problems. War, intemperance, sectarian education, Indian rights, woman's rights, and slavery remained central to ultraist endeavors. The last of these required ever greater attention as the Kansas-Nebraska crisis, the Fugitive Slave Law, the Dred Scott decision, and similar events heightened abolitionists' horror while at the same time seemed to promise the downfall of the corrupt system that sustained the cursed institution. In addition, the ultraist Friends of Human Progress announced in 1854 that "the land monopoly" was "the chief cause . . . preventing the masses from acquiring homes," thereby producing "poverty and crime."[34] The following year, the Friends resolved to work for health reform—including the education of "the young of both sexes" in "Anatomy and Physiology"—and for prison reform. On the latter topic, they concluded that "men are not invested by God with the right to *punish* those who violate the precepts of morality," but should seek to reform their character, exercising "only such a degree of non-injurious force as is absolutely indispensable."[35] Protests against capital punishment soon followed.

It was this last campaign that temporarily reunited male political abolitionists with ultraists. On 19 December 1857 Rochesterians re-

[31] Lucy Coleman to Amy Post, 5 March 1857, IAPFP.

[32] See esp. Susan B. Anthony to Amy Post, 2 June 1857, encouraging ultraist attendance at the annual meeting of the Friends of Human Progress, which ultraists had founded, IAPFP.

[33] S. E. Thayer to Amy Post, 23 December 1857, IAPFP. See also, Sarah Hallowell Willis, Obituary, 1914, Unitarian Society of Rochester Records, University of Rochester, and Lucy Coleman, *Reminiscences*, p. 18.

[34] YMCF, *Proceedings, 1854*, p. 6.

[35] YMCF, *Proceedings of the Annual Meeting of Friends of Human Progress, Held at Waterloo, N.Y., on the Third, Fourth, and Fifth of the Sixth Month, 1855* (Syracuse: Evening Chronicle Print, 1855), pp. 20, 23.

ceived the news of the sensational murder of lawyer Charles W. Little by his wife and her brother, Ira Stout. The next spring, Stout was brought to trial. More than 150 townsmen were questioned before a jury was seated, during which a number of ultraist men announced their "consciencious [*sic*] scruples against bringing a man in guilty of murder" if execution was to be his end. The trial itself proceeded rapidly, and on the day of the summation, the court house "was full and . . . the stairs wer[e] crowded (so full that the plastering on the under-side cracked) all the way down to the street by the Hack stand, and the street from Fitzhugh street Bridge wall full all around the Court House, all trying to get a sight of Ira Stout."[36] The accused was found guilty and sentenced to be hung on 18 June 1858.

Efforts were immediately begun to commute his sentence to life in prison. Appeals to the court and petitions to the governor were strongly supported by both political and moral suasion abolitionists. They drew on antislavery principles in asserting that "life is the great primary and most precious and comprehensive of all human rights," the "continued possession" of which is not to be assumed or destroyed "by individuals separately, or combined in what is called Government."[37] The concerned and the curious crowded the jail throughout the spring to observe or converse with the condemned man. Among the first visitors were Sarah Burtis and Jenny Post, Amy's daughter-in-law, who offered Stout books, spiritual and spiritualist solace, and conversation. He "observed" to them that "it was a strange way to reform one, to kill them," encouraging their efforts to orchestrate his commutation.[38] Ultraist women continued to visit the jail, and each time "sympathies were so aroused" that the whole circle "felt it the more." Some considered "the jury and Judge . . . equally guilty with Ira Stout," while others felt "as guilty as they," having not earlier "bestirred [them]selves for the abolition of so horrible a law." Whatever their particular sympathies in the case, most did not wish to suggest that their consideration was "for this man above others" but rather for the practice itself, which was barbarous in any circumstance.[39] The June

[36] Jacob Kirby Post to Amy Post, 25 April 1858, IAPFP. See also, John Dewey, comp., *Rochester and the Post Express: A History of the City from the Earliest Times* (Rochester: Post Express Printing, 1895), p. 33. Mrs. Little was tried separately for manslaughter, which did not carry a capital sentence.

[37] *Liberator*, 22 October 1858.

[38] Isaac Post to Amy Post, 29 April 1858, IAPFP.

[39] Sarah Hallowell Willis to Amy Post, 9 May 1858, IAPFP.

sentence was postponed, and a protest meeting in October brought together Frederick Douglass, Samuel D. Porter, William C. Bloss, Susan B. Anthony, and Amy Post among others to fight on for a full commutation. The battle was lost, however, and Stout was executed two weeks later.

A winter petition campaign to abolish the death penalty never materialized, and the abolition of slavery once again emerged as the paramount issue in both political and moral suasion camps. A series of antislavery lectures, by Antoinette Brown Blackwell, Parker Pillsbury, and others who appealed to a wide spectrum of abolitionists, ushered in the new year and strengthened the still uneasy alliance between third-party men and ultraists. Perfectionist women maintained their distance, however, as their ultraist sisters took increasingly visible and vocal stands on public platforms. Even in the fall of 1859 when Douglass was threatened with arrest in connection with John Brown's raid on Harper's Ferry, his LASS supporters did not speak out publicly but worked quietly behind the scenes while their male kin and female competitors expounded on Brown's martyrdom in a memorial meeting on the day of his execution. Despite their statements celebrating Brown's commitment and courage, however, both political abolitionists and ultraists were ambivalent about the martyr's use of violence, and they groped uncertainly for some nonviolent resolution to the national crisis.[40]

The Republican party offered one of the few alternatives. Its leaders promised, if elected, to end slavery's expansion into the territories, though they would not attempt to abolish it where it already existed. Would confining the institution to the South gradually expunge it altogether? Were there sufficient reasons for antislavery men to cast their ballots for Lincoln, knowing that in his victory, abolition was by no means assured and war was possible? Local abolitionists commiserated with each other as they struggled to weigh expediency and principle, to balance promises of nonextension with the potential for war. Frederick Douglass was a major force in bringing the two abolitionist factions together in 1860, as he had been central to their division a decade earlier. From his refuge in England after the Harper's

[40] In *Frederick Douglass' Paper,* 15 April 1859, Douglass praised John Brown's work in the antislavery movement and his personal courage. Douglass was later sought for questioning about the Harper's Ferry raid and friends feared for his safety in the panic of the moment. He escaped to Canada and then to England, where he remained until his name was cleared.

Ferry raid, Douglass wrote to Amy Post seeking to heal old wounds. She received his letter on the evening of 12 February and replied the following morning. Thankful for Douglass's words of reconciliation, Amy lamented "that we have lost five years of *beautiful, joyous* friendship," but begged Douglass not to despair "about all those scenes of the past, so unspeakably painful. . . . [We] shall resolve to be unspeakably good" now. "Please give my love to Mrs. Julia [Griffiths] Crofts," she added. "Tell her there is so much which we have known, to make us love each other and the rest should be forgotten."[41] While the exchange of letters could not heal the breach between the factions, it foreshadowed new efforts at cooperation between perfectionist and ultraist women.

The dramatic events of the late 1850s—revivals, recession and recovery, resurgences of proslavery legislation and antislavery sentiments, murder and "treason" and the execution of their perpetrators—reshaped the concerns of female activists. New institutions and associations were established, new issues and tactics introduced, and the potential for alliances resurrected. Yet in the same period there were also evidences of unrelenting estrangement. Throughout the 1850s, for instance, the CS had placed poor, sick women in the home and in 1858 had enlisted HF leaders in petitioning for a refuge for female juveniles. Then in 1859 the CS board rejected a merger proposal from the HF, resolving "that we will pursue our course as usual, noiselessly, economically, and consistently. . . ."[42] The HF soon assured its supporters that rejection by the city's benevolent leaders would not push the association into the arms of the ultraists. In a *JHF* article entitled "Common Sense," an anonymous contributor complained first of women "who prefer to be a little ridiculous for the sake of being patronized and protected" and therefore take no part in the world's affairs. She then turned to condemnations of "strong-minded" women who "fling themselves with heroic ardor into the work of abolishing . . . all mental difference between man and woman. They will confer equality upon us," she continued disapprovingly. "Fortunately," she concluded, "there is for sensible women, a medium between the doll and

[41] Amy Post to Frederick Douglass, 13 February 1860; Frederick Douglass to Amy Post, [1860], IAPFP.
[42] Amy Hanmer-Croughton, "The Rochester Female Charitable Society," Rochester Historical Society, *Publications* 9 (1930), p. 79.

the Amazon." These women, modeled no doubt on those in the HF, "understand what [their] powers are" and "take an intelligent interest in the great world."[43]

As though anticipating the critique, the female members of the Friends of Human Progress provided ample evidence of their Amazonian bent at the 1859 annual meeting. They insisted that both established religion and government were proslavery and antiwoman, designating the latter institution as an "abomination" and the former as "superstitious, idolatrous, and [full of] atrocious absurdities, . . . a wild hallucination and an utter futility." It was these institutions that branded blacks with the "awful curse of slavery—both physical and mental" and women with "false and depressing notions of dependence and inferiority." For the black, the Friends sought not only emancipation but also the end of "what is popularly called prejudice against color." For woman, they proclaimed her "right to engage in any and every useful vocation" since her "rights are co-extensive with her being, and are bounded only by her capacity." Indeed, the key point of debate was whether the enslavement of blacks or of women "was the greatest atrocity in the land."[44]

In general, it was differencs of emphasis that separated benevolent and perfectionist women, whereas it was differences of ideology that forestalled alliances between either group and ultraists. Nevertheless, within each network problems arose during this period that suggested the need for a broader appeal. Among ultraists, debates over the use of force and the relative importance of blacks' versus woman's rights divided the small circle of coworkers. Isaac Post, for instance, stood "his ground well on the peace question—amid all the warlike utterances of his Garrison friends," while Amy Post prayed for "the 'restoration of freedom of speech'" within ultraist convocations.[45] Both feared that zeal for one cause, especially if that cause was war, would fragment ultraist forces just at the moment of judgment. The LASS offered neither refuge nor competition to ultraist women as war ap-

[43]*JHF,* 1 September 1860.

[44]YMCF, *Proceedings of the Annual Meeting of the Friends of Human Progress, Held at Waterloo, Seneca Co., N.Y., on the Third, Fourth, and Fifth of June, 1859* (Rochester: C. W. Hebard, 1859), pp. 5–7, 18. Lucy Coleman and Frederick Douglass argued that the slave's oppression was worse; Lewis Burtis and a Dr. Wellington argued that women's oppression was worse. Others joined in the debate but were not identified as to their position on this question.

[45]William C. Nell to Amy Post, 8 July 1860, and Frederick Douglass to Amy Post, [1860], IAPFP.

proached. A small circle of evangelical and Unitarian women continued to meet monthly, claiming to be the "only Ladies' Society which makes help to fugitives a part of its duties." Without the presence of either Douglass or Griffiths, however, the association floundered.[46] Even LASS leader Mrs. Porter directed her greatest efforts toward assuring the HF's continued prosperity. After the CS's refusal to merge with the HF, Mrs. Porter and Mrs. Livingston suggested "altering the Constitution [of the HF] to admit Aged Women in to the Institution." By 1860 the home offered "lifetime care" to a "worthy and respectable class" of elderly women for the payment of one hundred dollars in advance.[47] Presenting far fewer problems than their younger coresidents, this new group of "friendless women" soon predominated in the home's population and completed the transition of the HF from perfectionist to benevolent institution.

Rochester's benevolent societies had their own problems to resolve. The growth of the city demanded the expansion of charitable efforts, annually increasing the pressures on the CS and OAA to find new funds and new workers, at the same time that the IS and the city hospital syphoned off resources in new directions. In 1860 the OAA suffered a major fire that damaged a barn, the roof of one wing, and the main building. Reciting the expenses entailed in repairs, the board noted that "contributions in money or supplies [would] be peculiarly acceptable" that year. Because of the fire, the OAA aided fewer children than usual and discontinued their infant school for several months; at the same time, the board recorded the largest number of deaths among its charges in a single year (five) and received the first serious complaints of their "matron's management of the family."[48] The CS's problems were less severe, resulting mainly from the retirement, illness, or death of the society's perennial leaders. There were also complaints in the 1860 annual report that several of the CS's eighty-four district visitors had neglected their duties, while some of the "most judicious and Valuable" workers failed to provide the board with written reports of their labors.[49] The board that year included "more than one of the [CS's] earliest members," whose lengthy and devoted service they hoped

[46]*Frederick Douglass' Paper*, 11 September 1859.

[47]HF, Minute Book, 6 April 1859, FHP; *JHF*, 1 September 1860.

[48]OAA, Annual Report, 1860, Scrapbook, HCCP. See also, OAA, Minute Book, 31 January and 28 February 1860, HCCP.

[49]CS, *Charter, Constitution, By-Laws, and Officers of the Rochester Female Charitable Society (for the Relief of Sick Poor), Together with Its History and Annual Reports for the Year 1860* (Rochester: C. D. Tracy, 1860), p. 15.

would offer "a valuable suggestion to those who are comparatively young in its service." Yet these new members were apparently too few, and the directors noted in 1860, as they had sixteen years earlier, that the "prosperity, nay the very existence of the Society" must "be committed to a new generation."

In November 1860 Lincoln was elected president of the United States, receiving only a minority of the vote nationwide but a clear majority in Rochester. Though no female activist cast a ballot for Lincoln and most deemed electoral politics either inappropriate or unworthy of their attention, the Republican victory dramatically affected the public as well as the private lives of Rochester women. The war that followed upon Lincoln's ascension to office increased the labor of women, North and South, in households, hospitals, fields, and factories. It demanded dollars as well as drudgery, created jobs as well as the widows to fill them, and pressed nonactive women into public service and activist women into choosing between increased competition or cooperation.

When Lincoln declared war in April 1861, ultraists immediately claimed a role for themselves in publicizing the abolitionist potential of the conflict. Two months after the firing on Fort Sumter, Amy Post invited western New York friends to a "4th of July celebration and Anti-Slavery Pic-Nic" in the city, featuring Parker Pillsbury, Giles Stebbins, Elizabeth Cady Stanton, and Frederick Douglass. Enjoining her sister laborers to attend, Amy contended, "The abolitionists surely have a work to do now, in influencing and directing this bloody struggle, that it may end in Emancipation, as the only basis of a true and permanent peace."[50] Douglass also pleaded for unity, congratulating his old foe Stephen Foster for attempting to "re-unite the scattered anti-slavery elements. . . ." He claimed it was essential not to consider blame for earlier divisions but to "produce one solid abolition organization, who will use all the powers of the Federal as well as the State Governments . . . for the abolition of slavery."[51] Yet many ultraists, especially female ultraists, were reluctant to abandon their pacifist principles. In a moving speech to the June 1861 meeting of the Friends of Human Progress, Catharine Fish Stebbins, who had lost an infant to disease just a year earlier, now confronted her brother's choice to face

[50] Amy Post to [?], 18 June 1861, IAPFP.
[51] Quoted in Philip Foner, ed., *The Life and Writings of Frederick Douglass, Pre-Civil War Decade, 1850–1860* (New York: International, 1950), p. 524.

death voluntarily in the Union army. Torn by "great and conflicting emotions," she argued in opposition to her brother's choice and her husband Giles's prowar pronouncements. The oppressive institution of slavery, she contended, could not be ended by the enslavement of thousands to the oppressive institution of war.[52] With war already under way, however, most ultraists fought to make it a war for emancipation while they aided "contrabands," those slaves who escaped into Union territory.

It was in this latter endeavor that ultraist women finally joined forces with their perfectionist counterparts. In October 1862 the LASS employed Julia Wilbur to serve as its agent among the contrabands. She was sent first to Washington, D.C., and from there was directed by the "Commissaries for the Contrabands" to Alexandria, Virginia. A few days before setting off on this journey, Julia Wilbur had stopped by the Post & Willis pharmacy, where she spoke to Amy Post. The latter offered to "make an effort to send" garments and other items to be distributed among the needy blacks in the South. After settling at the boardinghouse of Mrs. Kimball, a former acquaintance of the Posts, Wilbur wrote to Amy of conditions in Alexandria. She described an "old Slave pen" in which there were "20 women and children, many of them sick;" they were "huddling around" a little fire and "were wrapped in old rags." After further depictions of the misery there, she pleaded *"Do send something"* and asked Amy to circulate the letter among LASS members to save the time of her writing to all the various friends of the cause.[53] Amy Post immediately began to solicit goods for the LASS agent and tried to convince one of her single coworkers to join Wilbur in the field. Her willingness to labor for the Alexandria project may have been augmented by the news that one of Wilbur's coworkers in the city was ex-slave Harriet Brent Jacobs, a guest in the Post home ten years earlier.[54]

Through an informal network of sewing circles and collectors that stretched across central and western New York, ultraist and perfec-

---

[52] YMCF, *Proceedings of the Thirteenth Yearly Meeting of Friends of Human Progress, Held at Waterloo, Seneca Co., N.Y., on the Thirty-first day of May and the First and Second days of June, 1861* (Cortland: VanSlyck and Ford's Power Press Print, 1861), pp. 26–32.

[53] Julia Wilbur to Amy Post, 5 November 1862, IAPFP. For further descriptions by Wilbur, see LASS, *Twelfth Annual Report* (Rochester: A. Strong, 1863), pp. 9–11.

[54] Harriet Brent Jacobs's presence in Alexandria was noted in LASS, *Twelfth Annual Report*, p. 14. She was sent to Alexandria by the Hicksite branch of the New York City Society of Friends.

tionist women shared the burdens of caring for Alexandria's black population. In addition, for the first time these women gained some of the political support that had always been accorded benevolent enterprises. In Alexandria, Mr. Pierce and Dr. Ripley, both of Rochester, were among those appointed to direct contraband efforts, while Republicans at home felt that it was at least politically expedient to support Wilbur's labors. For two years Amy Post served as one of the major conduits for letters and supplies shipped from western New York to Virginia, though neither she nor the LASS could induce anyone else to join Wilbur in the distribution of those goods. The network of support stretched to Quakers Emily Howland and Anna Searing in central New York, to Post family members on Long Island, and to coworkers in Massachusetts and Philadelphia; at home it included the Porters, Foggs, Galushas, Cornells, Posts, Hallowells, Anthonys, and Fishes. With the assistance of church and government agents in Alexandria and of the National Relief Association for Freedmen in New York City, this band of western New York workers furnished freed men and women with clothing, food, medical care, housing, and education.

HF women also responded quickly to the demands of war, though initially they spent more time determining women's duty to the crisis than actually fulfilling it.[55] These women, along with their sisters in the OAA, IS, city hospital, and CS considered the soldier and his dependents, rather than the slave, the primary objects of concern. The *JHF* regularly printed war news, selections from the *Soldier's Hymn Book*, warnings of intemperance in army ranks, and notices of fund-raising events to sustain the war effort. Yet HF leaders simultaneously worried that the "present state of the country" would "lead our kind friends to forget us." The death of Mr. Selah Mathews, one of the HF's most devoted and wealthy supporters, in August 1861 heightened their fears, which were confirmed by the announcement of a three-thousand-dollar debt the next year.[56] The OAA faced similar difficulties, particularly as war boosted both the numbers of orphans and the cost of caring for them. In September 1862 the OAA admitted its first war orphan, Anna Spall, whose father was killed at Sharpsburg and whose mother was "enfeebled." Within two months, a committee was established by the

---

[55] *JHF*, 1 April 1861, reprinted an article entitled "Women's Duty to the Crisis" from *Century* magazine. Similar articles appeared throughout the next year.

[56] Ibid., 1 June and 1 August 1861, 1 June 1862.

OAA board to "solicit contributions to the amount of $3000 to remove the debt of the Institution."[57]

About the same time, the CS, IS, HF, and OAA renewed their appeals for a facility for female delinquents. While the financial situation was not auspicious, benevolent leaders apparently feared an increase in that class of public charges after fathers and brothers left for war. While this joint petition produced no better results than the prewar request for a similar institution, the appeals of individual associations received hearty responses. HF fears were calmed at their annual donation day in November 1861 when "war troubles" and "hard times" were seemingly forgotten as both "city and country" residents provided bountifuls gifts to the home. In January 1862, the *JHF* enthusiastically announced the engagement of Mr. Gough "to deliver *an old fashioned Temperance Address . . . for the benefit of the Home.*" Two months later, Rev. George Dana Boardman presented a course of lectures, the first on benevolent institutions in Paris, for the benefit of the city's "four principal Protestant Charitable associations"—the CS, OAA, HF, and IS.[58] In summer 1863 both the OAA and the HF reported with "heart-felt thanks" to God and "our beneficient citizens" the complete repayment of their debts. In addition, the OAA announced that during the year it had cared for 130 orphans, including "nine little ones whose fathers have gone forth to fight for their country."[59] During the same year, the CS increased its receipts while actually curtailing its expenditures. The *JHF* concluded by September of 1863 that the war effort, particularly the recent victories, actually heightened interest in local benevolent enterprises.[60]

It was not until the summer of 1863 that Rochester women outside antislavery circles first focused their full attention on the war effort. The previous summer, visitor Elizabeth Eaton wrote to her husband Amos that "every thing is war, war, war, except the wedding, the marriage of Miss Clark to the returned missionary, Rev'd. Mr. Marsh." A week later, she reported on a meeting "to glorify Gen. —— somebody. . . . Rochester is very zealous for the war, . . . money & men are freely given & there is much zeal & activity for the Union—*some zeal*

[57] OAA, Minute Book, 30 September and 25 November 1862, HCCP.
[58] *JHF*, 1 December 1861, 1 March 1862.
[59] OAA, Annual Report, 1863, Scrapbook, HCCP.
[60] CS, Minute Book, 1850–1860, summary of receipts and expenditures, CSP; *JHF* 1 September 1863.

for liberty."[61] The observations of Mrs. Eaton betokened the war enthusiasm in her native city but also indicated its limits in the early years. The juxtaposition of war and weddings suggests that some Rochesterians, most likely women, saw the war as an exciting but distant event. At the same time, the eager contribution of men and money and the zeal for Union over liberty revealed that Rochesterians' primary concern was military victories rather than military victims.

By 1863, however, local and national events converged to bring hundreds of Rochester women into war work as the war's casualties multiplied. Again, it was antislavery women who led the way in new organizations and projects. Lincoln's Emancipation Proclamation, put into effect in January, led directly to the organization of the National Women's Loyal League under the auspices of Elizabeth Cady Stanton and Susan B. Anthony. The association, the leadership of which was generally identified with the woman's rights movement, promised to suspend feminist activities and concentrate on petitioning Congress for a Constitutional amendment to abolish slavery. Amy Post was invited to direct the Rochester campaign, and she and her coworkers did convince large numbers of women to sign the appeal, adding their names to the national list of four hundred thousand women.[62] Lincoln's proclamation also boosted the morale of local laborers who were working on behalf of the freed men and women in Alexandria and coincided with ultraist efforts to transform zeal for union into zeal for liberty through a winter lecture series that featured ex-slave Sojourner Truth. It was the "remarkable interest in religion, manifested in Rochester" in spring 1863 that raised perfectionists' hopes of translating religious zeal into work for the freed people.[63] By the summer, the city was indeed flooded with new war workers, but rather than finding its ranks expanded by them, the LASS had its roster depleted by the call to join the new Soldier's Aid Society.

The reestablishment of financial security within the OAA and HF, the Emancipation Proclamation, the National Loyal League campaign, the winter lecture series, and the spring revivals together with a string

[61] Elizabeth Selden Eaton to Amos Eaton, 26 August and 2 September 1862, in McKelvey, "Letters," pp. 120–21.
[62] Susan B. Anthony to Amy Post, 13 April 1863, IAPFP; Ellen Carol DuBois, *Feminism and Suffrage: The Emergence of an Independent Women's Movement in America, 1848–1869* (Ithaca: Cornell University Press, 1978), pp. 53, 73.
[63] *JHF,* 1 May 1863.

of victories by Union forces heightened women's willingness to cloak themselves in the mantle of public patriotism. Yet like their male counterparts, most female Rochesterians had far greater interest in union than in liberty and in soldiers and their dependents than in slaves. The Rochester SAS was one of hundreds of Northern auxiliaries to the newly established United States Sanitary Commission, which was deemed more respectable to work for than the feminist-tainted Loyal League. Where the latter gained women's signatures on petitions, the new organization claimed women's *"head, heart, and hand"* in service to "the sick and wounded" on distant battlefields. *The Soldier's Aid,* a magazine published by the local SAS, printed news of the Sanitary Commission, of other New York aid societies, and of local soldiers. In its first issue of June 1863, the editor outlined the duties of women in the present crisis and demanded their immediate contributions of "money, materials, or labor" to offset the popular image of the northern woman as less devoted to the cause than her southern sister. The SAS was to be "co-existent with the war itself," its members, like the soldiers they assisted, recognizing "that the service required . . . is something more than the result of occasional spasms of patriotism; that it is *work,* undisguised, continuous work, that we must render."[64]

The SAS attracted many women into war work who had "hitherto avoided" such "positions and responsibilities before the public" as "altogether distasteful." The society was led, however, by experienced women from the IS, HF, and LASS. The 1 January 1864 issue of the *JHF* reported on a December bazaar at Corinthian Hall for the aid of sick and wounded soldiers. Some of the HF's members were prominent on the Ladies of the Bazaar committee along with representatives of the nearly complete city hospital and the IS. Their efforts were better rewarded than at any previous women's fund-raising event: ten thousand dollars was raised on this occasion. In the following months, the IS merged its editorial skills with those of the SAS to publish a monthly journal, the *Industrial School Advocate and Soldier's Aid.* The major fund-raising event of the IS, a summer strawberry festival, was quickly adapted to SAS service with an appeal made in the *Aid*'s 12 July 1865 issue on behalf of soldiers and the destitute children they left behind. In both the circulation of their journal and their fund-

64 *The Soldier's Aid* (Rochester), 19 June 1863.

raising appeals, the SAS worked through the network of rural and small-town auxiliaries that had aided first the FMRS and later the HF and IS.

Simultaneously, the HF pointed to its work with war widows to boost its own appeals. Before the home's annual donation day in 1864, the *JHF* ran an article "Martyrs at Home," which described the situations of wives, mothers, and daughters left by soldiers and reminded the public that the home aided those who gave their most precious offering to the Union cause. That year, the HF's annual report told of "blessed work accomplished—of an enlarged sphere of action—of great sources of encouragement in every department of labor—of increasing success and prosperity—and of abundant and unnumbered favors and mercies."[65] In the fall the IS added a fund-raising reception to its strawberry festival donation, and the proceeds allowed both the IS and the SAS to expand their labors.[66] The city hospital was formally dedicated in January 1864, though it had begun caring for returning soldiers a few months earlier. In the spring the *Hospital Review* appeared, serving as the editorial arm of the hospital and containing considerable news of its parent association, the CS.

During the war years, the expansion of benevolent efforts was paralled by the growth of efforts on behalf of the freed people. Though the LASS lost the labor of some to the SAS, those who remained intensified their efforts with the assistance of ultraists. "A retrospective view" of 1864 gave LASS managers "the comforting assurance that much [had] been done towards the destruction of Slavery." With funds supplied by western New York and British friends, Julia Wilbur established a freedmen's school and provided newly arrived contrabands with food, clothing, and medical care. Wilbur also distributed thirty-six "boxes, barrels, and packages of clothing and bedding" donated by the LASS, the Ladies Relief Society (probably the ultraist branch of the enterprise), and friends in central New York, Worcester, Massachusetts, and Philadelphia.[67]

During the same period that LASS labors were expanded, LASS members' faith in the government was declining in direct relation to their contact with federal officials. "It has seemed at times," wrote Maria Porter in the annual report, "that opportunities for striking effec-

[65] *JHF*, 1 November 1864.
[66] Peck, *Semi-Centennial History*, p. 424.
[67] LASS, *Thirteenth Annual Report* (Rochester: Rochester Democrat Steam Printing House, 1864), pp. 2–6.

tive blows for Freedom have not been embraced by the Government, and we who have labored so long and earnestly in the cause, and have it so warmly at heart, have chafed at the slowness of those in power." In the following pages, Julia Wilbur described her disgust at learning "that *colored women,* for punishment, were put naked into the shower bath" on the outside of the government holding facility and hearing "a young corporal there say 'we don't call them women. . . .'" Nor was Wilbur always pleased with government-appointed physicians and clergy, several of whom she labeled "racist."[68]

Yet perfectionist abolitionists retained their belief that government and church, when functioning properly, were essential to the slave's liberation. Along with stories of ineptitude, greed, and racism on the part of political appointees, Wilbur pointed to signs of improvement, some engineered by her own lobbying of government officials. In addition, partial blame was laid on the freed men and women themselves, many of whom Wilbur characterized as "ignorant and superstitious," though admitting that such characteristics were bound to result from lifelong enslavement. Her Rochester coworkers insisted they were "thankful for the past and hopeful for the future, sure that out of this terrible war which has made desolate so many hearts and homes, . . . out of the mistakes of Generals—will come forth at least a nation humbled by experience, purified by suffering, glorified by the blossoming of a new and truer Freedom, making our beautiful and widespread land indeed the 'Home of the Free.'"[69]

Even ultraists were somewhat hopeful of the war's ultimate effects. They saw "a great advancement in liberality" during the war years and, especially after the Emancipation Proclamation, were "sometimes amused" in hearing former foes assert "we are all abolitionists now." Such sentiments could be vexing as well as amusing, however, since "prejudice and intolerance" were "not entirely removed in respect to the negro;" many who claimed to be the slave's friend were nonetheless "weary in hearing equality spoken of." Indeed, speakers such as Theodore Tilton, Wendell Phillips, and Garrison, who "insisted on this [equality] as the duty of the country and the right of the colored man" were accused of "advocating amalgamation" and shouted down.[70] The ultraists seemed to believe that major advances in the direction of

[68] Ibid., pp. 3, 10–11, 13.
[69] Ibid., pp. 21, 3.
[70] Mary Robbins Post to Amy Post, 22 March [186-], IAPFP.

equality would have to await the war's end. In the interim, they donated labor and goods to the freed people, petitioned for the Constitutional abolition of slavery, sustained lecturers who advocated racial justice, and maintained women's right to work equally with men in these endeavors.

In the spring of 1865 the Civil War ended. The need for aid—for soldiers, orphans, widows, and freed people—did not. Indeed, the months after Lee's surrender at Appomattox were among the busiest for the LASS and SAS, and the situation was exacerbated by a severe Genessee River flood that submerged downtown Rochester in the spring, also necessitating major relief efforts. A three-man committee appointed by the common council collected nearly two thousand dollars to aid flood victims and turned the total amount over to the CS for distribution.[71] The CS's work in 1865 doubled their expenditures of either of the previous two years. Often the CS visitors found that flood and war relief were combined. "Mrs. Kenflick, a soldier's widow, lost a great deal" in the flood, and her oldest children were now "suffering from the Ague from exposure." Another soldier's wife who had "received no intelligence from her husband in nearly two years" was given clothing for herself and her children.[72] The cases multiplied rapidly.

It was, however, the very multiplication of cases that secured benevolent women's place in the community. In the post–Civil War years, CS, OAA, HF, IS, and city hospital efforts all expanded. The CS and HF continued to employ private donations and volunteer labor in providing social services to the community, while the two newest institutions were directed by boards of female volunteers but were more dependent on state funds and paid labor. The OAA combined these two modes of operation, appealing to local citizens for support but largely dependent on state funds for their actual expenses. The combination seemed to work well during the war years. In 1865 the OAA cared for 152 orphans, the largest number ever received in a single year, and they maintained these high levels of service for the next two years.

Moreover, all the city's benevolent institutions benefited from the demobilization of the SAS. In the final year of the war, the SAS noted that they had not at first included the word "annual" in their constitution because they believed their efforts would be short-lived. Having

[71] Hanmer-Croughton, "Rochester Female Charitable Society," p. 90.
[72] CS, Visitor's Report, 1865, CSP.

experienced " 'ways of peace and pleasantness' " in their youth, the younger members of the association recalled that when war began they "turned with aversion from this new order of things." Yet beginning with a sewing circle, they "imperceptibly glided into new channels of labor . . . which the exigencies of our rapidly increasing armies demanded of us." With the flowering of "large numbers of 'Aid Societies' in adjoining neighborhoods and towns," the Rochester SAS found itself "occupying the position of a *'Central Society'* connected with a noble band of *Workers* on the one hand, and *Receivers* on the other." These efforts, which produced "a feeling of awe and reverence . . . never felt for human labor before," led wartime workers into wider public services when the SAS disbanded in 1866.[73]

In their more high-flown moments, these new SAS workers claimed that the Lord and their Revolutionary foremothers called them into service as "the first traitorous shot reverberated from the distant wall of Sumpter [*sic*]." When Lincoln called for seventy-five thousand troops, "from every loyal woman's heart arose the cry, 'LORD, what wilt thou have *me* do, ...'" Then tales of grandmothers' "sacrifices in the memorable war of the 'Revolution' " were recalled and "with one accord we began to ply our needles . . . and to furnish comforts and delicacies for the days of sickness and suffering, of which we began to have a dim foreshadowing."[74] The sickness and suffering, however, were nearly two years old when the SAS was formed, the Lord apparently being heard more clearly in the local revivals of 1863 than upon Lincoln's call for recruits in 1861. Moreover, for most of the young SAS leaders, the Misses Whittlesey, Gould, Selden, Starr, and others, the sight of their own mothers' public service must have been more compelling than memories of their grandmothers.

The entry of this new generation of women into charitable enterprises changed the collective character of benevolent leadership. Partly because of their youth, former SAS workers introduced a contingent of single women into societies dominated for three decades by married or widowed women. With the retirement or death of early workers, the new activists shifted the balance in the societies toward locally born and bred leadership. Yet more of these young women would leave the city for a period of their adulthood—to travel, teach, or obtain a college education. With the building of new churches and

---

[73] *Industrial School Advocate and Soldier's Aid,* 12 July 1865.
[74] Ibid.

the movement of elites into outlying wards and towns, the new leaders would also prove more religiously and residentially diverse, but their ties to local centers of power were in no way weakened. Indeed, the concentration of that power, especially economic power, in the hands of a few families, increased after the war. The need for material support from male kin would lessen in the late nineteenth century as local, state, and federal governments began to assume more of the expenses for social welfare services, but at least into the 1890s local benevolent leadership would remain within the hands of the most affluent.

Those circles of affluence contained more families in the 1820s than in the 1850s yet comprised a smaller portion of the city's population. Since all benevolent societies drew officers from the same circle, the network of benevolent leadership remained tightly woven. As early leaders were removed from office, their daughters and daughters-in-law stretched their talents across the CS, OAA, HF, IS, and city hospital. The Wards, Strongs, Chapins, Brewsters, Buells, Rochesters, Elys, Pecks, Bissells, Goulds, and Whittleseys along with newer families bound to the city's pioneers by business or marital partnerships, directed urban charity.

Despite the increase in volunteers, funds, and state support, and the intergenerational continuity of leadership, benevolent societies faced a number of problems in the post–Civil War years that limited or redirected their efforts. The OAA and HF faced these problems first, foreshadowing dramatic changes in social welfare practices in the last decades of the century. Especially for those associations that managed institutions but depended on private donations, finances remained a perennial problem. In one important way the situation worsened after the war. The development of a market economy that had released affluent women for benevolent labors in the first half of the century now so dominated the exchange of goods and services that cash became absolutely critical to institutional management. The home and asylum, which in the 1840s and 1850s had supplied their tables with produce and meat donated by rural supporters, budgeted increasingly large cash outlays for such items after the war. During the war emergency and under the relative prosperity it bestowed on benevolent institutions, the HF and OAA along with the IS and city hospital expanded their services and became more dependent on hired help. In the late 1860s the curtailment of services and the release of hired help seemed essential as economy measures but often generated criticism from employees and the public. The alternative of maintaining services and keeping on help frequently led to declines in the quality of work performed and in the hours and wages of employees, which proved equally distressing to the community and placed some benevolent institutions on the defensive for the first time since their founding.

Management problems were rarely only a matter of finances. In some cases, the clientele needing assistance changed; in others, it was the expectations of relatives, supporters, or city and state officials that underwent a transformation. Just before the Civil War, the HF had decided to offer a permanent residence for elderly women while retaining its initial program of providing a temporary refuge for young women. By 1865 the association began to phase out its original plan, claiming that "the times have brought great changes in the class which this institution was designed to benefit." Having discovered that several "servant girls and young women" who came to the home seeking employment had proved a disappointment to their employers, the HF board concluded that any girl who could not find employment on her own and therefore needed HF intervention "to procure work" was probably "unworthy." In addition, too many woman came to the home without recommendations or character references and many refused to take jobs as domestics if it meant moving to the country. This caused annoyance to HF supporters and led some to denounce the home. The HF board thus resolved to close their employment service for "friendless women" and to emphasize the care of the elderly over the rescue of the young.[75]

Because the OAA's charges were younger, they had fewer problems of discipline and employment. Rather, complaints about the OAA originated with parents, the city's overseer of public welfare or the Poor Master, and the city physician and spread to the larger community. At the beginning of the war the OAA had received its first complaints about the practices of its matron, Mrs. Clark, who was in charge of household management and discipline.[76] Whether for this or other reasons, a few cases occurred of mothers wishing to remove their children from the asylum, which the OAA board fought each time on the basis of the parent's unsuitability. In December 1866, however, the city's Poor Master accused Mrs. Clark of being an unsuitable guardian and "refus[ed] to send any more children to the Asylum." He claimed

[75] *JHF,* 1 October 1865.
[76] OAA, Minute Book, 31 January 1860 and 31 May 1864, HCCP.

"that a very strong prejudice exists in the community against its interior management."[77] An investigation by an OAA committee revealed that many people in the community did, indeed, think "Mrs. Clark was too severe and did not give" the orphans "a sufficient quantity of nourishing food."[78] Mrs. Clark agreed to mend her ways, and the board was satisfied. Yet by 1868 the number of orphans cared for annually had dropped to sixty-nine and complaints resurfaced, this time from Dr. David Little, the city physician. Dr. Little threatened to resign from the OAA's service but was convinced instead to submit a report detailing proper dietary and medical care for children. In the fall, however, Mrs. Clark's resignation was finally obtained by the OAA board. Two years were then spent acquiring a new matron and re-establishing local credibility. During that period, however, a state investigation of the earlier complaints was finally launched, disrupting the OAA's attempt to put their difficulties behind them.[79]

By 1872 the OAA had recovered its reputation, its clientele, and its funds. During the process of recovery, however, the society was shunned by other benevolent organizations in the city and thus became more dependent on and responsible to state agencies.[80] At the same time, the OAA itself took a less charitable attitude toward anyone who tried to interfere in its internal management, especially "officious mothers coming to see [their children]," and decided to accept only full orphans over whom the OAA would have complete guardianship.[81] Thus, like the HF, the OAA tried to rid itself of its most troublesome charges and to place at least partial blame for its failings on those it assisted. At the same time, the HF and OAA found it necessary to assure local supporters and state investigators that they were not wasting funds on unworthy clients. As early as 1860 the CS had made a distinction between worthy and unworthy poor a part of its official report to the public. Its successes, the society claimed, derived from "its adherence to these two general rules: First, That it *affords* relief where relief is a public benefit. Secondly, That it *refuses* relief where

[77] Ibid., 26 December 1866. For cases of parental feuds, see 29 July 1862 and 31 May 1864.
[78] Ibid., 29 December 1866 and 4 January 1867.
[79] Ibid., 29 January, 26 May, and 30 June 1868 and 26 October 1869. Because the investigation was not begun until Clark's resignation had already been accepted by the board, it was generally inconclusive.
[80] Ibid., 31 May 1864 and 20 February 1867 provide examples of disputes with the HF and IS.
[81] Ibid., 25 January 1870.

relief is a public detriment." Thereby the community could be assured that their charity was not misdirected, nor "their sacred sympathies imposed upon."[82] With the growth of the city, the influx of immigrants, and the resurrection of community concern over intemperance, crime, and delinquency in the postwar years, benevolent associations found that the "unworthy" poor multiplied at a far faster rate than the "worthy." Limiting their services to the latter restricted the growth of the CS and HF. The OAA, IS, and city hospital, all of which needed state funds to expand their operations and the latter two of which could not limit themselves to "respectable" clients, maintained their vitality as organizations but lost some of their local and voluntary character. By the last quarter of the century they were making far fewer appeals to local philanthropy and replacing female volunteers with service workers and professionals.[83]

By the late 1860s the OAA, HF, and IS, all of which had been infused with perfectionist zeal at their founding, had become thoroughly benevolent institutions. None would ever achieve the status of the city's premier charitable society, but all now offered amelioration rather than perfection to their clients and the community. Only with the resurgence of revivalism in the late 1800s would religious zeal again dominate social reform movements the way it had in the 1830s. Nevertheless, some perfectionists retained more of that zeal than others, and in Rochester it was these women who sustained efforts on behalf of freed blacks. While the women of the LASS wished to improve the lot of blacks generally, the small circle of dedicated workers decided to concentrate their limited resources on the blacks of Alexandria. Julia Wilbur remained in that city for at least two years after the war's end, distributing goods, teaching school, and helping newly arrived families get settled. In Rochester the LASS turned to the private sale of its fund-raising items to known supporters, "as it [was] no longer deemed advisable to hold Fairs." The workers were not all discouraged, however, hoping that those who shifted their energies to the SAS in 1863 would now return to "the truly missionary duties of relieving the Freed people."[84]

[82] CS, *Charter*, p. 15.
[83] Female volunteers served as the managers of the OAA, IS, and city hospital into the twentieth century, but daily chores and care of inmates and patients were increasingly taken over by paid staff.
[84] LASS, *Fifteenth Annual Report of the Rochester Ladies' Anti-Slavery Society and Freedmen's Aid Society* (Rochester: William S. Falls, 1866), pp. 1–5.

Their hopes were not realized. By 1867 moves from the city and death left few members in the LASS, and few new women had been recruited. Meetings were still held every other week and collections of clothing and other items continued, though apathy increased with distance from the war, and LASS women were convinced that lectures and fairs were now generally better avoided if the object was aid to free blacks. The last annual report (1867) contained little news of Rochester activities, being almost exclusively a summary of conditions in Alexandria. Julia Wilbur observed that freedom and the vote were insufficient alone to improve the lot of newly emancipated slaves. Without changes in the attitudes of Southerners and of government officials, without economic assistance and education, and without blacks' own acceptance of new (white, middle-class) ideas about marriage, religion, and work, Wilbur saw little hope for true advancement. Despite these discouraging prospects, LASS members continued to assist free blacks by whatever means came to hand and rejoiced in every small triumph.[85]

With few resources to aid blacks, the LASS had to rely on Radical Republicans fulfilling promises to ensure blacks citizenship, suffrage, and economic assistance. Yet, having accepted subordination within third-party politics, perfectionist women could do little more than hope for such changes. Not only did perfectionist women have no leverage within the Republican party, most of their male kin lost out in postwar party battles to more pragmatic, experienced, and conservative politicians. The usually charitable Samuel D. Porter castigated the party's new leadership, calling them "chicken hearted white livered republicans" as he rejected political activity for religiously based reform efforts in the 1870s.[86]

A few perfectionist women began to voice, albeit indirectly and hedged with qualifications, the notion that women might be as well qualified as men to make political decisions after all. As early as 1856 former Rochester perfectionist Elizabeth Atkinson Finney revealed to Susan B. Anthony that the woman's rights movement had "the sympathy of a large proportion of the educated women. . . . In my circle," she confided, "I hear the movement much talked of & earnest hopes for

---

[85] See, for instance, Wilbur's moving account of a "colored woman" destroying the "old Slave Pen" with an axe, in ibid., p. 25.

[86] Samuel D. Porter to Lewis H. Morgan, Esq., 15 January 1869, in McKelvey, "Letters," p. 138. See McKelvey's note, ibid., on Porter's return to religious activism within Plymouth Congregational Church.

its success expressed. But," she added, "these women dare not speak out their sympathy," apparently for fear of being labeled "Infidels."[87] After observing numerous instances of governmental ineptitude during the war, Elizabeth Eaton came to a similar conclusion. Having complained to her husband about Secretary of War Stanton's lack of statemanship, Mrs. Eaton proclaimed it "an insult to *go by* E. C. Stanton *a woman* & take up the nomination for President" of Secretary Stanton "altho' he happens to wear a man's apparel." She quickly added, "do not mistake your wife however for a woman's rights woman. I am not, I only meet that fraternity at some points. I cannot swallow & digest the whole dish—without reservation."[88] Julia Wilbur, who also observed governmental ineptitude, never evidenced an interest in political power until she watched black men vote in municipal elections. "I confess," she wrote in her 1867 annual report, "to feeling a little jealous—the least bit humiliated. But, nevertheless, I looked on and rejoiced. . . ."[89]

Ultraists, however, refused to be spectators any longer. Having suspended woman's rights activities during the war in order to support black emancipation, they returned to the struggle for their own rights with high expectations. They immediately had those expectations lowered by former allies within the American Anti-Slavery Society. At the first post-Civil War meeting of the association, in May 1865, Garrison announced the end of his work, believing that the society had completed its task with the achievement of freedom for slaves. Wendell Phillips led the faction that disagreed and, upon Garrison's resignation, became the new president of the organization. Feminists hoped that Phillips's concern for black equality would be extended to women, especially since he had been a woman's rights advocate in the prewar period. Now, however, Phillips declared, "This hour belongs to the Negro." The majority of the American Society concurred, seeking the adoption of the Fourteenth Amendment to guarantee black citizenship

[87] Susan B. Anthony to Elizabeth Cady Stanton, 26 May 1856, Scrapbook, vol. 1, Elizabeth Cady Stanton Papers, Vassar College, Poughkeepsie, N.Y. This conversation took place privately between Anthony and Mrs. Finney after the latter sat through a discussion between her husband and Anthony in which Rev. Finney denounced woman's rights advocates as "infidels."

[88] Elizabeth Selden Eaton to Amos Eaton, 29 August 1867, in McKelvey, "Letters," p. 134.

[89] LASS, *Sixteenth Annual Report of the Rochester Ladies' Anti-Slavery Society and the Freedman's Aid Society* (Rochester: William S. Falls, 1867), pp. 17–18.

despite the fact that the wording of it limited women's citizenship rights for the first time.[90] Clearly, the woman's rights battle had just begun.

The first postwar woman's rights convention was held the following spring in New York City. On a motion by Martha Wright the convention participants agreed to demand universal suffrage. They formed the American Equal Rights Association and launched campaigns to achieve racial and sexual equality through state legislation. In December 1866 the Equal Rights Association held a convention in Rochester. The audience was small but demonstrated that many of the old WNY-ASS workers were interested in the new organization or at least in the speeches of its agents, Parker Pillsbury, Charles Remond, and Sojourner Truth. Susan B. Anthony, who returned home to attend the meeting, was encouraged. Six months later she appeared before the New York State Senate Judiciary Committee to testify on behalf of universal suffrage. At the close of the session, she reported that Mr. Reynolds of Rochester presented his "cheerful face and cordial hand" to her while Mr. Ely came up to be introduced, as he "knew my father and brother well, but had never had the pleasure of my acquaintance." Noting that her " 'wild heresies' " were becoming " 'fashionable orthodoxies,' " Anthony headed west to take her suffrage campaign to Kansas.[91]

It seemed plausible that local ultraists, willing to walk the line between wild heresies and fashionable orthodoxies, might attract wider support. Most of their potential recruits were members of the newly resurrected Unitarian congregation. Always an abolitionist stronghold, the Unitarian church had burned to the ground in 1859, and services were suspended until after the war. Then in 1865 the Reverend Frederick W. Holland, who had led the congregation in the late 1840s, returned to the city and initiated a successful rebuilding campaign. The new church was financed by private donations, including a four-thousand-dollar gift from Mrs. Jonathan Watson, who was to attend the Equal Rights Association meeting the next December. Her coworshipers included Emily Collins, Laura Wilcox Ramsdell, Sarah Colman Blackall, and Mrs. L. C. Smith, all of whom moved to Rochester in the late 1850s and became committed suffragists by 1870. With local free meetings discontinued, the Unitarian Society also attracted members

[90] DuBois, *Feminism and Suffrage*, pp. 56–64.
[91] Ida Husted Harper, *The Life and Work of Susan B. Anthony*, 3 vols. (Indianapolis: Bowen-Merrill, 1899), 1: 279.

of the Anthony, Hallowell, Willis, Post, Kedzie, and Burtis families to its pews.

Yet alliances were made almost exclusively on the issue of suffrage rather than on the broader pre–Civil War ultraist platform. Moreover, local women who had been long active in the cause were more distraught than Anthony and new coworkers were over divisions with former allies. The closing of the *Liberator*'s office and the decision to publish the *National Anti-Slavery Standard* monthly instead of weekly were two of the most visible results of the deterioration of abolitionist ranks and solidarity. As soon as Amy Post heard the news of the *Standard*'s curtailment of publication, she wrote to editor Aaron M. Powell, "The thought of not . . . see[ing] the Standard entering our door, but once a month, fell upon my living, earnest soul like the death-knell of a dear, and ever welcom [*sic*] friend who had . . . ever kept the chane [*sic*] bright, that has bound the coworkers so pleasantly together." She also feared that "our Waterloo meeting" would not get "advertised without the Stand" and begged Powell to attend that gathering in the summer.[92]

Though wishing to maintain her ties with former American Anti-Slavery Society colleagues, Amy Post assured Powell that she was "supprized [*sic*] that all you speakers [at the 1865 American Anti-Slavery Society meeting] should touch the *Woman question* so gingerly, when *so many* of the speakers, *so well understand* the fearful danger of the procrastination of that theme. It was only this," she concluded, "that made me feel that we could possibly *spare* the organization."[93] Thus she and her daughter Mary Hallowell served as agents of the *Standard* after the war but simultaneously joined the Equal Rights Association. When that organization disbanded, and Anthony and Stanton formed the National Women's Suffrage Association, Amy Post and Mary Hallowell entered its ranks along with Catharine Fish Stebbins, Sarah Hallowell Willis, and Rhoda DeGarmo. Still, work within a single-sex association that focused on a single political goal did not hold as strong an appeal as earlier organizations through which ultraists had sought a "thorough re-organization of Society."[94] A number of the most ardent early workers, including Lemira Kedzie and

[92] Amy Post to Aaron M. Powell, n.d., IAPFP.
[93] Ibid.
[94] YMCF, *Proceedings of the Yearly Meeting of Congregational Friends, Held at Waterloo, N.Y., from the Fourth to the Sixth of the Sixth Month, Inclusive, with An Appendix, 1849* (Auburn, N.Y.: Oliphant's Press, 1849), p. 6.

Sarah Burtis, virtually disappeared from activist circles. Others, such as Rebecca Sanford, moved west and reappeared as suffrage and temperance advocates in their new homes. A few attempted to work for suffrage while also supporting broader platforms that embraced racial and economic as well as sexual and political equality. Thus Amy Post, as a local leader of the National Liberal League in the 1870s, circulated the association's pamphlets "amongst our hopeful freethinkers." She praised the league's work in promoting an antisectarian spirit and mounting a campaign against the Victorian sexual mores embodied in the Comstock Law. Yet within the league's broader platform, the cause of women sometimes was lost. In the league's proposed "Liberal compact for government," Amy Post discovered "one omission which seemed to me unworthy [of] the thoughtful and conscientious men by whom it was signed—that omission was the word *woman*." As she warned suffrage workers that true reform embraced more than just women, she cautioned the league not to "forget that we—Women—are the long downtrodden [*sic*] class of National Citizens. . . ."[95]

In general, the ultraists did no better in the 1860s than the perfectionists in attracting SAS workers to their cause, though for a brief moment in 1868 the concerns of ultraists, perfectionists, and former SAS leaders seemed to converge. In that year a society was organized in the city "for the reformation of abandoned women."[96] This new Female Moral Reform Association, part of a nationwide "Magdalen Movement," attracted several SAS leaders as officers, including Mrs. L. C. Smith, Mrs. E. A. Nelson, and Mrs. B. L. Hovey. Their bonds to former perfectionist movements were revealed in their meeting places—evangelical churches—and in their tactics—prayer meetings at houses of prostitution. "The ladies who have undertaken to cure society of [this] social evil" apparently feared that their efforts might not be well received by the community, for they refused "to allow their proceedings to be reported" by the press.[97] It is known, however, that Amy Post and suffrage coworker Emily Collins attended at least one of the

[95] Amy Post to A. L. Rawson, 9 September 1879, IAPFP. Anthony Comstock was the leader of the Society for the Suppression of Vice. At his urging, Congress passed Section 211 of the Criminal Code, the so-called Comstock Law, which banned the mailing, interstate transportation, or importation of any "obscene, lewd, or lascivious" matter. Free love literature and birth control information were the focus of most prosecutions under this law.

[96] Emily Collins, "Reminiscences," in Elizabeth Cady Stanton, Susan B. Anthony, and Matilda Joslyn Gage, *The History of Woman Suffrage,* 4 vols. (New York: Fowler and Wells, 1881), 1: 93.

[97] *Union and Advertiser* (Rochester), 17 and 22 April 1869.

meetings. On that occasion, the question was raised of where "fallen women could go" if they wished to be rehabilitated as two such women were seeking asylum that very night. The evangelical women present were at a loss what to do when Amy Post "spoke up and said, 'I will take one, and if there is no second place for the other, I will take her too.' "⁹⁸ The evangelical leaders then discussed the possibility of establishing a house of refuge for future converted prostitutes. Emily Collins, however, "endeavored to show how futile all their efforts would be, while women, by the laws of the land, were made a subject class; that only by enfranchising woman and permitting her a more free and lucrative range of employments, could they hope to suppress the 'social evil.' "⁹⁹

The association as a whole was apparently not swayed, though no further notice exists of its proceedings after 1869. At least one of the leaders, however, Mrs. L. C. Smith, was convinced by Emily Collins's arguments and perhaps by those of others among her Unitarian coworshippers. In 1872 Mrs. Smith joined fifty other Rochester women in registering to vote for the fall presidential election. In the eighth ward, Susan B. Anthony led her sisters Mary Anthony, Guelma McLean, and Hannah Mosher, early ultraist Rhoda DeGarmo, and eleven neighbors to Robert Renfew's West End News Depot to register on 1 November. In the first ward, Amy Post, Mary Fish Curtis, Mrs. L. C. Smith, and Dr. Sarah Adamson Dolley were among the most well-known registrants.¹⁰⁰ Four days later, only the eighth ward women were allowed to vote. Inspectors of Election W. Baugh Jones and Edwin T. Marsh, the latter a long-time abolitionist, received the votes against the instructions of the United States inspector. Both inspectors were prosecuted along with Susan B. Anthony, and each was fined one hundred dollars. Jones paid the fine after a short stint in jail; Marsh refused to pay and remained behind bars. He was "deluged with bouquets and a vast variety of elegant foods and drinks" during his incarceration and was finally released, without payment of his fine, to the cheers of his feminist supporters.¹⁰¹

Anthony was tried in the United States District Court in Canandai-

⁹⁸ Coleman, *Reminiscences*, p. 85.
⁹⁹ Collins, "Reminiscences," 1: 93.
¹⁰⁰ *Democrat and Chronicle* (Rochester), 1 November 1872. For Anthony's recollections of the event and a list of voters, see Harper, *Life and Work*, 1:423–429.
¹⁰¹ Mary Hebard, "Female Suffrage," 1873, n.p., Pamphlet Collection, New York State Historical Library, Cooperstown.

gua in June 1873. According to the prosecutor, she had "voted for a representative in the Congress of the United States" on 5 November 1872, and at "that time she was a woman." Not "arguing the question, but simply stating the reasons why sentence [could] not, in justice, be pronounced against [her]," Anthony reiterated her arguments regarding women's subject status and claimed the denial of her right to vote as "the denial of my sacred rights to life, liberty, [and] property. . . ." Fined one hundred dollars by Judge Hunt, who evidenced exasperation at her pleadings for her sex, Anthony ended by assuring him that she would "earnestly and persistently continue to urge all women to the practical recognition of the old revolutionary maxim, that 'Resistance to tyranny is obedience to God.' "[102]

Anthony's trial was a turning point in the woman's rights movement, the starting point of its transition into the woman's suffrage movement. The new cause was radical in its attack on the most well-protected bastion of male privilege—political office—yet conservative in its acceptance of the existing power structure so long as women were allowed equal access to its benefits.[103] Anthony's stirring rhetoric of Revolutionary antecedents and Godly admonitions appealed more strongly to other female activists, particularly as her goal was the specific one of suffrage, than had ultraists' earlier appeals for a revolution in social, sexual, and familial relations. The Rochester papers, for instance, were more neutral than hostile during Anthony's trial, and her lawyer was Henry R. Selden, of the pioneer family that spawned activist Elizabeth Selden Spencer Eaton. Anthony received the support of a number of local residents who had not previously spoken out on behalf of woman's suffrage, and by the 1880s she was being toasted as a local heroine by the Porters, Farleys, Goulds, and Seldens, as well by her ultraist coworkers.

Yet many of those who would look back on Anthony's trial and tell of their support on her behalf were not those who actually stood beside her to cast their ballots in 1872. Of the fifty women who registered that November, only some two dozen had their names recorded in the local press or the annals of the women's movement. Of these, four were relatives of Susan B. Anthony, three were founding members of the

---

[102] Stanton, Anthony, and Gage, *History,* 2: 628, 687, 689.
[103] For a provocative argument on the character of the suffrage movement, see Ellen DuBois, "The Radicalism of the Woman Suffrage Movement: Notes toward the Reconstruction of Nineteenth-Century Feminism," *Feminist Studies* 3 (1975): 63–71.

WNYASS and organizers of Rochester's 1848 Woman's Rights Convention, at least three were Unitarian coworshipers, and two appeared on Amy Post's list of persons wishing to employ freed slaves after the Civil War. Of the registrants who were married, a few had professional or merchant husbands, including a newspaper publisher, a physician, a lawyer, a miller, and a pharmacist. But the majority were considerably less affluent, having married salesmen, insurance agents, farmers, artisans, or laborers. Three of the women were single and at least a half dozen were widows, including Amy Post, whose husband Isaac had died only months earlier. A few of the women supported themselves by teaching or sewing. Three were physicians, though only Sarah Adamson Dolley had a regular medical degree; Drs. Wheeler and Dutton listed themselves as hydropaths, dispensers of water cures that attracted numerous feminists in the mid-1800s.[104]

At least a dozen of the women who registered, including members of the Anthony, Fish, and Hallowell families, became the core of a new countywide organization, the Women's Taxpayers Association. Formed in the spring of 1873, the WTA organized support for Anthony's trial and, immediately upon its conclusion, held a meeting at the mayor's office that was addressed by Anthony and WTA vice-president, Mary Hebard. Hebard noted that "might is right is the one great pillar of masculine authority," and claimed that women sought "in beautiful majesty the principle of universal justice luminating every organic entity." She then described the role that slavery played in awakening Americans to the fact that "the garments of the godess [*sic*] of liberty were dripping with human blood." It was only when "the fog of American slavery was lifted from this land," she continued, that "this subtle and refined slavery, this dominance of man over woman became apparent. . . ."[105] The rest of her speech was a combination of ultraist arguments for equality and more traditional claims for woman's natural moral superiority. This contradiction in the rationale for giving women the vote was dressed in the guise of female socialization, which served alternately to account for woman's present limits and for her universal virtue.

It was perhaps these ambiguous claims allowing women to advocate

[104] The data on 1872 voters and registrants and the organizers of the WTA was collected primarily from Rochester city directories for 1872, 1873, and 1874; the Unitarian Society of Rochester Records, University of Rochester, and the First Unitarian Society Records, First Unitarian Church, Rochester.

[105] Hebard, "Female Suffrage," n.p. See also Stanton, Anthony, and Gage, *History*.

suffrage on the basis either of equality or of superiority that brought new women into the suffrage ranks in the postwar period. In addition, the very name chosen for the new association may have reassured some women that the feminist ranks did not extend below property owners and that the leaders were concerned primarily with specific economic and political protections rather than more fundamental rearrangements of gender roles. The actual number of feminist activists did not increase significantly until the 1890s, but the forty to fifty women in the WTA included a more heterogeneous group than did early ultraist circles.[106] Mary Fish Curtis, Sarah Hallowell Willis, Catharine Fish Stebbins, and Mary Post Hallowell, the younger members of the WNYASS set, were among the first fourteen officers of the WTA. They were joined by five other women who registered to vote in 1872, including two Anthony relatives and Magdalen Movement leader Mrs. L. C. Smith, who served as the WTA's first president. The newest suffrage coworkers were Unitarians Mrs. Laura Ramsdell and Mrs. Sarah Blackall, the former an abolitionist and recent widow, the latter an abolitionist turned social worker. These suffrage pioneers drew on three decades of ultraist agitation but in their own work modified ultraist arguments and expanded their alliances in the fight for the single right of suffrage.

In 1872 as in 1848, female ultraists were the most visible, because the most controversial, of local women activists. Yet they were still a minority largely at odds with community sentiment. The attraction of a few Unitarian perfectionists to their ranks may have resulted in part from a lack of alternatives as the HF became a bastion of benevolence and the LASS and SAS disbanded. In 1874, however, perfectionists would reemerge and, in the context of evangelical zeal and extralocal support, form the Women's Temperance Union. Laboring "to suppress temperance by every laudable means" in their power, Rochester's new temperance band was led by lawyers' wives with experience in the HF, OAA, and IS and filled with affluent and middle-class evangelicals from Baptist, Methodist, and Presbyterian churches.[107]

The bastion of female public service in Rochester in the 1870s, as in each of the previous four decades, was, however, the CS. Serving

---

[106] The WTA and the WNYASS had equivalent numbers of members, but the latter included men and included individuals from a much larger geographical area.

[107] *The Rochester Directory for 1874* (Rochester: Drew and Allis, 1874), p. 428. The Women's Temperance Union was, or was soon to become, the local auxiliary of the Women's Christian Temperance Union.

seventy-three districts with one hundred visitors, fourteen collectors, and twenty-five managers, the CS was "an institution invested with peculiar glories." On its fiftieth anniversary, in February 1872, the Reverend William Shaw of Brick Presbyterian Church preached an evening sermon to packed pews. In it he claimed that it was Christ's withdrawal from the world that allowed for the development of philanthropic institutions. The CS and its sister organizations thus stood "as witnesses that the Messiah has been on earth." Yet the CS stood highest because it had never made "invidious distinctions" by religion or nationality among those it aided and because "its members like the Divine Redeemer, go forth to look for and minister to" the needy. Moreover, the society "look[ed] after those most needy and most worthy—those who are too modest to make their wants known—who suffer in silence rather than let the world know these wants."[108] Unostentatious victims cared for economically and efficiently by unostentatious women: the CS was a fifty-year success story.

By 1872 women's activism was securely embedded in the community consciousness and public paths of Rochester. Thousands of women had walked those paths in fifty years, providing social services and promoting social change. No question remained as to whether or not women should have a public role, but debate still raged over what that role should be. Thus female activists left two legacies, one to the city of Rochester and one to future activists. The former embraced all the labors performed by activist women—individuals aided, services rendered, institutions established, alms distributed, fugitives hidden, funds collected, lectures sponsored, meetings held, consciousnesses raised. The latter included the lessons these women learned and passed on—the forms and styles of activism pursued and their effectiveness, the choices made in issues, emphases, and alliances, and the balances achieved among principles, tactics, and actions. It is these legacies that constitute the final chapter of women's public service in nineteenth-century Rochester.

[108] *Union and Advertiser,* 26 February 1872.

[7]

Never Another Season of Silence

Through their wartime work, the members of the SAS came to appreciate "better than ever before" women's capacity for "heroism and self-sacrifice" and for long hours of labor with few resources.[1] CS leaders had learned this lesson decades earlier, but in 1860 they felt compelled to remind the community. Noting that more than fifteen thousand dollars had been expended on the sick poor in the previous fifteen years, CS vice-president Mrs. Samuel Selden assured her neighbors "that the *real* burden of effort and self-denial, which the use of this seemingly large sum involves, has fallen upon the dispensers rather than the donors of this bounty."[2] For half a century, those female dispensers provided the bulk of social services to the poor, sick, orphaned, homeless, and destitute as Rochester grew from a village of two thousand to a city of fifty thousand inhabitants.

"In reviewing the action of this Association" over past years, the CS leaders of 1860 noted, "it is pleasant to find in it the germs of more than one important public institution." By 1872 the CS could claim the OAA, HF, IS, and city hospital among its progeny. In addition, in 1844 the CS had presented the common council with the "first petition for the establishment of a Work House" and pursued the matter until the "Penitentiary, with its fine buildings and its excellent management" was completed.[3] Finally, the joint petitions for a refuge for female

[1] *Industrial School Advocate and Soldier's Aid* (Rochester), 12 July 1865.
[2] CS, *Charter, Constitution, By-Laws, and Officers of the Rochester Female Charitable Society (for the Relief of Sick Poor), Together with Its History and Annual Reports for the Year 1860* (Rochester: C. D. Tracy, 1860), pp. 5–6.
[3] Ibid., pp. 6–7.

juveniles begun in 1858 resulted in the erection of the Girls' Reformatory in 1876.

The CS also claimed that the program of district visiting had *"originated* with its founders" and had "since been adopted by numerous similar Associations in other places. . . ." It was adopted as well by other women's organizations in Rochester. House-to-house canvasses for those in need as well as for those willing to donate goods, pay membership dues, or sign petitions provided an important basis for the permeation of female activists into the larger community. During the 1850s and 1860s, most associations that followed the CS into the benevolent network discontinued door-to-door solicitations, believing that local citizens would now go directly to the established institutions to obtain or offer aid. Only the CS, which had no institutional base, continued to employ personal visitation as the primary means of relief. Yet this was by no means simply the continuation of an outmoded practice, since it provided the model for privately and publicly funded visiting nurse and social work programs in the early twentieth century.[4]

Benevolent women had entered the public domain with a specific clientele in mind. In 1822 the CS considered fifteen district visitors sufficient to aid the village's sick poor; in 1837 the OAA counted some twenty orphan children in need of asylum; and in 1849 the HF believed that a home for fifty residents could shelter the city's friendless females. Most of the needs of the societies themselves could be met by donations of goods rather than cash, and most of their services were counted in qualitative rather than quantitative terms. Major financial outlays were only necessary for the construction of institutions and even then the land and labor were often donated. By mid-century the total annual expenditure of the CS, OAA, and HF combined amounted to only five thousand dollars, two thousand of which went to construction and repair on the asylum. Thus approximately three thousand dollars was extended to provide emergency relief to 430 sick poor and room and board for 56 orphans and 74 friendless women.[5]

After mid-century, benevolent women collected and expended ever larger sums for relief work—$5,855 by the city hospital in 1855, $3,234 by the CS in 1860, over $7,000 by the OAA in 1863, and $3,700 by the

[4]Amy Hanmer-Croughton, "The Rochester Female Charitable Society," Rochester Historical Society, *Publications* 9 (1930), pp. 66, 81–82.

[5]Ibid., p. 70; OAA, *History of the Rochester Female Association for the Relief of Orphan and Destitute Children, Together with Its Organization, By-Laws, &c.* (Rochester: Shepard and Strong, 1839), p. 3; HF, Minute Book, 28 March 1849, FHP.

home in 1865. Yet these monies were stretched over a rapidly multiplying population during a period of significant inflation, so that the amount expended per person remained relatively low. Claiming that between 1844 and 1860 they had needed less than $1,000 per year to relieve the wants of the sick poor, the CS observed that this sum "will suggest a large amount of relief to those who know how much can be provided by the judicious expenditure of a few dollars."[6] "Judicious" and "few" were supremely accurate terms. An average of 80 visitors supplied districts of about 650 persons each with clothing, bedding, and medical care for approximately $12.50 per year per district. In 1860 itself, the CS reported 500 to 600 cases of relief offered for the sum of twenty-five cents to several dollars each.

Frugality, however, could not keep economic problems at bay. Benevolent societies complained of empty and near empty treasuries throughout the 1860s, and they no longer could pretend to meet the needs of the entire population. Throughout the war years the CS aided 500 to 700 persons annually, the asylum housed 130 to 160 orphans, and the home, 80 to 100 friendless women. These services could not possibly have exhausted the needs of a city of 50,000. After the war these institutions, along with the IS and city hospital, remained important sources of social welfare, but they no longer dominated charitable enterprises the way they had in the prewar years. Catholic and Jewish benevolent societies began easing pressures on their predominately Protestant predecessors. As early as 1843 a Catholic orphan asylum for girls was established in the city, but a wider network of associations did not develop until the 1860s, when in rapid succession two Catholic and a Jewish orphanage, a Catholic Home of Industry, a Ladies' Hebrew Benevolent Society, and a Ladies' Hebrew Aid and Hospital Association were founded. The Episcopalians also established their own church home for "destitute children and aged communicants" in 1869. In addition, publicly funded institutions were established or expanded in the 1870s and 1880s. In 1872, for instance, the alms house increased its capacity from one hundred to four hundred occupants, and a new insane asylum was built. Soon after, an institute for deaf mutes and a society for the prevention of cruelty to children were begun with public assistance.[7]

[6] CS, *Charter*, pp. 5–6.

[7] William Farley Peck, *A Semi-Centennial History of Rochester with Illustrations and Biographical Sketches of Some of Its Prominent Men and Pioneers* (Syracuse: D. Mason, 1884), pp. 415–418, 425–428.

The primary function of the city's benevolent societies between 1822 and the Civil War was to ameliorate the problems of urban growth until the lower classes were better able to care for themselves or were provided care by the state. During this period, city fathers were neither willing nor able to provide such services with public funds. The alms house, established in 1823 and having seventy to one hundred occupants, and the Western House of Refuge, for delinquent youths, were the only pre–Civil War institutions supported by city or county funds other than the county jail. Since city fathers were likely to be the male kin of benevolent women, they often applied private donations to labors they refused to fund publicly. Yet the CS rarely expended more than three hundred dollars per year in its first fifteen years of operation, and thus placed little financial pressure on male donors. In 1837 the OAA began making greater economic demands on local philanthropists, soliciting donations from local gentlemen of fifteen hundred to three thousand dollars per year, and at mid-century the HF and the CS's city hospital committee added their appeals. Yet city leaders still preferred to sustain private benevolence rather than subscribe public funds. The economic rationale for this choice was made particularly clear in 1849.

In that year two institutions were founded, one by male and one by female activists. Following the appeals of the men's Prison Discipline Society, the Western House of Refuge "was erected by the state . . . on a 42-acre farm at the northwestern edge of the city" to house delinquent boys and keep them away from the bad influences of the county jail.[8] The HF was opened the same year in half of a double house on Edinburgh Street in the city's center. Between the original proposal for the House of Refuge in 1846 and its opening three years later, state and city governments appropriated $53,000 for its construction. The state legislature appropriated an additional $12,000 in 1849 for operational expenses. No funds were made available to the HF in the three months between the proposal for a home and its opening, which was formalized by the payment of $50 for a six-month lease to the building's owner.

It was clearly a combination of ideology and necessity, then, that led HF leaders to hope that their institution "as far as practicable" would be "a self-supporting one." The revenue made by HF inmates through "washing, ironing, & needlework" would be augmented by yearly

[8] Blake McKelvey, *Rochester: The Water-Power City, 1812–1854* (Cambridge: Harvard University Press, 1945), p. 338.

membership fees or "not less than 50 cents" per person and life members' donations of ten dollars.[9] This amount proving insufficient for initial expenses, it was proposed in June that officers "try to obtain members and get what they can." In July a committee of one or two ladies from each church was appointed to solicit aid; in August it was voted that "a notice of the Home embracing its locality, its designs and accomplishments be published in one or more of our City papers" to increase public interest. Four months later, HF directress and matron Mrs. Ingersoll was requested to "call upon Mr. *Champion*," a well-known local philanthropist, "and make known the history of the Home, its wants &c. and solicit aid in its behalf from him."[10]

Mrs. Ingersoll lived with her husband, the Reverend Mr. Ingersoll, in the other half of the double that housed the home. As the sole salaried employee of the home, she received less than $200 for her services from May 1849 to April 1850.[11] For the same period, Mr. Ingersoll, the second-lowest paid of six salaried employees at the House of Refuge, received $250 for his part-time services as chaplain. Only the gatekeeper received less—$200 per year. The superintendent, Samuel S. Wood, received $1,500 annually, and total salaries for the House of Refuge amounted to $3,500 a year. One year later the HF's total financial resources were $494, with the "gentlemen of the city" donating only $70 and the sole government allocation being $36 from the Overseer of the Poor.[12]

The OAA was considerably more successful than the HF in securing private donations and public funds, particularly by 1849, when it was a dozen years old and had completed the transition to a thoroughly benevolent institution. Yet its financial status was far closer to that of the HF than that of the Western House of Refuge. When the latter received its final state grant of $12,000 in 1849, the OAA received its first state grant ever of $851.[13] The total of salaries paid by the OAA that year, for a "Matron and Assistant and labor in and about the Asylum," was

[9] HF, Minute Book, 28 March 1849, FHP.

[10] HF, Minute Book, 5 June, 18 July, 21 August, and 17 November 1849, FHP.

[11] The exact salary paid Mrs. Ingersoll is uncertain, but figures for other expenses and for receipts indicate that $200 is the maximum amount that could have been paid to the matron.

[12] Salaries at the Western House of Refuge are listed in the *Daily American Directory of the City of Rochester, for 1849–1850* (Rochester: Jerome and Brothers, 1849). The meagreness of men's contributions to the HF is noted in the home's annual report, printed in the *Daily Advertiser* (Rochester), 12 April 1851.

[13] OAA, Annual Report, 1849, Scrapbook, HCCP.

$500, a mere 14 percent of that paid to House of Refuge employees. By a number of economy measures, including the use of orphans as workers within the asylum, the OAA cared for an average of sixty-three children in 1849 at a cost of 67 cents per child per week. Per-person expenses at the refuge were approximately double that amount despite the greater availability of land and labor to supply the inmates' needs.[14]

City fathers had struck a sound bargain in choosing private, female-directed over public, male-directed charity. Moreover, the most intense period of female benevolent activity coincided with popular idealizations of women's moral devotion and consumer sense, so that women themselves placed a premium on their frugality in charitable enterprises. Thus they claimed in self-congratulatory tones that it was female labor rather than male dollars that was the key to women's success as community caretakers.[15] The extent of that female labor increased as the number of benevolent associations and the population to be cared for multiplied. In the CS alone, visitors were to visit their districts at least once a month and report their activities on the first Tuesday of the month to the society-at-large. The president and secretary directed daily business in the first five years, after which they were aided by a board of directresses. The charity school also required the daily attention of several members and periodic visits by CS officers, while all the society's members were encouraged to attend the annual fall meeting and the annual spring sermon. As other benevolent associations emerged, their activities were arranged to harmonize with those of sister organizations, allowing women to serve each in turn. Thus OAA meetings were scheduled for the last Tuesday of each month and HF meetings for the third Tuesday. Annual meetings, sermons, and fund-raising events were also staggered, and individual workers determined their own calendar of district, asylum, and home visitations, solicitations, church and ward collections, and begging expeditions into nearby towns. During the Civil War, SAS labors were added to the

[14]This figure is quoted in ibid., and fits with other figures noted in the budget. Figures for the House of Refuge were estimated from operating costs minus salaries, assuming a full capacity of 150 inmates. As late as 1872 OAA leaders noted that tickets for a benefit could be priced at one dollar if sold by male trustees but at only fifty cents if sold by female managers.

[15]On the development of the ideology of consumerism, see Ann Douglas, *The Feminization of American Culture* (New York: Knopf, 1977). For the clearest expressions of this ideology in benevolent records, see *JHF*, 1 July 1861, 1 August 1862, and 1 June 1863; and CS, *Charter*, p. 6.

schedule for many women, with the second ward branch sustaining "its *regular weekly meetings*" every week for *"nearly three years."*[16]

The translation of organizational schedules into individual labors may best be illustrated by tracing one woman's work for a year. In 1837, when the OAA joined the CS in benevolent labors, Mrs. David Scoville served as a district visitor in the latter and a directress of the former. She attended CS monthly meetings the first Tuesday of each month and OAA meetings the last Tuesday of each month. The OAA made it "the duty of two of the Managers and one Directress to meet once a week at the Asylum to inquire into its condition, and to transact such business as may be necessary."[17] As one of four directresses, Mrs. Scoville undertook this duty once a month. Extra meetings of the OAA were called in its early years for sewing clothing and bedding for the asylum; in addition, committee meetings, expeditions into the country for supplies, membership campaigns, bookkeeping, and the consideration of applications for admission required regular attention. Mrs. Scoville also toured her CS district once a month and presented reports to the CS board. She applied to the CS board periodically for clothing, bedding, and other items for her charitable charges, distributed the same, and eventually tried to collect the items for use elsewhere. She undoubtedly attended the annual sermon and probably the public examination of the charity school. On October 30, Mrs. Scoville presided over the OAA's annual meeting, presenting the annual report she had earlier helped to write. One week later, she presented a summary of her monthly visitations to the CS's annual meeting. The year ended with her reelection to office in both societies.

Between 1837 and 1872 dozens of women held posts in two or three organizations simultaneously. Six of fifteen OAA founders and twelve of fourteen HF founders were already serving as officers in another benevolent society when they decided to establish new institutions. Thus Mrs. Scoville's experience was duplicated by many other women, who formed the core of benevolent efforts and the public image of the benevolent activist.

Charitable organizations adopted not only parallel schedules but also similar administrative and, with the exception of the CS, institutional forms. The replication of these forms, even by associations initially dominated by perfectionists, eased the entrance of women into social

---

[16]*Industrial School Advocate and Soldier's Aid,* 12 July 1865.
[17]OAA, Minute Book, 21 March 1837, HCCP.

activism and resulted in an increasing acceptance of certain public roles as particularly suited to women's skills and character. The support of male kin and community leaders, formalized as benevolent societies appointed male boards of trustees in the 1840s and 1850s, reinforced that acceptance by Rochester's citizens. Through frugal management, intensive labor, essential services, and male endorsements, then, benevolent ladies successfully challenged the Godly admonitions and popular literature that attempted to relegate women to the private sphere in the second quarter of the nineteenth century and, instead, legitimated women's extensive public labors.

Yet the legitimation accorded female benevolence was not wholly transferred to other groups of women activists. Perfectionist and ultraist labors were not always deemed equally essential and did not always involve significant economic benefits to the city. The primary role of perfectionist women's antislavery, moral reform, and temperance societies, in tandem with similar male associations, was to alert the community to the moral dangers of material success. They introduced new techniques of activism as well as new issues, employing prayer meetings, the press, and petitions to publicize their work. Yet all of these associations also attempted to rehabilitate the victims of the vices they fought, thus serving the interests of the local community while participating in national campaigns to eradicate the vices themselves. Initially, the most time-consuming labor for women may have been spreading their views to other women as they marched from house to house carrying petitions, pledges, the *Advocate of Moral Reform* or the *Liberator*.

Yet few nonevangelical men ever supported perfectionist women's labors and even a few benevolent women voiced their disapproval.[18] The downfall of the first phase of perfectionism resulted from the attacks of unsympathetic editors and clergy and the attendant withdrawal of evangelical men's, including clergy's, support from perfectionist women. When these women reappeared, they redirected their efforts by institutionalizing their concerns (in the HF) or subordinating themselves to male allies (in the LASS). In altering their approach to social change, they were able to pursue some of their original goals—the salvation of vulnerable women and assistance to blacks—with the wider resources provided by a more approving community.

[18] Sophia E. [Mrs. Jonathan] Child to Mrs. Sarah D. Fish, 14 May 1835, BFFP.

Nevertheless, the experience of the HF founders demonstrated the difficulties of overcoming their moral reform roots. The OAA, which contained a healthy share of perfectionist leaders, was nonetheless free of any direct association with FMRS or FASS labors. In its first two years of existence, the OAA raised $3,800 despite the onset of a financial panic. The HF, though founded in more prosperous circumstances, collected only $700 in the same period of time. Given the relatively equivalent services provided by the two institutions, HF women were forced to develop a number of new fund-raising techniques to offset the discrepancy in initial support. These techniques included an employment agency for domestic servants and prospective employers, a donation day at the home, and a journal to publicize HF activities in surrounding towns. HF members also found it necessary to hold fund-raisers more frequently, to aid the matron and inmates more regularly, and to make begging expeditions into the country more often than their OAA peers.[19]

The LASS, attracting the less affluent members of early perfectionist organizations, demanded an even wider range of labors from its members. The society's constitution stated that it was "the duty of the Directress to make all purchases and to cut and prepare all work for the Society"; home and asylum leaders delegated the bulk of these tasks to a hired matron.[20] To raise funds, LASS women also organized an annual fair, which required significantly more preparation than either annual sermons or donation days. Antislavery women attracted donations by the sale of articles they manufactured themselves or solicited from other female antislavery societies and then utilized the monies gained to organize lectures, aid fugitive slaves, and subsidize men's political efforts. At least seven of the thirty or so women who performed these labors in 1851 and 1852 combined them with paid labor as teachers or boardinghouse keepers.

Perfectionists' male colleagues, like their benevolent counterparts, recognized the benefits of female voluntarism. Female moral reformers dominated the local movement against licentiousness, while abolitionists secured petition signatures and raised funds.[21] In the 1850s this last

[19] HF, Minute Book, FHP, contains numerous examples of these labors, especially from 1849 to 1854.
[20] LASS, "Circular, the First Report of the Rochester Ladies' Anti-Slavery Sewing Society, 1852," SDPFP.
[21] For an excellent discussion of women's roles in these labors, see Gerda Lerner, "The Political Activities of Anti-Slavery Women," in Lerner, ed., *The Majority Finds Its Past: Placing Women in History,* (New York: Oxford University Press, 1979), pp. 112–128.

function was more important to local men as publication and campaign costs escalated. Frederick Douglass, Gerrit Smith, Samuel D. Porter, and their coworkers readily admitted that it was to women "that [they] looked for great services to the cause."[22] Still, female perfectionists gained far greater moral than financial help from their male advocates. Their male kin were less affluent than those of benevolent women and, too, were ensconced in their own associations to fight slavery and intemperance in the 1850s; they thought far more in terms of receiving funds from than depositing funds in female associations. Because they viewed the backing of male efforts as one of the only means open to them for influencing the antislavery cause, perfectionist women accepted the burdens it entailed.

At least by the mid-1850s, HF and LASS labors were increasingly well rewarded. They had subdued many of their earlier opponents and thereby gained the latitude to extend their sphere of activity beyond the bounds defined by their benevolent forerunners. They had made moral reform and abolitionism and women's participation in campaigns for both palatable to large numbers in the community. They had increased women's use of and community access to the press by subsidizing the home's *Journal* and *Frederick Douglass' Paper*. For fugitive slaves, the LASS provided essential aid—hiding places, clothing, and more—to speed their escape to Canada, despite the illegal nature of such activities. Among Rochesterians, LASS and HF women reached out to needy populations that were largely neglected by benevolent ladies and provided friendless women and free blacks with the means to sustain themselves. Perfectionists clearly accepted the basic institutions of their society, though neither naively nor uncritically. By trying to make churches and the state as well as the community at large conform to the spirit of evangelical and Constitutional doctrines, perfectionists ultimately helped assure the survival and improvement of the existing order and women's legitimate if subordinate place in it.

Ultraist women had little faith in the existing order, so when they experienced the hostility of the community, they took it as a demand for more radical endeavors. The notion that the righteous were often persecuted by the powerful, a legacy of Quakerism, sustained ultraists in the face of public censure, yet they hoped that their worldly labors would eventually transform opprobrium into approbation. Collective and continuous labor was their weapon, for they had few familial and

[22] Frederick Douglass to Mrs. Samuel D. Porter, president, LASS, 27 March 1852, printed in LASS, "Circular," SDPFP.

no public resources to employ. The multiplicity of their concerns and the limits of their numbers assured each ultraist a full day's and a full life's work. While ultraist women shared far more labors with men than their benevolent or perfectionist counterparts, a life's work in activism was still more arduous. They performed many of the same tasks as other activist women—fund-raising, publicity, petitioning—but many fewer people were spread over more causes. As in perfectionist circles, limited resources were divided between men and women in the same campaigns, though ultraist women, working in joint-sex associations, did maintain some control over the use of the funds they raised. At the same time they were expected to and wanted to participate more fully in the organization and direction of public events. They were in fact more likely than other activist women to take on new, and often so-cially unacceptable, roles as itinerant lecturers, presiding officers in public meetings, delegates to state and national conventions, and au-thors of pamphlets, resolutions, and policy statements. Because they pursued unpopular causes by unwomanly means, ultraists had to work harder to gain the resources necessary to the continuation of their campaigns. In 1844 Paulina Wright of Utica wrote to Amy Post that their antislavery fair "was more opposed than anything that had been started in our goodly citty [*sic*] for years." While assuring her Roches-ter colleagues that, because of the opposition, the money collected "is *simon pure Antislavery* money," Wright also observed that it was a very small sum.[23]

Small sums collected at many separate events was the only way for ultraists to maintain their principles and the cause simultaneously, and since fund-raising was largely women's work, that meant continual labor. In 1849, for instance, the women's sewing circle of the WYNASS met weekly to make sale items for their fairs, while some women also met on Tuesday evenings with the WNYASS executive committee. These meetings were often held in the homes of members, so that women may have been called on simultaneously to perform domestic and public duties. Two members of the sewing circle alter-nated as directors of the antislavery reading room, and others jour-neyed to neighboring towns to manage or assist at antislavery fairs. Several women worked long hours to organize the annual meeting and fair in Rochester in December, a women's meeting in January, and the

[23] Paulina Wright to Amy Post, 12 February 1844, IAPFP.

winter lecture series. These women could not rely on the support of local editors or clergy so they were more responsible for publicizing the events they scheduled. In addition, the very women who performed these myriad labors for the WNYASS also performed them on behalf of woman's rights, the Congregational Friends, working women's rights, temperance, and the anti-capital punishment movement.

In dollars and cents and individuals aided, ultraist contributions to social amelioration or social reform in Rochester were far less obvious than those of either benevolent or perfectionist women. In part, the lack of visibility resulted from ultraists' failure to keep systematic records of those they helped. Many ultraists worked on the Underground Railroad helping fugitive slaves, but no records were kept of the number working or the number aided. An Indian from the Cattaragus reservation wrote the Posts periodically, thanking them for medical treatments; there may have been others who did not write. Ultraist women worked to organize local seamstresses, took unemployed and abandoned women into their own homes, hired ex-slaves as domestic servants or farm laborers, hosted itinerant lecturers, distributed reform literature, circulated petitions, and collected funds; but they kept no annual summaries of labors performed as did the other women's associations in the city. Moreover, because ultraists did not restrict their efforts to the local arena, their contributions to social change could not be measured only within the perimeter of Rochester.

What did result from ultraist labors was a reshaping of community attitudes about race relations, women's roles, and similar issues. Rochester's ultraists never came close to converting large numbers of their neighbors to the views they held, but they moderated hostility to such views. Woman's rights conventions, for instance, generally received less strident and satirical critiques in Rochester papers than in those of other cities. Antiabolitionist mobs never attacked abolitionist meetings in Rochester, even in years noted for the virulence of such attacks elsewhere.[24] According to Susan B. Anthony, bloomer wearers were less subject to public ridicule and physical harassment in her home town than in other upstate New York communities.[25] Ultraists

[24] Elizabeth Cady Stanton, "Reminscences," in Elizabeth Cady Stanton, Susan B. Anthony, and Matilda Joslyn Gage, *The History of Woman Suffrage*, 4 vols. (New York: Foster and Wells, 1881), 1: 468.
[25] Ida Husted Harper, *The Life and Work of Susan B. Anthony*, 3 vols. (Indianapolis: Bowen-Merrill, 1899), 1: 116.

believed that in the future, their small circles of association, which were now like a "green spot in the desert," would "cover the earth as the waters do the sea," and Rochester would become "the Model City" to which the whole country would turn for progressive ideas.[26]

Rochesterians gradually adopted apathy rather than antipathy in response to ultraist demands, and a few, such as William Reynolds, Alfred Ely, Elizabeth Eaton, Julia Wilbur, and Samuel D. Porter, began to consider ultraist claims worthy of serious consideration. Indeed, ultraist women's greatest contribution to social change may have been that they expanded Rochesterians vision of the possible by extending the spectrum of social, religious, and political views in the direction of ever more radical critiques and solutions. They thereby lent a semblance of moderation to what otherwise, and in other places, would have been deemed extreme. By presenting their fellow Rochesterians with Amazons, they made the efforts of other activists seem supremely womanly, allowing local benevolent and perfectionist women to step farther beyond the bounds that defined woman's proper role than would have been possible in other communities.

Though Rochester's three groups of activist women defined their roles differently from each other and were each perceived differently by the community, they shared a commitment to public labor and, together, contributed work, money, services, institutions, and ideas to the city. The exchange of skills and experiences within each network and among networks revitalized women's activism and pushed it into ever expanding arenas of labor. Over time, this associated effort provided activist women with an autonomous identity—though one that generally complemented that of their male kin. For affluent women, community service became a symbol of their family's social standing and moral superiority. For upwardly mobile women, perfectionist campaigns contributed to the establishment of a social and moral order commensurate with the economic order pursued by their male kin. For newly arrived agrarian Quakers, ultraism assured the maintenance of their community heritage in a new urban setting. All of these women began their campaigns with altruistic motives and succeeded in extending aid to large segments of the population, but they simultaneously

[26]YMCF, *Proceedings of the Yearly Meeting of Congregational Friends, Held at Waterloo, N.Y., From the Third to the Fifth of the Sixth Month, Inclusive, 1850* (Auburn, N.Y.: Henry Oliphant, 1850), p. 8; Phebe Thayer to Amy Post, 8 May [185–], IAPFP.

carved out more fulfilling roles for themselves as a legacy for daughters and granddaughters.

Benevolent women, because of their early starts in public arenas, established the lengthiest records of service in mid-nineteenth-century Rochester. Paralleling the professional, mercantile, and manufacturing careers of their male kin, these women dedicated themselves to long years of service, a regular and busy work schedule, and the formalities of vacations, leaves-of-absence, resignation, and retirement. Fully one quarter of CS charter members continued their efforts for fifteen years or more, and between 1822 and 1872 forty-nine women served twenty years or more in benevolent associations. In an era characterized by high geographical mobility and a rapid turnover in male jobs and occupations, these statistics appear even more unusual. Mrs. Elizabeth Atkinson, for example, was superintendent of the charity school in 1821 and a charter member of the CS who served the society as vice-president and then president. She was elected a directress of the OAA in 1837 and continued her services to both societies until her marriage to Charles G. Finney in 1848. Mrs. Edwin Scrantom joined the CS in 1822 as Mary Ann Sibley. Active in that society until 1837, she then turned her attention to orphans for the next twenty-five years and ended her career in the 1860s as an officer of both societies. The benevolent career of Mrs. Thomas Rochester, also a CS charter member, spanned a dutiful forty-five years. During that period, she served as secretary-treasurer, vice-president, and directress of the CS and as treasurer and directress of the OAA. She was removed from this last office by death in 1868.

Other benevolent women began their careers later but pursued them as avidly. Mrs. James K. Livingston first appears as president of the CS in 1827, though she must have been a member earlier, and served as a directress until 1859. During these twenty-two years she also served variously as president, secretary, and directress of the OAA and as secretary of the HF. Mrs. Maltby Strong joined the CS in 1836 where she soon became involved in the society's effort to establish a hospital. Having served on several committees to promote the venture, she became president of the Board of Lady Managers of the city hospital upon its incorporation in 1863. She also served in the HF during the 1850s and as a directress of the OAA into the 1860s. In 1872 she was serving her twelfth of twenty-four years as CS president. Mrs. Chester

Dewey began her benevolent career as a manager of the OAA in 1837 and was president by 1841, holding this post for twenty-five out of the next thirty years. She put her leadership skills at the disposal of the CS as well, as directress for nine years, as president for a year, and as vice-president for ten years. Upon her retirement in 1870, the members of the OAA resolved that "our Institution sustains a positive loss in the retirement of our zealous and efficient President," but the loss was not permanent: Mrs. Dewey returned as a member of the honorary executive board in 1872.[27] Mrs. Silas O. Smith's fiftieth year of service, 1872, was likewise noted with a series of resolutions as well as with her election as a directress of the HF, a position she first held in 1855.

By the 1860s perfectionist and ultraist leaders demonstrated that they, too, considered public service a lifelong duty. Mrs. Samuel D. Porter entered worldly labors upon her arrival in Rochester in 1836, laboring for thirty-five years in a wide range of associations and most prominently in the FASS, OAA, LASS, and HF. When she died in 1880, her obituary noted her long years of service to this last society, promoting its work "during all the term of its existence up to the very day preceding her death, (when she attended a meeting of the Board of Directors)."[28] Her sister-in-law, Maria G. Porter, also entered perfectionist circles in 1836, from which she was removed only by death sixty years later. Mrs. Selah Mathews was among the initiators of perfectionist activism in the city. Following her conversion under Charles Finney, she helped found prayer circles and maternal associations and then the FMRS and FASS. In the 1840s she hovered between perfectionist and benevolent enterprises, finally assuming the presidency of the HF in 1851, a position she held for twenty years. Among her ultraist competitors, Amy Post, Mary Hallowell, Sarah Hallowell Willis, Catharine Fish Stebbins, Sarah Burtis, Mary Fish Curtis, and Rhoda DeGarmo all served three decades or more. Each of these women entered the WNYASS in 1842, attended the Rochester Woman's Rights Convention in 1848, entered the ranks of the Congregational Friends the same year, worked for racial and sexual equality through the 1860s, and supported the woman's suffrage campaign in the 1870s.

Both DeGarmo and Curtis died in 1873, having closed their activist careers by voting in the 1872 elections. Amy Post worked for the

[27] OAA, Minute Book, 25 October 1870, HCCP.
[28] *Union and Advertiser* (Rochester), 25 September 1880.

National Liberal League, the National Woman Suffrage Association, and in a variety of local campaigns until her death in 1889 at age eighty-seven. The others stretched ultraist careers into the twentieth century. On the death of ninety-year-old Sarah Burtis in 1900, a coworker recalled that at "the great [suffrage] gatherings in Washington, the young women . . . made much of the delightful old lady, who, it is believed, was the oldest suffrage advocate in the country."[29] Her example would be surpassed by Sarah Hallowell Willis, whose ultraist career of seventy-two years was finally ended by death at age ninety-six in 1914. More than a half century earlier, sixty-four-year-old Sarah Thayer had written to Amy Post, "[My] bodily and mental *Woman* is ever renew'd. The call I have had for my powers has seemed to brighten and toughen my nerves."[30] So it seemed for many of Rochester's most active female leaders.

Rochester's women activists shared their commitment to public labors and to long years of service, but they did not share the same vision of the world in which they lived or in which they hoped to live. Their legacy is the richer for their differences and, even in their own era, their contributions may have been the greater for having to prove the value not just of women's activism but of their particular brand of women's activism. Benevolent women were primarily concerned with ameliorating the hardships inherent in rapid economic and demographic growth. Such amelioration seemed essential to their families' continued control of the political and economic order, control that both fostered and reaped the benefits of Rochester's expansion. Perfectionists were not satisfied with amelioration alone. They sought to cleanse both individuals and institutions of the evils attendant on urban development. The fortunes of their families rested on the tenets of Evangelicalism, the work ethic, and Constitutional democracy, all of which assumed that the channels to salvation as well as to wealth and power would remain open to those who followed the path of righteousness. Ultraists, more critical of existing institutions, envisioned the formation of democratic and egalitarian social, political, and economic relations as the key to re-forming society. Sharing with perfectionists an emphasis on individual conversion, they diverged from them on its

[29] Obituary of Sarah Anthony Burtis, 30 October 1900, in William Farley Peck, Scrapbook, vol. 2, Rochester Public Library.
[30] S[arah] E. Thayer to Amy Post, [?] June 1856, IAPFP.

content and meaning. For ultraists, collective conversion would lead, at the least, to the defusion of hierarchies of power and authority in existing institutions and, at best, to those institutions' fundamental restructuring.

These differing perceptions of social change were derived from differing assumptions about the nature of social order and authority and were reflected in differing attitudes toward class, race, and gender relations. In part, those perceptions were produced by the broad sweep of cultural and intellectual currents, particularly as woman's proper moral and social role was redefined by preachers, physicians, and popular writers in the early decades of the century. Yet women's attitudes were simultaneously shaped by their immediate circumstances, including the churches they attended, the literature they read, the families they lived in, the material resources at their disposal, and the political power and support offered them. In their forms of organization, in the types of activities they pursued, in the roles they assigned to men, working-class women, and blacks, and in the style and content of their public appeals, activist women translated lived experience into visions of and vehicles for social change.

Women modeled their associations on existing institutions, especially religious institutions. The Presbyterian and Episcopal churches from which benevolent leaders emerged were characterized by definite hierarchies of authority, by institutionalized associations such as Sunday schools and missions, and by clear definitions of women's spiritual responsibilities and subordinate status. Benevolent societies were, in turn, hierarchically structured and relatively routinized in administration, while they pursued amelioration through missionary excursions into city neighborhoods or the institutionalization of the needy. While benevolent women uniformly established all-female associations over which women themselves presided, they asserted women's subordinate status through deference to male political and financial advisers and to clerical spokesmen.

Within each association differentiation of tasks among members was clearly defined; to carry out these tasks, a large portion of CS and OAA activists served in some official capacity during their benevolent careers. Filling the offices of these associations in the early years required the participation of at least one third of the members each year. In the CS, for instance, an ever expanding number of directresses, collectors, and visitors broadened the leadership base in tandem with the increased population of the city and of the society itself. At the same time, there were distinctions made between a relatively small number of CS leaders who held major and multiple offices over an extended period and a much larger number who served more briefly in minor offices. Substantially different tasks were assigned to women in these various positions. Major officers set associational policy, dealt with hired personnel, dispensed funds, and acted as liaisons with male advisers and community leaders. Collectors worked in churches or wards to recruit members and collect dues, thus coming into contact primarily with members of their own social circle. It was primarily district visitors, then, who came into direct contact with the poor and needy whom the CS sought to aid.

Minor officers were required to report to the CS executive board to gain access to funds and goods to be distributed. In the OAA, administrative channels were established that restricted the power of most members by making a directress's approval necessary to the admission of any orphan to the asylum. Over time, an expanding hierarchy removed benevolent officers even further from the poverty, illness, or distress they sought to ameliorate, while increasing their control over the resources for that amelioration. The high turnover or hired status of those most immediately in contact with the recipients of aid diminished these workers' impact on associational policy. Benevolent leaders were not unaffected by the social problems they hoped to alleviate, but they, like their male business and political counterparts, created structural as well as social distance between themselves and the unfortunate. Only CS visitors maintained direct contact with the needy. By mid-century, these CS workers were the only female activists other than perfectionist abolitionists and ultraists who preferred to aid individuals in their own homes rather than relocate them in institutions.

Initially, all perfectionists pursued noninstitutional means of reforming society. When universal perfection was the goal, it was essential to reach out to and discover every hidden perpetrator of vice and every reluctant convert to virtue. Drawing on evangelical forms, perfectionists of the 1830s adopted moral suasion, on a mass scale, as the means to change society. While the FASS and FMRS elected leaders annually, they did not establish the differentation of tasks among major and minor officers and members that their benevolent counterparts drew. The early emphasis in antislavery and moral reform work on personal conversion and individual salvation meant that members could perform the most important duties without the approval of superiors. Lesser access to and need for funds in such projects also diffused the authority that might have inhered in hierarchy, as did the geographical dispersion of members throughout the city's agricultural hinterland.

Perfectionist leaders' primary tasks involved the coordination of activities, the hiring of agents and the distribution of pamphlets, tracts, and other items to members, correspondence with parent associations and with rural and small-town auxiliaries, and contact with male clergy and editors. Yet perfectionist associations were managed by a small core of women who were less easily replaced than benevolent leaders when they suspended their activities for any reason. It was this core of leaders who initially determined that petition campaigns, prayer circles, pamphleteering, and direct confrontations with evil-doers were the proper weapons to be used in improving imperfect conditions and gaining community support. In the 1840s, as this core of leaders came under attack from conservative community leaders, they focused increasing attention on their own spiritual and moral perfection through prayer meetings and addresses by gentlemen.

Throughout the first phase of perfectionism, most activists came into contact with members of their own neighborhoods and churches—as they collected signatures on petitions and pledges and circulated copies of reform journals—far more often than with the blacks, drunkards, or prostitutes they aimed to save. As with benevolent workers, the distance of activists from their public charges increased over time; only two visitors of the FMRS and eighteen members of the temperance Vigilance Committee devoted as much time to reclaiming the victims of vice as to reconfirming their own salvation. The establishment of the HF brought activist and client back into close contact, but now those clients were supposedly all virtuous and the meeting place was not the private residence of the needy but the public home of her benefactors.

The LASS retained more of the appearance of its perfectionist predecessor but in truncated form. The small core of leaders remained, but the numerous and far-flung membership had devolved into auxiliary sewing circles in nearby towns that were both distinct from and subordinate to the Rochester association. All of the society's officers resided in the city and all of its major events were held there. Among the circle of directors, tasks were widely shared. The clearest distinction was between those women, like Julia Griffiths, who worked nearly full time for the cause and those who participated primarily in fund-raising for the LASS while also working for other causes or for wages. It was evident by the 1850s that LASS leaders hoped to expand their ranks by attracting benevolent supporters. Accordingly, at their anti-slavery fairs, less emphasis was placed on obtaining simon-pure anti-slavery money than on attracting the best class of citizens through ornamental sale items, eloquent speakers, and elegant entertainment. These fairs were held annually and modeled on church and charitable, rather than earlier abolitionist, bazaars.

Compared with benevolent and perfectionist women, ultraists seemed decidedly disorganized. Their associations were characterized by fluid forms of authority, event-oriented selections of leaders, and decentralized decision making. In the early 1840s, when ultraist women and men joined evangelical men in the WNYASS, the organizational forms they adopted were closer to those of other activist groups. Yet in practice hierarchy was generally diffused, and hierarchical forms began disappearing again in the following decade. By 1854 a coworker wrote to Amy Post, "I too with thee have turned my face from all 'organizations.' "[31] Conventions, fairs, and meetings rather than formal associations became the basis for ultraist endeavors until the suffrage era. Within each arena of activity, men and women shared equal labors in principle even when they performed distinct activities. In the small circles of association in which ultraists worked, only small differences in tasks developed between leaders and members. Some women served more frequently and over a longer period, but if this gave them greater control over policy or resources it was only in an informal way. Such women were more likely to visit and correspond with extralocal workers and with national leaders and to attend meetings and fairs outside Rochester, but these efforts were largely on their own initiative rather than at the direction of sister workers. After mid-century, urban women played the most prominent role in ultraist endeavors, though in principle rural activists were accorded equal status.

Ultraists, especially within the Hicksite meeting, had first concentrated their efforts on relieving their own oppression, as religious sectarians or women. Beginning in the 1840s, however, with the WNYASS, they began extending their reach into the larger community, fighting racial prejudice and then sexual and class exploitation. Choosing neither to institutionalize those whom they sought to aid nor to provide

---

[31] Esther Titus to Amy Post, 26 February [1854], IAPFP.

male colleagues with the means of acting in the world, female ultraists offered immediate and individualized attention to free blacks, working women, and others of disparate social and economic circumstances. In these endeavors, their differences from benevolent and perfectionist women were clear: blacks and workers were not so much victims to be aided as coworkers to be organized. The assumption that persons of lesser social and economic status could be coworkers set ultraists apart from sister activists and from the community at large.

The CS claimed that all classes were welcome to lend a hand in its efforts, but the rhetoric was belied by the CS's attitudes toward their own labors and toward those they aided. During the society's first decade, fortunes could be quickly made and lost in the village's boom-town economy, so class distinctions were difficult to maintain. These frontier conditions and the fact that visitors could actually acquaint themselves with most families in their districts may have blurred lines between almsgivers and the recipients of aid. By the mid-1830s, however, the residential segregation of the poorer classes and tales of abuse and intemperance within their neighborhoods encouraged CS leaders to make clear distinctions between worthy and unworthy and between themselves and those they aided. By 1860 the society proudly announced that under its auspices "the rich and poor, the prosperous and the unfortunate, the hale strong ones and the pining invalids, may meet without any intervening mockeries or delusions. . . ." Certain that its visitors were rarely deceived, the CS assured the community that professional vagrants, beggars, and indolent persons were refused relief. To be worthy, "the sick and suffering poor" must be "the smitten and shrinking victims of misfortune and disease, . . . who but for our aid were ready to perish." One particularly deserving woman "suffered intensely, but bore all her pain with patience" and often expressed her gratitude "for the assistance and consolation she had received from the Society." This worthy woman died a quiet and exemplary death.[32] The worthy poor bore their burdens in the same manner as did the benevolent lady—noiselessly.

Perfectionist women, emerging from the most dynamic economic sector, claimed that conversion and salvation were available to all, regardless of gender, race, or class. Yet their horror of vice and intemperance suggests that they did make distinctions between themselves

[32]CS, *Charter*, pp. 13, 14.

and the victims of vice, most of whom they assumed were from the poorer classes. Indeed, they assured themselves and their neighbors that anyone who lived a life of licentiousness and intemperance would sink to the depths of destitution, thus removing from suspicion any upstanding middle-class family, or at least its successful members. Initially, the character of perfectionists' class distinctions remained implicit since early perfectionists did express sympathy for the victims of vice, especially female victims, and looked to religious rather than economic forces to explain and expunge social problems. In the 1850s moral reformers and abolitionists expressed their class concerns more explicitly, seeking the aid of those with "influence, wealth, [and] talent" while aiding the "poor and industrious."[33] HF and IS members most frequently came into direct contact with young working-class women. They sought to aid these women by teaching them domestic skills and preparing them for jobs as seamstresses or servants, which they considered the proper and pragmatic route to salvation for laboring women.

The influx of large numbers of immigrants in the 1840s and 1850s sharpened class issues for some activist women, including a majority of those in the OAA and HF. Fed by the nativist fears that swept the country in the early 1850s, the asylum and home were closed to Catholic priests and their parishioners, however needy. This was a specific change in policy, written into the bylaws of the two associations, and revealing a departure from the more ecumenical spirit of their early years. Anti-Catholicism might have arisen earlier, in the midst of Protestants' revivalistic zeal, except that it was not until mid-century that "Popish religion" was linked with poverty and intemperance in the minds of Rochesterians. It was at this point, though with the vocal dissent of a minority, that the OAA and HF chose to banish the working-class Catholics from their houses of refuge.[34] Among the Protestant poor, moral uplift and domestic training continued to be used as the primary means of salvaging the destitute.

Ultraists followed a decidedly different course. In the formation of the Working Women's Protective Union, ultraist women revealed their faith in organizing laboring women to meet the workers' own needs. The first four officers of the union included two seamstresses. Member-

[33] LASS, "Circular," SDPFP.
[34] See OAA, Minute Book, 26 July, 29 November, 27 December 1853 and 28 February 1855, HCCP; HF, Minute Book, 29 March 1854, FHP.

ship dues for women were set at one cent weekly to allow working women "to associate together for . . . [their] individual and collective benefit and protection." Men were also allowed to join the organization but for the sum of two cents weekly, "this inequality of assessment" to cease when "women receive an equal remuneration for the same labor performed as men."[35] Ultraist women recognized differences of class within their own ranks and asked that the more affluent take particular cognizance of the terms by which they employed help. They also asked working women to articulate their grievances to ultraist gatherings as well as to the community.[36]

At the 1848 convention, several reports detailed the conditions of laboring women in Rochester, the author of one denouncing "the *castes* and *ranks* existing in society."[37] In Congregational Friends meetings and private correspondence, ultraist women also discussed the relation between "capital & labor."[38] They condemned women's lack of control over their own earnings, noting that if a wife needs "some addition to her wardrobe," her husband, "must be the judge before he will allow her to have the means to make the purchase." Yet, "in -reality," ultraists argued, the money "as rightfully belongs to her as to him—she either recev'd [*sic*] it from her inheritance or contributed her full share of labour to produce it."[39] To eradicate this exploitation of working women, ultraists not only organized the union but in 1854 appointed a committee "to prepare an address to capitalists and industrialists of New York on the best modes of employing and remunerating the energies of women."[40] They also constantly petitioned for woman's property rights, including the control of land, personal and household goods, and wages and the right to sue for the same in court.

Ultraists also individually aided abused, abandoned, and widowed women, whose harrowing tales strengthened the belief that poor women needed not only assistance but also the means of fighting their own battles. Nancy Hassey, abandoned by her husband, wrote to an ultraist friend in Rochester after resettling with her children in Buffalo. She thanked the woman for her "kindness to me . . . and my child."

[35] *North Star* (Rochester, 15 September 1848.
[36] See *Daily Advertiser* (Rochester), 3 August 1848; Sarah D. Fish, "A Word for Domestics," *Liberator* (Boston), 22 August 1852.
[37] *Daily Advertiser,* 3 August 1848.
[38] Mary Robbins Post to Amy Post, n.d., IAPFP.
[39] [Amy Post], "Resolution for the Rochester Woman's Rights Convention," written on the back of a prospectus for *North Star,* 2 August 1848, IAPFP.
[40] *The Lily,* 2 January 1854.

Now "I will exert myself for a living," she continued, "as long as I have strength to do so."[41] Another woman wrote to Amy Post, "I am worse than a *widow* for the one that should be my *Protector* is changed to a cruel *Enamy* [*sic*] and that is harder to be reconciled to than my extreme destitution."[42] Yet a third claimed that a widow's lot was harder, reporting that a friend had lost her husband and "like many others . . . was compelled to commence a struggle with the cold world."[43] Ultraists were certain that only legal protections, equal access to and pay for employment, and the organization of the exploited could ultimately relieve these problems.

The perception of the working class by benevolent women as charges to be aided, by perfectionists as persons to be saved or rehabilitated, and by ultraists as individuals to be organized was paralleled in many ways by their perception of blacks. Yet racism and a relative lack of contact with free blacks complicated these general patterns. Two CS charter members were daughters of slave owners and, though aid was apparently given to free blacks, some resistance may have arisen from these and other female relatives of Rochester's Southern-born founders. Few benevolent leaders were married to active abolitionists in this period, and few joined women's antislavery efforts in the 1830s. Upon the establishment of the asylum, a number of OAA board members voted to exclude black children from its services.

It was the perfectionists sitting on the same OAA board who insisted on black orphans' admission to the asylum. In many Northern cities, even the establishment of separate asylums for black orphans was considered so radical that few supporters could be found. Thus FASS women's willingness to mix black and white orphans in the asylum and to improve the "character and condition" of the city's free blacks by their own efforts suggested that they were far in advance of most Northerners on racial issues. Their main concern, however, was the immediate emancipation of the enslaved of the South—a concern that required little direct contact with blacks in the city. In the 1850s some of these same activists joined black women in the management of the Thompson antislavery festival, and reasserted their concern for the "improvement and elevation" of the enslaved race.[44] The society's major contact with free blacks, however, was not in Rochester but in

41 Nancy Hassey to [?], n.d., IAPFP.
42 E. Bowen to Amy Post, 19 November 1857, IAPFP.
43 Jenny Dods to Amy Post, n.d., IAPFP.
44 LASS, "Circular," SDPFP.

Canada and Alexandria, Virginia. Julia Wilbur's reports on her labors in the latter city reflected a missionary concern with the "instruction and encouragement" of blacks similar to that demonstrated by HF women toward working-class females.[45] LASS members, with their attention focused on fugitives and ex-slaves and their subsidies given to male political abolitionists, were able to avoid the severe criticism that had disheartened their forerunners and to sustain their activities over many more years.

The context of women's antislavery labors had changed between the two periods of perfectionist abolitionism. More women were speaking out publicly against slavery, and a variety of positions from third-party politics to disunionism had been hammered out among opposing camps of activists. While perfectionist abolitionists in the FASS had advocated the most radical doctrines of their era—immediate emancipation without compensation—their sisters in the LASS focused on more pragmatic and specifically political solutions. While still more progressive on race issues than most Rochesterians, perfectionist abolitionists of the 1850s were no longer in the vanguard of antislavery thought. Ultraists, who referred to enslaved women as "OUR SISTERS" and sought to live out such relationships with local free blacks, now held that vanguard position.[46]

While ultraists' formal ties with black antislavery societies were only slightly more extensive than perfectionists', their personal associations with local blacks seem to have been considerably wider. Visits with black families, correspondence with fugitives briefly met, invitations to social events at the homes of blacks and at the Methodist Episcopal Zion Church, the placement of newly freed blacks in jobs after the war, and the admission of black women to antislavery sewing circles all reflected ultraists' everyday commitment to racial integration. In antislavery, Congregational Friends, and woman's rights meetings, ultraists demanded complete equality and sought the eradication of racial prejudice in themselves and the world at large. A number of blacks testified to the ultraists' success in their personal battles. Frederick Douglass wrote to Amy Post before he settled in Rochester, "Your family was always Dear—very dear to me, you loved me and treated me as a brother before the world knew me as it does & when my friends

---

[45] LASS, *Thirteenth Annual Report* (Rochester: Rochester Democrat Steam Printing House, 1864), p. 19.
[46] *Daily Democrat,* 4 April 1848.

were fewer than they now are."[47] Harriet Brent Jacobs addressed Amy Post as "my dear friend" whose "purity of heart and kind sympathies" convinced Jacobs to write her autobiography.[48] William C. Nell constantly praised the commitment of the WNYASS workers. He wrote an open letter to the *Liberator* in 1852 while he was a "sojourner with Isaac and Amy Post," claiming that their names were "synonymous with Truth and Zeal in Humanity's cause."[49]

Attitudes toward blacks and the working classes revealed activists' differing conceptions of social order, conceptions that were crucial in determining the means by which they pursued social change. Benevolent women, from first-settled families with deep roots in the commercial towns of New England or the plantation aristocracy of Maryland, assumed that different social roles were assigned to rich and poor and whites and blacks as well as to men and women. CS women forgot neither their Savior's admonition that "the poor ye have always with you" nor his promise " 'With what measure ye mete, it shall be measured to you again.' "[50] Their vision of society as composed of a ranked order of classes demanded their acceptance of their responsibilities as almsgivers. The fortunes of their families seemed bound to both the order and the duty, and should they not mete out alms to ameliorate social ills, the measure returned might not be welcome.

While perfectionist women also accepted a hierarchically ordered society, their own experience of mobility in the midst of rapid economic change made them sensitive to the "trial and temptation" of urban society.[51] They wished to minimize the worst effects of social and economic dislocation on the community at large and on their own families and neighborhoods. They were anxious first to rehabilitate the fallen and the needy and later to provide them with moral instruction and material resources that would allow them to become "self-supporting" within the confines of their proper social role.[52] Their concern was not to establish equality among races or classes but to assure that those determined "to be free and enlightened" might "arise from

---

[47] Frederick Douglass to Amy Post, 28 April 1846, IAPFP.

[48] Harriet Brent Jacobs to Amy Post, 21 June [185–] and n.d., IAPFP. Amy Post wrote the foreword to Harriet Brent Jacobs, *Incidents in the Life of a Slave Girl, Written by Herself,* ed. by Lydia M. Child (Boston: privately published, 1861).

[49] *Liberator,* 5 March 1852.

[50] CS, *Charter,* p. 15.

[51] HF, Minute Book, 28 March 1849, FHP.

[52] LASS, *Thirteenth Annual Report,* p. 5.

[their] degraded condition."[53] Believing that as Evangelicals and as women they were already among the chosen, perfectionists sought the proper and uncorrupted functioning of the institutions of church, state, and economy through which they and their families might improve their own place in the community.

Ultraists, emerging from relatively homogeneous villages characterized by religious precepts of sexual equality and limited class stratification, did not invest the institutions of commercial and urban society with the same God-given status accorded it by their peers. Confronting a more stratified, sex-segregated, and bureaucratized community upon their arrival in Rochester, ultraists became sensitized to the distinctiveness of their own social experiences. Knowing from that experience that sharp differences in the roles of men and women were not ordained by nature, ultraists increasingly questioned the supposed naturalness of other divisions and distinctions. Ultraists were excluded from the city's centers of power and authority but unlike blacks and working women still had sufficient resources to challenge some of the worst abuses of power and authority; and for them, change was more promising than stability and order.

Seeking to reorder society, female activists of necessity reached beyond the boundaries of their particular associations. They formed alliances with other organizations and groups, appealed for more general support, and encouraged the translation of moral into pecuniary favor. Benevolent women generally forged alliances only within the boundaries of their own kinship and church circles in Rochester itself. Perfectionists, with visions of a millennium that crossed community boundaries, allied themselves with coworkers in surrounding towns and other urban centers in the 1830s. The delimitation of their millennial perspective also led to the circumscription of their extralocal alliances, which were continued but in modified and restricted forms. Ultraists found few allies in Rochester outside their own circles of association. Local apathy and the continued hopes of ultraists for a universal re-formation led them to alliances with kindred spirits— whether Quakers in Ohio and Michigan, disaffected Evangelicals in New England and New York, free blacks in Boston, Philadelphia, Rochester, and Canada, or the spirits of ancestors.

Both perfectionists and ultraists reached beyond the city limits to find coworkers and supporters, yet they touched few of the same com-

[53] LASS, "Circular," SDPFP.

munities. Perfectionists looked to female residents of Rochester's agricultural hinterland whose farmer, artisan, and shopkeeping kin were closely tied into the urban commercial network, while ultraists appealed to those in agrarian Quaker communities who were largely isolated from the city, economically as well as geographically. By the 1850s perfectionists and ultraists in the antislavery movement also reached across the Atlantic for coworkers. According to Julia Griffiths, "the cause of *human freedom*" could be "bound by no geographical or national lines." It demanded the "co-operation of the universe."[54] For perfectionists, however, the antislavery universe only embraced the British Isles. It was ultraists who took Griffiths at her word, and though they did not forge working relations with Europeans outside Britain, they followed revolutionary events throughout the world. At mid-century, Sarah Owen, removed to the wilds of Michigan, wrote to the Posts, "I have just been reading the result of the Hungarian effort for freedom, and it will deeply effect [*sic*] the heart of every lover of liberty."[55]

Commitment to a wide array of revolutionary causes was an important principle among ultraists, but most activist women were more concerned with finding allies who could provide practical support—laborers, publicity, or funds. Since women were not expected to speak out in public, female activists were faced with special difficulties in publicizing their goals and achievements. Even the CS claimed that it encountered the perennial problem of "calling the attention of the public to the wants of this society."[56] Sermons were the means first used by the benevolent ladies to announce their presence to the community, while all activists employed speeches, pamphlets, reports, and public meetings—some written or read by women activists themselves. Yet these forms were most effective only when an association had gained the popular ear. The founders of the CS had devised an efficient way to introduce themselves simultaneously to the needy and to the affluent—the district visiting plan. Beginning in the 1830s, however, the segregation of city neighborhoods by class and ethnicity limited personal visitation as a vehicle for meeting a cross-section of the city, and other means had to be developed, especially to catch the attention of the affluent.

The OAA found that the location and appearance of the asylum itself

[54] Ibid.
[55] Sarah [C. Owen] to Amy Post, 24 September [?], IAPFP.
[56] CS, Minute Book, 3 October 1848, CSP.

was an important advertisement. A Greek Revival mansion in an idyllic landscape could attract both attention and investment. After barely two years of existence, members of the asylum board publicly congratulated themselves on having acquired a "suitable home . . . in a healthy and retired part of the city, on Corn Hill, with a garden attached." They moved to a "spacious and delightful building" nearer the city's center in 1844. Several years later they added a new carriage entrance and a fence with "the words 'Protestant Orphan Asylum' . . . printed distinctly" on it, and to assure the fullest attention, they attached "additional boards . . . during the time of the State Fair, with the words, open from 9 A.M. to 6 P.M."[57]

Antislavery, moral reform, and temperance advocates competed with the OAA for funds but lacked an institutional vehicle for their appeals. Consequently, they returned to the practice of house-to-house solicitation that had been utilized by the CS. They were less interested in meeting the needy, however, than in obtaining the membership dues and signatures of middle-class women. They were generally more successful in getting the signatures. When perfectionists reemerged in the 1850s, they had learned a good deal about public relations and appealed to the community through less personal but more publicly palatable means. The HF adopted the institutional weapons of the OAA. They painted "Home for the Friendless" across the portal, believing that "the virtue of its touching appellation" would direct "the minds of the public to it as they spelled its letters on the sign over the door. . . ."[58] Thus passersby would be immediately inspired to offer aid to the institution. Antislavery perfectionists were not so eager or so able to adopt benevolent forms, and they continued personal solicitations. Yet their primary means of gaining attention was the annual antislavery bazaar in which they showcased women's domestic skills, female abolitionists's connection to British allies, and male political abolitionists oratorical powers.[59]

Ultraist abolitionists had held fairs for almost a decade before the LASS did, believing that such events served to awaken the public. They also employed more dramatic means to overcome local apathy. To gain wide attention with few workers, they employed popular polit-

[57] OAA, Minute Book, 28 May 1839; Annual Report, 1844, Scrapbook; and Minute Book, 28 July 1851, HCCP.

[58] HF, Annals of the Home, 1849–1858, FHP.

[59] Clearly these events were organized to raise funds, but the dissemination of information was always noted as an important secondary function of fairs.

ical forms—rallies, demonstrations, and parades in the city's public parks. Fourth of July picnics might also lure potential recruits who, once in attendance, would hear not proclamations on American freedom but denunciations of American slavery. Individual women forced their ultraist politics into the public eye by strolling down city streets in the company of free blacks or in the costume of Turkish trousers.[60] Since the ultraists primary concern was raising community consciousness rather than donations, they were willing to be far bolder in their publicity tactics.

Having gained attention, activists still had to convince Rochesterians to accept their particular programs and policies. Private conversation and correspondence were the most intimate and unostentatious forms of persuasion and were thus the favored means of benevolent leaders. In 1855, for instance, a CS committee was selected to petition the common council, reminding them of "the duties of the city physician . . . to the sick poor." Finding it "difficult to prepare a document that shall contain the necessary facts . . . without expressing more than might be prudent to write," they suggested that a few ladies obtain the opinion of the city leaders, privately, as to "the expedience and usefulness" of such an action. As a result, the mayor agreed to discuss the matter informally with the city physicians "and the desired results were secured without the drafting of the memorial."[61] OAA and HF leaders similarly laid "subjects before the gentlemen" of the city, yet such intimate discussions could not meet the needs of all activists.[62]

When the groups presented their arguments to a wide audience, differences in style and content were even more conspicuous. For example, when the CS announced its entry into organized civic activity, it did so through the sermon of Rev. Francis H. Cuming at St. Luke's Episcopal Church, the spire-capped tower of which adorned the city's center. Woman's rights advocates, on the other hand, announced their cause to the community in their own "faltering tongues" from the front of the Unitarian church, a small frame structure on Fitzhugh Street at the border of the first and second wards.[63] Perfec-

[60] Numerous examples of such acts appear in the *North Star* and the IAPFP. It is certain that Susan B. Anthony and Lucy Coleman wore bloomers, and the approval of such dress is voiced by several other ultraists. See Harper, *Life and Work,* 1: 115–119.

[61] Quoted in Hanmer-Croughton, "Rochester Female Charitable Society," p. 67.

[62] OAA, Minute Book, 18 February 1837, HCCP; *Canfield and Warren's Directory of the City of Rochester, for 1845–1846, with a Map* (Rochester: John Canfield and Ansel Warren, 1845), p. 9.

[63] WRC, Minutes, 2 August 1848, PPWP.

tionist women combined these forms, calling on evangelical clergy to proclaim their virtues to the community while they articulated their own views in ladies' meetings and reform journals. Indeed, the primary perfectionist innovation was the establishment of a local institutional publication, the *Journal of the Home,* which combined local activist news with fiction, poetry, advice, and other elements borrowed from religious, reform, and popular periodicals. Through the *JHF* home women were able to express their views to a wide audience in Rochester and the surrounding area without retreating behind male spokesmen or advancing onto the public platform themselves. Their example was followed by the IS, SAS, and city hospital.

Women's exclusion from public platforms had never been absolute, but the hearing they received varied dramatically depending on the style and content of their presentations and the audience they faced. CS women prided themselves on never ascending such platforms, having pursued four decades of service "noiselessly, economically, and consistently."[64] The author of their 1860 history claimed that the records of the society "present no striking occurrences or extraordinary achievements" but bear testimony instead to "perseverance in well doing."[65] This image of the quiet and patient almsgiver contrasts sharply with that presented by mid-century ultraists. In an "Address to the Women of the State of New York," ultraists claimed that in order to free woman to fulfill her real role in life, it was necessary to enumerate past wrongs "however harshly [they] may grate upon the delicate and perverted sensibilities of the public ear." Such wrongs will continue, they claimed, "unless woman, by emphatically demanding and maintaining her rights, shall prove she is worthy of them."[66]

Benevolent women certainly claimed a large sphere of activity for themselves, engaged in financial and political affairs, and administered sweeping social welfare programs and institutions. One way they preserved an image of proper feminine submissiveness in the midst of such activities was using an anonymous passive voice in their public pronouncements. When they did not channel their public appeals through men, benevolent women spoke as the "Society," the "Board of Managers," the "Asylum," or simply as the indefinite "We." They were not actors but "instruments".[67] Rather than particular leaders, it was the

[64] Quoted in Hanmer-Croughton, "Rochester Female Charitable Society," p. 79.
[65] CS, *Charter,* p. 5.
[66] YMCF, *Proceedings, 1850,* pp. 15, 16.
[67] This language appears repeatedly in associational records and published reports of the CS and OAA.

"Institution" or the "Society" that sought support. Indeed, the only mention of the names of individual workers in the reports of these societies, other than the list of officers, was of those who had been "called away by death."[68]

Having emphasized silent meditation within Quaker meetings, worldly activists came to view silence as an unworthy *"IDOL"* and quickly labored to get rid of the burden.[69] They prided themselves on their "straight-forward common sense" and rarely pulled punches in their fight for the public mind.[70] Ultraists claimed they were justified in speaking "more boldly" in the antislavery cause because "those for whom we plead cannot plead for themselves." Perhaps referring to perfectionist women's retreat from abolitionism, ultraist women chided former advocates whose "ears seem to have grown heavy so that they do not hear the clanking of the bondsman's chains." Ultraists had not only to present their own views but also to drown out "the slanderous tongue of negro haters."[71] They were equally vocal in the cause of women. Noting that woman's "name and her being . . . have scarcely a recognition upon the Statute Book, or the Historic Page," feminists of the period pleaded for woman "to build unto herself a name for her talents, energy, and integrity."[72] Ultraist women's names uniformly appeared in the published proceedings of conventions, the announcement of fairs, and the reports of meetings. Moreover, in stark contrast to their benevolent counterparts, ultraist women employed their first and last names unadorned by titles of marital status or office. Clearly, these women were "not deterred from prudent conscientious action by the felt pressure of public sentiment," nor, even though they sought the support of their neighbors, did they shrink from condemning "the men in [their] own county and city" who had become "too imbued with the i[dea] of man's superiority."[73] Ultraists rarely called for aid; rather they called for action on the basis of the "high uncompromising ground of right."[74]

The two perfectionist associations that emerged at mid-century,

[68] For a few of many examples see OAA, Annual Report, 1844, 1846, 1847, and 1859, Scrapbook, HCCP.

[69] Mary W. WIllis to Amy Post, n.d., IAPFP.

[70] Announcement of a lecture by Sojourner Truth, n.d., IAPFP.

[71] *North Star,* 9 November 1849, 16 November 1849.

[72] YMCF, *Proceedings, 1850,* p. 15; WRC, "Proceedings," in Mari Jo and Paul Buhle, eds., *The Concise History of Woman Suffrage* (Chicago: University of Illinois Press, 1978), p. 101.

[73] YMCF, *Proceedings, 1850,* p. 18; WRC, "Resolution, IAPFP.

[74] *North Star,* 29 December 1848.

fearing they would be lost between the quiet power of female benevolence and the harsh din of ultraism, sought to combine elements of assertion and submissiveness in their public appeals. The founders of the HF assumed much of the anonymity of their benevolent counterparts, speaking as the voice of the "Home Association" or the "Board." The home's "baptismal name was its chief recommendation," and its success was rooted in the "marked sympathy of the community and the evident tokens of the favor of Providence."[75] Yet HF women were less passive in their assertions than such anonymity might suggest. In their annual report of 1851, published in the local papers, the HF board complained of the paltry contributions from the gentlemen of the city. Moreover, once disguised as anonymous and collective spokespersons of an "Institution," HF women periodically detailed dramatic cases of the abuse, abandonment, and ruin that awaited unprotected females.

Similarly, the leaders of the LASS began their first report by claiming their "indebted[ness] to the kind co-operation of friends on both sides of the Atlantic" and trusting that their reports would be "acceptable to the friends of the slave."[76] Soon, however, they proclaimed that the society's business was "urgent and imperative" and called upon "the friends of freedom *everywhere*" to fulfill the "duty of increasing their activity."[77] In the 1860s the members still disclaimed personal recognition—or responsibility: "as individuals we have done little" though "as a Society we may feel that our influence has been felt for good." Yet they also "chafed at the slowness of those in power" and chided the president for his "disastrous Colonization scheme."[78] LASS women, like HF women, combined their gratitude for any "tokens" of "sympathy" with revelations about the results of inaction and urgent demands for public attention to the needs of their society. They thus relied on the "better feelings of the community" while they avoided the harsher tones of ultraist Amazons and demonstrated a "well directed interest in the world's affairs."[79]

[75] HF, Annals of the Home, 1849–1858, FHP; *Daily Democrat,* 23 April 1853.
[76] LASS, "Circular," SDPFP.
[77] LASS, "The Third Annual Report of the Festival Held by the Rochester Ladies' Anti-Slavery Sewing Society," n.d., n.p., WHSP.
[78] LASS, *Thirteenth Annual Report,* pp. 2, 3, 19.
[79] Julia Griffiths to Mrs. William Henry Seward, 4 August 1854, penciled note on copy of the LASS, "Third Annual Report," WHSP; OAA, Annual Report, 1838, Scrapbook, HCCP; *JHF,* 1 September 1860.

The styles of argument chosen by activist women are products of both their location in the community and the forms of social change they espoused. The noiseless activity of benevolent women was indicative, in part, of the mild changes they sought to effect, while the collective anonymity of "the Society" or "We" was rendered powerful by the well-known social and economic circumstances of those who stood behind it.[80] The bolder and louder assertions of ultraists reflected both their commitment to radical change and their distance from the public ear. Realizing that apathy and opposition often combined to muffle or distort their messages, ultraists had little choice but "to tell *plainly what we want,* so plainly that it will admit of no two inter[preta-tions]. . . ."[81]

Activist women had clear economic motives for appealing to the public, though only a small number of events were formally designated as fund-raising affairs. Since these endeavors entailed women's entrance into public and specifically economic domains in ways that often challenged community standards of propriety, activist women tended to be highly self-conscious regarding to whom and how they directed their applications for aid. The necessity for and the delicacy of this task among nineteenth-century female activists meant that in this domain the various elements of each group's activism—organization, programs, class and racial attitudes, alliances, and appeals—converged in particularly vivid ways.

Benevolent women depended on their personal ties to community leaders to provide a buffer between economic needs and overt public appeals. Sermons and private solicitations of gentlemen were the most acceptable means by which benevolent ladies garnered funds. The OAA found these sources insufficient, however, and gradually developed a series of events that proved financially fruitful and conformed to dominant notions of women's proper role. The "orphans' concert" was the most popular. The "buoyant spirit and healthy beaming faces" brought before the community at the concert in 1855 "sp[oke] eloquently of the Orphan's home." The managers hoped that

[80] A suggestive essay on the power of this form of language is R. Brown and A. Gilman, "The Pronouns of Power and Solidarity," in Pier Paolo Giglioli, ed., *Language and Social Context* (New York: Penguin, 1972), pp. 252–282. See also Dell Hymes, *Foundations of Sociolinguistics: An Ethnographic Approach* (Philadelphia: University of Pennsylvania Press, 1974).

[81] Amy Post to Howard Harrison, 2 November 1852, IAPFP. On Quaker modes of plain speaking, see Richard Bauman, "Aspects of Quaker Rhetoric: An Essay in God's Truth" (Ph.D. diss., University of Pennsylvania, 1968).

"citizens and strangers" would be encouraged by this performance to visit the asylum, where they could "witness the practical results of their charity."[82] Benevolent societies also tried to limit the apparent frequency of their appeals, identifying fund-raising events as the annual sermon, annual donation day, or annual concert. Thus they minimized their visibility in the more material aspects of moral pursuits. They were aided by wealthy Rochesterians who left substantial legacies to benevolent associations and by visiting lecturers and entertainers who offered to perform benefits on their behalf.

Perfectionist associations, including the HF in its early years, could not be assured of similar benefits. The late entry of the LASS and HF into competition for community resources and their need for large sums of money led to certain commonalities in their financial appeals. The LASS clearly sought to interest "a class of Rochester citizens" not previously reached by abolitionist appeals. The HF, while gaining some benefactors from benevolent ranks, also hoped to attract a wider circle of "friends and patrons."[83] That many of these friends and patrons were members of the nouveau riche is suggested by HF and LASS women's interest in publishing the names of their donors, often accompanied by specific descriptions in dollars or the goods of the donations.[84] Only the OAA's 1839 publication of its building-fund subscribers provides a parallel among benevolent enterprises. Indeed, the anonymity of benevolent benefactors was so frequently proclaimed that it was certainly a sign of status to be sufficiently affluent to offer alms without public recognition. Donors to perfectionist campaigns were upwardly mobile citizens pleased to announce their entry into philanthropic ranks.

The HF and LASS reached into the ranks of new wealth primarily via its female members. The list of British articles sold at LASS fairs— "finely wrought baby linen, the exquisite sea-weed baskets, the drawings, the collection of Irish sea shells, and the beautiful embroidery"— were meant to attract a female clientele.[85] The home, too, supplied a table of "fancy goods" at its donation day. It also supplied a visitors' book and a refreshment table, creating the equivalent of a private calling day in a public space.[86] The language of perfectionist publica-

[82] OAA, Annual Report, 1855, Scrapbook, HCCP.
[83] *Daily Democrat*, 23 April 1853.
[84] For a particularly detailed example, see the *JHF*, 1 December 1860.
[85] LASS, "Circular," SDPFP.
[86] For a description of one such day, see *JHF*, 1 November 1860.

tions was also directed at a respectable female audience. It was bolder and more dramatic in tone than that used by benevolent publicists, yet perfectionists offset that boldness by appealing specifically to women and by couching the evils of slavery and friendless women in the rhetoric of moral and religious sentimentalism. While in its annual report, the LASS did periodically describe slavery as a "heinous crime" and "deep disgrace," it generally employed more uplifting language to discuss the cause, especially in fund-raising appeals. The organizers of the LASS fair appealed to their audience, for instance, by pointing to the individual success of "a colored man," Frederick Douglass, who "burst thro' the thick incrustations of ignorance" and arose "from his degraded condition." Performing a "missionary work," they "humbly [relied] upon *'the God of the oppressed,'* to bless their labors" and awaited the day "when rejoicing millions, redeemed from thrall-dom, shall attest that *'He who sitteth in the Heavens, and ruleth the destinies of men is merciful and just.'*"[87] At times the LASS seemed bent on disguising the identity of those it sought to aid—Southern blacks—by describing them in terms generally reserved for the needy in their own midst. In 1855, for instance, the LASS described its objectives in purely benevolent terms: to " 'deal out its bread to the hungry,' 'bring the poor that are cast out to its house,' assist the wayfaring man, and help homeless exiles to a place of safety."[88] Such language sounded even less bold when compared with the shocking terms employed by ultraists.

The women of the WNYASS managed antislavery fairs throughout the 1840s. They appealed to "women and men," to "the old and the young, the farmers, the mechanics, and the merchants" to "devote what they [could] spare either of money or of the fruits of their labor." The fair organizers requested items both "useful and ornamental," but their emphasis on the former was evidenced in the list of goods they sought for the 1847 fair: "eggs, butter, cheese, cream, turkeys, hams, dried beef, pickles, and fruits" and other items of "small as well as large value." After an 1849 fair that garnered only eighty dollars, the fair committee explained that "the goods were altogether too ornamental to meet the ideas of hard-handed, industrious farmers." Nor could ultraists' concern for slaves be mistaken for benevolent interest in the worthy poor. Ultraists labored on behalf of "more than a million of our

[87] LASS, "Circular," SDPFP.
[88] *Frederick Douglass' Paper,* 12 January 1855.

sisters, crushed, abused, and bleeding under the lash."[89] While LASS leaders shielded the public from such harsh images, ultraists believed that "all who feel bound to improve the precious time allotted to them here" must be "brought to painfully remember . . . the oppressed and suffering bondmen who still remain toiling unrequited in the southern prison house." No uplifting tales of emancipation appeared in ultraist publications, but instead tales of woe—of "labor wrested from them unremunerated," of "suffer[ing] from intense hunger and cold," and of "the females . . . subject to the cruel and passionate outrages of their tyrannical masters and overseers."[90]

Ultraist women shied away neither from shocking images nor from shocking issues in their promotion of antislavery labors. They invited notorious agitators such as William Lloyd Garrison and Abby Kelley Foster to speak at their conventions. They constantly identified the slave's oppression with their own and were frequently asked why their brand of abolitionism led "into everything—unbelief, skepticism and infidelity, Spirit rapping."[91] By presenting harsh images, appearing with unpopular agitators, and espousing unpopular causes, ultraists winnowed out the coworkers in the community as they solicited aid. The ultraist antislavery fair was not an annual appeal for funds as much as a repeated attempt to "agitat[e] the public mind" in the "cause of truth and righteousness."[92]

Whereas economic resources and elite support were essential to the amelioration sought by benevolent women, moral agitation was primary for ultraists who sought a restructuring of society. An entirely local focus was appropriate to the former, but a societywide vision was necessary for the latter. Early perfectionists preceded ultraists in the use of moral suasion tactics and the belief in universal change; yet, ultimately, perfectionists did not wish fundamentally to alter basic institutions but rather to institutionalize certain rights and privileges supposedly guaranteed by evangelical and constitutional doctrines. Thus they turned to the establishment of model asylums and the approval of principled politicians.

Activists' definition of community as well as their location in a par-

[89] *North Star*, 3 December 1847, 26 January 1849, and 14 January 1848.
[90] *Daily Democrat*, 4 April 1848.
[91] Mary Robbins Post to Isaac and Amy Post, 5 December 1852, IAPFP.
[92] *Daily Democrat*, 4 April 1848; Amy Post to Frederick Douglass, 2 February 1850, IAPFP.

ticular community shaped these patterns of activism. Benevolent women perceived community as a place; perfectionists's definition vacillated between community as a set of spiritual bonds and community as a set of institutions; and ultraists saw the primary meaning of community in the network of lived social relations. Thus the CS prided itself on having "long constituted a most agreeable bond of union amongst our citizens" as it wove through the city a dense web of almsgiving and amelioration.[93] Perfectionists formed bonds of sisterhood and public domesticity that linked the "unprotected female" with her more fortunate sister and connected the country with the city.[94] By the 1850s they had institutionalized "parental discipline" and "maternal care" for virtuous females, orphans, the ill, and the uneducated while they carried the tenets of middle-class respectability and domesticity into the newly established homes of free blacks, North and South.[95] Ultraists, with their agrarian heritage, viewed the world as a "moral vineyard" in which men and women must labor side by side to cultivate "that Tree of Life, . . . the fruit of which is for the healing of the nations—Justice, Mercy, Love, Purity, Fidelity." Thus would the seeds of exploitation—of slaves, women, and workers—be replaced by " 'fruits of the spirit' " to create a "healthful, united, and happy" human family.[96] If any man or woman was oppressed, ultraists felt "as bound with them."[97] Yet they were also linked "in the bonds of progression" with the forces that might free all humankind, with freethinkers, spiritualists, agitators, and revolutionaries.[98]

Benevolent women's sense of community was the most stable and geographically grounded. Rochester was their home; they were its founders and its leaders. They had established the city's order and they wished to sustain it. They did not, in fact, seek social change at all but continuity, and amelioration was the best means of assuring that stability and continuity. The circumstances under which perfectionists entered Rochester were quite different and made them far more concerned with their own mobility and with the effects of mobility on

[93] CS, *Charter*, p. 4.
[94] HF, Minute Book, 28 March 1849, FHP.
[95] See, for example HF, "Rules of the Home," n.d., FHP; OAA, "By-Laws," in OAA, *History*, pp. 9–15. There are numerous descriptions of parental and familial care in OAA and HF minutes, annual reports, and public appeals.
[96] YMCF, *Proceedings, 1850*, p. 6.
[97] This was a common Garrisonian expression and appeared repeatedly in the WNYASS reports, the *North Star*, and in private correspondence.
[98] B. G. Bushnell Marks to Amy Post, 16 January 1854, IAPFP.

the population at large. In numerous communities throughout the North, rapid growth and change catalyzed attempts by upwardly mobile Evangelicals to control sexual and other appetites as a way of controlling the emerging bourgeois order. As late as 1865 a writer for the *JHF* revealed continued ambivalence about that new order. Describing Rochester homes as "humble and simple," she described this city of fifty-thousand as "an overgrown country village" and assured her readers, "we are content it should be so."[99]

Though most ultraists were raised in country villages, they were not content to remain or return there. At the same time, their attachment to Rochester was minimal compared with that of other activists. Ultraists believed that people must "begin and prosecute the work of reform on their own souls—thence, working outward" to the larger community. But their goal was to "exert an influence on the world."[100] Because of both their desire for fundamental change and their reliance on extra-local sources of support, ultraists focused their gaze beyond the local community. Although they attended closely to local manifestations of societywide problems—the wages of local seamstresses, the hanging of a local murderer, the plight of local blacks—their notions of a new social order were not easily confined to a single community. This extralocal orientation and ultraists' insistence on racial, class, and sexual equality clearly distinguished them from their benevolent and perfectionist counterparts.

It was the issue of woman's equality that most often served as the dividing line within the ranks of female activism, isolating ultraists from their benevolent and perfectionist peers. While the latter two groups did not share the same definition of woman's role, they both rejected women's right to pursue every and all public labors equally with men, and they both saw barriers to equality as a matter of natural selection rather than of socialization or oppression. Even when pursuing public labors, Rochester's benevolent women rarely wandered far from the threshold of the private household. Thus it could be said of

[99] *JHF*, 1 June 1865. For examples from other communities, see Mary P. Ryan, *Cradle of the Middle-Class: The Family in Oneida County, New York, 1780–1865* (Cambridge: Cambridge University Press, 1981), and Carroll Smith-Rosenberg, "Sex as Symbol in Victorian Purity: An Ethnographic Analysis," in John Demos and Sarene Spence Boocock, eds., *Turning Points: Historical and Sociological Essays on the Family* (Chicago: University of Chicago Press, 1978), pp. 212–247.

[100] YMCF, *Proceedings of the Annual Meeting of Friends of Human Progress, Held at Waterloo, N.Y., on the Third, Fourth, and Fifth of the Sixth Month, 1855* (Syracuse: Evening Chronicle Print, 1855), p. 14.

Mrs. Jonathan Child upon her death that no one had "ever had the interests of the Society more at heart, or labored more faithfully for its welfare" even though she herself had condemned any combined public effort by women.[101] Similarly, the obituary of Mrs. Silas O. Smith noted her many accomplishments in the field of public charity but concluded that "the consistent beauty of her life was best known in the private circles in which she moved."[102]

Perfectionist women, who were the initial target of debates over woman's role, were acutely self-conscious about legitimating their public endeavors. At first unsuccessful in convincing the community of the propriety of their labors, perfectionists found one solution in the formation of a series of institutions behind the walls of which they could more quietly pursue the salvation of various classes of the needy. These institutions, dotting the city's landscape with replicas of Christian domesticity, brought benevolent and perfectionist women together in ever more tightly interlocked networks of leadership. This largely female world employed metaphors and models of home and family, with God as the father and the woman activist as the mother. Yet these were not simply translations of private into public forms; they were also public models for private life. The rules of the asylum and the home, for instance, proclaimed a regimen of sleeping, eating, instruction, prayer, and work that few private households could have replicated, but which institutional leaders described as proper domestic arrangements. The inmates of these institutions were to be trained as domestics, carrying the regimens they learned into private families. Unlike their CS counterparts, who could define their benevolent labors almost exclusively in private terms, the benevolent and perfectionist founders of institutions had to move between private and public domains. Yet, simultaneously, they sought to create a female world in both so that the labors of men and women would be separate but complementary. During the Civil War, SAS members proclaimed their work as the perfect example of the proper division of public labors into "masculine and feminine elements" harmonized "in the mercy of God."[103]

Complementary roles were also developed within those perfectionist campaigns that defied institutional structures. Like their HF and SAS

[101] CS, Minute Book, 5 March 1850, CSP.

[102] Obituary of Mrs. Silas O. Smith, n.d., William Farley Peck, Scrapbook, vol. 2, Rochester Public Library.

[103] *Industrial School Advocate and Soldier's Aid*, 12 July 1865.

counterparts, perfectionist abolitionists clearly differentiated themselves from male laborers by subsidizing rather than attempting to share directly in the electoral efforts of third-party men. By working under male auspices and reinforcing existing political institutions, LASS leaders could justify auxiliary involvement in some political activities. LASS women noted that "the perpetuity of Slavery" deprived "one portion of the people of the inestimable blessings of Liberty" and the Constitution and endangered "the Domestic Tranquility." In order to assure liberty to all by Constitutional means, women might form themselves "into a Society," they concluded, to "raise funds for Anti-Slavery purposes."[104] For LASS members and other perfectionist women, the separation of men's and women's roles did not conform to a division between public and private spheres but rather to a division of each of these spheres into male and female domains.

Ultraists were far less committed to Constitutional traditions, horrified by "what laws our Fathers and brothers have enacted for mothers and sisters and wives to [wear] as galling chains."[105] Marginal both to male-dominated centers of economic and political power and to the proliferation of evangelical and popular definitions of true womanhood and domesticity, the Hicksite settlers of the 1830s necessarily turned to men and women in their own circles as coworkers. A background of joint labors in work, meeting, and community and the relatively small numbers of committed individuals fostered alliances between male and female ultraists. At the same time, the primacy given to moral suasion, noninstitutional means, and democratic organizations allowed women and men to share public labors. As ultraists sought wider support, they found those who were marginal for other reasons—usually race or class—the most willing coworkers. Within this community of the disfranchised and disaffected, new models of political and social relations were developed.

The practices of everyday life were the most accessible means by which ultraists could demonstrate these models, so that social mingling of the races and joint labors of the sexes became political statements whether performed in public or private domains. Moreover, ultraists invited the community to scrutinize their private lives. Once again, public and private met in women's activism, but for ultraists public statements were primary and ideally were made by men and women jointly. This lifestyle politics had a different ideological origin from the

---

[104] LASS, "Circular," SDPFP.
[105] Sarah E. Thayer to Amy Post, 23 December 1857, IAPFP.

politics espoused by perfectionists. Ultraists drew on Quaker axioms of equality, on the doctrines of such European radicals as the Anti-Corn Law League, and on the American political traditions voiced by Thomas Paine. Not the Constitution but the Declaration of Independence was their favorite document. Their radical interpretation of its words was attested by the special role played in their Revolutionary memories by Tom Paine whose grave the Posts visited in 1860, "so as to *pass our feet* upon the soil this gifted man so oft had trod."[106]

The exigencies of material progress, urban growth, religious change, and the Civil War fostered myriad changes in the patterns of female activism between 1822 and 1872. Yet even in the latter year, benevolence—expressed in its purest form by the CS—and ultraism—most visible in the feminism of the Post family—still formed the two poles of the activist spectrum. In between, a variety of institutions and associations battled for primacy and became intertwined with each other, with male associations, with the state, and with national organizations. In the midst of alliances and realignments, three general forms of activism continually reemerged: amelioration by those citizens at the center of power and authority to sustain the status quo; reform by activists seeking entry into those centers to institutionalize free and open access to economic and political as well as spiritual salvation; and agitation by those persons marginal to power and authority to defuse the very meaning of those terms.

The long battle among the advocates of amelioration, reform, and agitation was crucial to establishing public roles for women in the nineteenth century and to expanding the social and political vision of their neighbors. Division and disagreement among women served as catalysts to increase women's efforts, multiply their associations, improve their techniques, sharpen their arguments, and strengthen their commitments. Still, within each network, association, and circle, sisterhood was essential to brace women for breaking new ground and fortify them in the face of mounting social problems, public criticism, and hours of work.

Near the end of her career Elizabeth Cady Stanton proclaimed that there must "never be another season of silence" for women and urged the next generation to maintain women's place in the world.[107] Yet there had never been a season of silence in Rochester. And among

[106] Amy Post to Frederick Douglass, 13 February 1860, IAPFP.
[107] Quoted in Elaine Partnow, ed., *The Quotable Woman, 1800–1975* (Los Angeles: Corwin, 1977), p. 26.

those women whose voices rang out most clearly was Amy Post. As Amy was laid in her grave, Lucy Coleman asked that friends and family not simply mourn her death but learn from her life. "Do you not remember of whom it was said, 'being dead, yet speaketh!' Let us listen, my sisters, possibly we may find echo in our own hearts."[108] Many of Rochester's women activists, weary in well-doing, must have hoped that they would be laid to rest in the same way—with praise by their peers and with pleas for future generations to follow in their footsteps.

[108] Lucy Coleman, *Reminiscences,* p. 85.

Tables

Table 1. Birthplace of women officeholders in benevolent organizations, 1822–1872

Birthplace	Charitable, 1822 (N = 60) Number	Percent	Charitable, 1827–1832 (N = 43) Number	Percent	Orphan Asylum, 1837 (N = 18) Number	Percent	Charitable/Orp▮ 1837 (N = 29) Number	Perc
New England	20	33	12	28	8	44	16	5
Eastern/Central New York	13	22	3	7	5	28	4	1
Western New York	0	0	0	0	0	0	0	
Long Island and Mid-Atlantic states	0	0	0	0	0	0	1	
South (Maryland)	2	3	2	5	0	0	0	
Great Britain	1	2	0	0	0	0	0	
Unknown	24	40	26	60	5	28	8	2

[a]The HF is included in tables for both benevolent and perfectionist women since both networks were re▮ sented among its founding members and continued to comprise the organization for a significant period of t▮

[b]Long-term benevolent women are those who served twenty years or more. Date-specific items for t▮ women are based on information from 1850.

Table 2. Religious affiliation of women officeholders in benevolent organizations, 1822–1872

Religious affiliation	Charitable, 1822 (N = 60) Number	Percent	Charitable, 1827–1832 (N = 43) Number	Percent	Orphan Asylum, 1837 (N = 18) Number	Percent	Charitable/Orp▮ 1837 (N = 29) Number	Per▮
First Presbyterian	33	55	13	30	4	22	8	2
Reform Presbyterian[c]	0	0	7	16	5	28	5	1
St. Luke's Episcopal	12	20	12	28	3	17	8	2
Other Episcopal[d]	0	0	3	7	1	6	2	
Methodist	0	0	1	2	1	6	1	
Baptist	0	0	1	2	3	17	4	1
Unitarian	0	0	0	0	0	0	0	
Orthodox Quaker	0	0	0	0	1	6	1	
Hicksite Quaker	0	0	0	0	0	0	0	
Hicksite/Progressive Quaker[e]	0	0	0	0	0	0	0	
Reform Presbyterian/ Unitarian	0	0	0	0	0	0	0	
Hicksite Quaker/ Unitarian	0	0	0	0	0	0	0	
Unknown	15	25	6	14	0	0	0	

[a]See note a, Table 1.

[b]See note b, Table 1.

[c]Reform Presbyterian churches are those significantly affected by the revivals of Charles Grandison Fir▮ and other Evangelicals. This category also includes members of First Congregational Church, which was fo▮ ed in 1841 by Finney converts.

[d]Category includes St. Paul's Episcopal Church founded in 1827 and Trinity Episcopal Church founde▮ 1855.

[e]All religious affiliations with slashes indicate that the persons in that category changed church affiliat▮ during their activist careers. Progressive Quaker was another name for Congregational Quaker and is used ▮ to distinguish this group from members of First Congregational Church.

for Friendless,[a] 1849 (N = 14)		Charitable/Orphan, 1849 (N = 36)		Industrial School/ Soldier's Aid/Hospital, 1863 (N = 31)		Long-term[b] (N = 49)	
er	Percent	Number	Percent	Number	Percent	Number	Percent
	57	16	44	3	10	24	49
	36	12	33	10	32	15	31
	0	1	3	0	0	0	0
	0	2	6	0	0	0	0
	0	1	3	0	0	2	4
	0	0	0	1	3	2	4
	7	4	11	17	55	5	10

for Friendless[a], 1849 (N = 14)		Charitable/Orphan, 1849 (N = 36)		Industrial School/ Soldier's Aid/Hospital, 1863 (N = 31)		Long-term[b] (N = 49)	
er	Percent	Number	Percent	Number	Percent	Number	Percent
	14	11	31	8	26	19	39
	50	7	19	6	19	7	14
	7	10	28	7	23	11	22
	7	2	6	3	10	2	4
	0	0	0	1	3	0	0
	0	2	6	0	0	4	8
	14	2	6	1	3	3	6
	0	0	0	0	0	0	0
	0	0	0	0	0	0	0
	0	2	6	0	0	0	0
	0	0	0	0	0	0	0
	7	0	0	5	16	3	6

Table 3. Marital status of women officeholders in benevolent organizations, 1822–1872

Marital Status	Charitable, 1822 (N = 60)		Charitable, 1827–1832 (N = 43)		Orphan Asylum, 1837 (N = 18)		Charitable/Orph 1837 (N = 29)	
	Number	Percent	Number	Percent	Number	Percent	Number	Per
Single	6	10	0	0	0	0	0	
Married	39	65	39	91	17	94	28	
Widowed	5	8	3	7	1	6	1	
Unknown	10	17	1	2	0	0	0	

[a] See note a, Table 1.
[b] See note b, Table 1.

Table 4. Occupational status of women officeholders in benevolent organizations, 1822–1872

Father's or husband's occupation	Charitable, 1822 (N = 60)		Charitable, 1827–1832 (N = 43)		Orphan Asylum, 1837 (N = 18)		Charitable/Orp 1837 (N = 29)	
	Number	Percent	Number	Percent	Number	Percent	Number	Pe
Banker/Merchant/ Manufacturer	18	30	18	42	9	50	12	
[Flour miller][c]	[7]	[12]	[6]	[14]	[4]	[22]	[6]	[
Professional	16	27	9	21	7	39	13	
Artisan	5	8	0	0	0	0	2	
Shopkeeper	1	2	1	2	0	0	0	
Clerk	0	0	2	5	0	0	1	
Farmer	0	0	0	0	0	0	0	
Commercial farmer	0	0	0	0	0	0	0	
Unknown	20	33	13	30	2	11	1	

[a] See note a, Table 1.
[b] See note b, Table 1.
[c] Flour miller is included in the figures for Banker/Merchant/Manufacturer but is also listed separately bec it was the most prestigious occupation in Rochester until 1845.

e for Friendless[a], 1849 (N = 14)		Charitable/Orphan, 1849 (N = 36)		Industrial School/Soldier's Aid/Hospital, 1863 (N = 31)		Long-term[b] (N = 49)	
ber	Percent	Number	Percent	Number	Percent	Number	Percent
	7	1	3	4	13	2	4
	93	31	86	25	81	45	92
	0	2	6	2	6	2	4
	0	2	6	0	0	0	0

e for Friendless[a], 1849 (N = 14)		Charitable/Orphan, 1849 (N = 36)		Industrial School/Soldier's Aid/Hospital, 1863 (N = 31)		Long-term[b] (N = 49)	
ber	Percent	Number	Percent	Number	Percent	Number	Percent
	50	18	50	13	42	26	53
]	[7]	[2]	[6]	[2]	[6]	[7]	[14]
	29	16	44	12	39	21	43
	0	1	3	0	0	0	0
	0	0	0	0	0	0	0
	0	0	0	0	0	0	0
	0	0	0	0	0	0	0
	0	0	0	0	0	0	0
	21	1	3	6	19	2	4

264   *Tables*

Table 5. Composition of households of women officeholders in benevolent organizations, 1849

Composition	Charitable/Orphan Asylum (N = 36)		Home for Friendless (N = 14)	
	Number	Percent	Number	Percent
Single with parents	1	3	1	7
Nuclear	11	31	3	21
Complex[a]	10	28	6	43
Extended[b]	4	11	1	7
Complex/Extended	5	14	2	14
Unknown	5	14	1	7

NOTE: Figures are based on 1850 United States Census.
[a] Complex households are those that contain nonrelated individuals such as boarders, servants, or laborers.
[b] Extended households are those that contain related individuals outside the nuclear family. Complex/Extended households contain both extra kin and nonrelated household members.

Table 6. Number of children per family of women officeholders in benevolent organizations, 1849

Number of children per family	Charitable/Orphan Asylum (N = 36)		Home for Friendless (N = 14)	
	Number	Percent	Number	Percent
0 (single women)	1	3	1	7
0 (married women)	4	11	0	0
1	6	17	4	29
2–3	7	19	4	29
4–5	11	31	4	29
6 or more	2	6	0	0
Unknown	5	14	1	7

NOTE: Figures are based on 1850 United States Census. The average number of children per family is 2.8; per family of married women only is 2.9. The mode is 1 and 5.

Table 7. Number of persons in households of women officeholders in benevolent organizations, 1849

Number of persons in household	Charitable/Orphan Asylum (N = 36)		Home for Friendless (N = 14)	
	Number	Percent	Number	Percent
2–3	4	11	1	7
4–5	6	17	2	14
6–7	11	31	7	50
8–9	7	19	3	21
10 or more	2	6	0	0
Unknown	6	17	1	7

NOTE: Figures are based on 1850 United States Census. The average number of persons per household is 6.4. The mode is 7.

Table 8. Religious affiliation of Charitable Society members in selected years, 1822–1852

Religious affiliation	1822 (N = 60)		1832 (N = 171)		1842 (N = 117)		1852 (N = 365)	
	Number	Percent	Number	Percent	Number	Percent	Number	Percent
First Presbyterian	33	55.0	50	29.2	35	29.9	71	19.5
Reform Presbyterian[a]	0	0.0	40	23.4	22	18.8	69	18.9
St. Luke's Episcopal	14	23.3	38	22.2	35	29.9	74	20.3
Other Episcopal[b]	0	0.0	9	5.3	11	9.4	64	17.5
Methodist	0	0.0	2	1.2	4	3.4	33	9.0
Baptist	0	0.0	1	.6	9	7.7	38	10.4
Congregationalist[c]	0	0.0	1	.6	0	0.0	0	0.0
Unitarian	0	0.0	0	0.0	0	0.0	16	4.4
Unknown	13	21.7	30	17.5	1	.9	0	0.0

[a] See note c, Table 2.
[b] See note d, Table 2.
[c] The one person in this category was a member of Brighton Congregational Church, which was outside the Rochester city limits.

Table 9. Birthplace of women officeholders in perfectionist organizations, 1834–1867

Birthplace	Female Anti-Slavery, 1834–1836 ($N = 23$)		Moral Reform, 1836–1845 ($N = 29$)		Home for Friendl 1849–1854 ($N = 40$)	
	Number	Percent	Number	Percent	Number	Per
New England	11	48	9	31	17	4
Eastern/Central New York	5	22	9	31	13	3
Western New York	0	0	0	0	0	
Long Island and Mid-Atlantic states	0	0	1	3	0	
South (Maryland)	0	0	0	0	1	
Great Britain	0	0	0	0	0	
Unknown	7	30	10	34	9	2

Table 10. Religious affiliation of women officeholders in perfectionist organizations, 1834–1867

Religious affiliation	Female Anti-Slavery, 1834–1836 ($N = 23$)		Moral Reform, 1836–1845 ($N = 29$)		Home for Friendle 1849–1854 ($N = 40$)	
	Number	Percent	Number	Percent	Number	Per
First Presbyterian	4	17	5	17	9	2
Reform Presbyterian[a]	7	30	13	45	12	3
St. Luke's Episcopal	1	4	0	0	6	1
Other Episcopal[b]	0	0	0	0	1	
Methodist	0	0	1	3	0	
Baptist	3	13	1	3	1	
Unitarian	1	4	1	3	2	
Orthodox Quaker	2	9	2	7	0	
Hicksite Quaker	1	4	0	0	0	
Hicksite/Progressive Quaker[c]	0	0	0	0	0	
Reform Presbyterian/ Unitarian	0	0	0	0	1	
Hicksite Quaker/ Unitarian	0	0	0	0	0	
Unknown	4	17	7	24	5	1

[a] See note c, Table 2.
[b] See note d, Table 2.
[c] See note e, Table 2.

Ladies' Anti-Slavery, 1851–1852 ($N = 30$)		Ladies' Anti-Slavery, 1853–1867 ($N = 63$)	
Number	Percent	Number	Percent
7	23	14	22
10	33	24	38
0	0	0	0
1	3	1	2
0	0	0	0
6	20	6	10
6	20	18	29

Ladies' Anti-Slavery, 1851–1852 ($N = 30$)		Ladies' Anti-Slavery, 1853–1867 ($N = 63$)	
Number	Percent	Number	Percent
2	7	9	14
7	23	14	22
0	0	0	0
0	0	0	0
2	7	6	10
2	7	2	3
5	17	10	16
0	0	1	2
0	0	1	2
0	0	0	0
1	3	0	0
0	0	1	2
11	37	19	30

Table 11. Marital status of women officeholders in perfectionist organizations, 1834–1867

Marital status	Female Anti-Slavery, 1834–1836 (N = 23)		Moral Reform, 1836–1845 (N = 29)		Home for Friendle 1849–1854 (N = 40)	
	Number	Percent	Number	Percent	Number	Per
Single	3	13	2	7	2	
Married	19	83	20	69	36	9
Widowed	0	0	4	14	2	
Unknown	1	4	3	10	0	

Table 12. Occupational status of women officeholders in perfectionist organizations, 1834–1867

Father's or husband's occupation	Female Anti-Slavery, 1834–1836 (N = 23)		Moral Reform, 1836–1845 (N = 29)		Home for Friendle 1849–1854 (N = 40)	
	Number	Percent	Number	Percent	Number	Per
Banker/Merchant/ Manufacturer	3	13	8	28	12	3
[Flour miller][a]	[0]	[0]	[1]	[3]	[1]	[
Professional	3	13	9	31	12	3
Artisan	6	26	1	3	0	
Shopkeeper	2	9	0	0	1	
Clerk	2	9	2	7	4	1
Farmer	2	9	1	3	1	
Commercial farmer	0	0	0	0	0	
Unknown	5	22	8	28	9	2

[a] See note c, Table 4.

Ladies' Anti-Slavery, 1851–1852 (N = 30)		Ladies' Anti-Slavery, 1853–1867 (N = 63)	
Number	Percent	Number	Percent
7	23	11	17
16	53	39	62
2	7	8	13
5	17	5	8

Ladies' Anti-Slavery, 1851–1852 (N = 30)		Ladies' Anti-Slavery, 1853–1867 (N = 63)	
Number	Percent	Number	Percent
5	17	15	24
[0]	[0]	[1]	[2]
2	7	8	13
2	7	7	11
5	17	5	8
3	10	3	5
1	3	1	2
2	7	2	3
10	33	20	32

Table 13. Composition of households of women officeholders in perfectionist organizations, 1849–1852

| Composition | Home for Friendless/Ladies' Anti-Slavery Society (N = 52) | |
	Number	Percent
Single with parents	4	8
Nuclear	14	27
Complex[a]	16	31
Extended[b]	3	6
Complex/Extended	6	12
Unknown	6	12

NOTE: Figures are based on 1850 United States Census. There were also 3 perfectionist women (6 percent) who boarded with nonrelated families.
[a]See note a, Table 5.
[b]See note b, Table 5.

Table 14. Number of children per family of women officeholders in perfectionist organizations, 1849–1852

| Number of children per family | Home for Friendless/Ladies' Anti-Slavery Society (N = 52) | |
	Number	Percent
0 (single women)	5	10
0 (married women)	4	8
1	10	19
2–3	16	31
4–5	10	19
6 or more	1	2
Unknown	6	12

NOTE: Figures are based on 1850 United States Census. The average number of children per family is 2.2; per family of married women only is 2.6. The mode is 3.

Table 15. Number of persons in households of women officeholders in perfectionist organizations, 1849–1852

| Number of persons in household | Home for Friendless/Ladies' Anti-Slavery Society (N = 52) | |
	Number	Percent
2–3	8	15
4–5	7	13
6–7	18	35
8–9	9	17
10 or more	2	4
Unknown	6	12

NOTE: Figures are based on 1850 United States Census. The average number of persons per household is 5.8. The mode is 6.

Table 16. Birthplace of women active in ultraist movements, 1842–1860

Birthplace	Western New York Anti-Slavery, 1842–1848 (N = 23)		Anti-Slavery and Woman's Rights, 1848–1860[a] (N = 39)	
	Number	Percent	Number	Percent
New England	1	4	6	15
Eastern/Central New York	11	48	9	23
Western New York	3	13	7	18
Long Island and Mid-Atlantic states	2	9	7	18
South (Maryland)	0	0	0	0
Great Britain[b]	0	0	3	8
Unknown	4	17	7	18

[a] Category includes those women who were active in the Western New York Anti-Slavery Society and also in the formal woman's rights movement between 1848 and 1860. The category Western New York Anti-Slavery, 1842–1848, includes women who were active in this organization in its early years but who did not necessarily join in woman's rights conventions in 1848 and after.

[b] Category includes two women born in Canada.

Table 17. Religious affiliation of women active in ultraist movements, 1842–1860

Religious affiliation	Western New York Anti-Slavery, 1842–1848 (N = 23)		Anti-Slavery and Woman's Rights, 1848–1860[a] (N = 39)	
	Number	Percent	Number	Percent
First Presbyterian	0	0	0	0
Reform Presbyterian[b]	1	4	1	3
St. Luke's Episcopal	0	0	0	0
Other Episcopal[c]	0	0	0	0
Methodist	0	0	0	0
Baptist	0	0	0	0
Unitarian	2	9	5	13
Orthodox Quaker	0	0	1	3
Hicksite Quaker	13	57	8	21
Hicksite/Progressive Quaker[d]	0	0	11	28
Reform Presbyterian/ Unitarian	1	4	3	8
Hicksite Quaker/ Unitarian	2	9	4	10
Unknown	4	17	6	15

[a] See note a, Table 16.
[b] See note c, Table 2.
[c] See note d, Table 2.
[d] See note e, Table 2.

Table 18. Marital status of women active in ultraist movements, 1842–1860

Marital status	Western New York Anti-Slavery, 1842–1848 (N = 23)		Anti-Slavery and Woman's Rights, 1848–1860[a] (N = 39)	
	Number	Percent	Number	Percent
Single	5	22	6	15
Married	14	61	29	74
Widowed	1	4	3	8
Unknown	3	13	1	3

[a] See note a, Table 16.

Table 19. Occupational status of women active in ultraist movements, 1842–1860

Father's or husband's occupation	Western New York Anti-Slavery, 1842–1848 (N = 23)		Anti-Slavery and Woman's Rights, 1848–1860[a] (N = 39)	
	Number	Percent	Number	Percent
Banker/Merchant/ Manufacturer	4	17	5	13
[Flour miller][b]	[0]	[0]	[0]	[0]
Professional	4	17	5	13
Artisan	5	22	6	15
Shopkeeper	1	4	5	13
Clerk	3	13	1	3
Farmer	1	4	11	28
Commercial farmer	0	0	3	8
Unknown	5	22	3	8

[a] See note a, Table 16.
[b] See note c, Table 4.

Table 20. Composition of households of women active in ultraist movements, 1842–1860

Composition	Western New York Anti-Slavery, 1842–1848 (N = 23)		Anti-Slavery and Woman's Rights, 1848–1860[a] (N = 39)	
	Number	Percent	Number	Percent
Single with parents	1	4	4	10
Nuclear	9	39	18	46
Complex[b]	1	4	6	15
Extended[c]	3	13	6	15
Complex/Extended	1	4	3	8
Unknown	7	30	2	5

NOTE: Figures are based on 1850 United States Census. There was also 1 Western New York Anti-Slavery Society member (4 percent) who boarded with a nonrelated family.
[a] See note a, Table 16.
[b] See note a, Table 5.
[c] See note b, Table 5.

Table 21. Number of children per family of women active in ultraist movements, 1842–1860

Number of children per family	Western New York Anti-Slavery, 1842–1848 (N = 23)		Anti-Slavery and Woman's Rights, 1848–1860[a] (N = 39)	
	Number	Percent	Number	Percent
0 (single women)	0	0	6	15
0 (married women)	3	13	5	13
1	2	9	4	10
2–3	7	30	13	33
4–5	2	9	6	15
6 or more	0	0	0	0
Unknown	8	35	5	13

NOTE: Figures are based on 1850 United States Census. The average number of children per family is 2; for married women only is 2.2. The mode is 0 but for married women only is 3.

[a] See note a, Table 16.

Table 22. Number of persons in households of women active in ultraist movements, 1842–1860

Number of persons in household	Western New York Anti-Slavery, 1842–1848 (N = 23)		Anti-Slavery and Woman's Rights, 1848–1860[a] (N = 39)	
	Number	Percent	Number	Percent
2–3	5	22	10	26
4–5	2	9	9	23
6–7	6	26	12	31
8–9	0	0	3	8
10 or more	0	0	0	0
Unknown	10	43	5	13

NOTE: Figures are based on 1850 United States Census. The statistics for Western New York Anti-Slavery, 1842–1848, are ambiguous because of the large number of unknowns. The average for Anti-Slavery and Woman's Rights is 4 persons per household with modes of 5 and 6.

[a] See note a, Table 16.

Index

Library of Congress Cataloging in Publication Data

Hewitt, Nancy A., 1951–
  Women's activism and social change.

  Includes bibliographical references and index.
  1. Feminism—New York (State)—Rochester—History—19th century.
2. Rochester (N.Y.)—Social conditions.   I. Title.
HQ1439.R62H48   1984   305.4′2′0974789   83-45940
ISBN 0-8014-1616-7 (alk. paper)